Jordan

This Book Socks

enjoy!

Gene Zaluny

KINDERGARTEN CHATS
and OTHER WRITINGS

LOUIS H. SULLIVAN

Dover Publications, Inc.
New York

Published in Canada by General Publishing Company,
Ltd., 30 Lesmill Road, Don Mills, Toronto, Ontario.

This Dover edition, first published in 1979, is an
unabridged republication of the revised (1918) edition as
published by Wittenborn, Schultz, Inc., New York, 1947.

International Standard Book Number: 0-486-23812-1
Library of Congress Catalog Card Number: 79-52523

Manufactured in the United States of America
Dover Publications
180 Varick Street
New York, N.Y. 10014

Editorial Note

The printing of the unpublished revision of *Kindergarten Chats* in this volume carries out at last Louis Sullivan's wish that his work be issued in book form — his Foreword, written in July 1918, is our authority. That no publisher was found during the six remaining years of his life, and that a good deal of vagueness and misunderstanding arose concerning Sullivan's attitude to this work — as well as with regard to the existence and condition of a revised manuscript — reflects the commonplace that human nature and scholarship are inextricably bound together.

Sullivan believed that a building represented an act, and that such an act revealed the man behind it, the mind and ethics of the architect, more conclusively and unerringly than any statement. In this sense, the fifty-two consecutive essays entitled *Kindergarten Chats* are an act, requiring no officious introduction or interpretation. Nevertheless, a few general remarks should be made to suggest the nature and significance of Sullivan's editing of 1918, particularly since the first version published serially in 1901 is available only in a few obscure files, and that edited by Claude Bragdon in 1934 is out of print.

From June to October 1918, Sullivan worked over the manuscript and produced the text which follows, and which therefore represents its definitive form. The actual manuscript gives the impression that Sullivan revised in the exact meaning of the word, that he gave attention to every sentence and paragraph, that his alterations of word and phrase, his cutting and rewriting, were the product of genuine reconsideration and a desire for greater clarity. The redundant or unprecise adjective was discarded; the specific term was substituted for the more general or the vague one; repetitive passages were deleted. Throughout this revision — and the text here published was prepared directly from the original manuscript — it may be said that the secondary has been sacrificed to the primary. For instance, many words, phrases and sentences expressing emotion strong enough to convey prejudice (rather than conviction) have been either cut or modified so as not to deflect the force of rational and organic exposition. Thus the revision is in no sense a compromise, or a recantation of criticisms concerning architects or architecture, or a softening of attitude because of advancing age; on the contrary, it is sharper, clearer, more logical. (In length, the text is shorter by about 30,000 words; chapters, or parts of chapters, completely or largely rewritten are so indicated by footnotes.) It should, however, be pointed out that part of the 1918 *Kindergarten Chats* stands as written in 1901, especially in the earlier sections; certain passages deleted for the 1934 edition, as dated or distasteful, appear here unaltered. The extent and nature of Sullivan's editing is in itself extremely indicative of the man as well as of the thinker and writer.

Seven essays have been added, at the suggestion of Mr. George Grant Elmslie, and selected by him, so that the reader may study the development of Sullivan's ideas from early in his career — the first was written when he was 29 — till near the close of his life. Most of these essays consist of papers read before architects' conventions, certain of them having been revised and certain having appeared in professional magazines, now defunct; most of them may be assigned to the years of Sullivan's greatest success and precede *Kindergarten Chats*. Finally, miscellaneous material, of biographical and interpretative interest, has been placed in Appendices which are self-explanatory. It has thus been the intention to make the whole volume a human as well as an intellectual and artistic document, and a basis for further study.

The photographs accompanying *Kindergarten Chats* illustrate buildings to which Sullivan was referring in fact if not by name, or to which he might have been referring. A few examples of Sullivan's work were chosen to provide a balance and also to serve as illustrations of his own principles.

In the matter of punctuation, spelling and capitalization, the style of the manuscripts has been preserved, except for a few changes; slight modifications, for instance in the use of dashes and colons, have seemed justified by variations that exist in the sources themselves, the result of copying and of publication, (the holograph manuscript of *Kindergarten Chats* differs from the serial text; there are differences between successive printings of some of the essays). Certain apparent inconsistencies in capitalization — of such words as Democracy, Man, Architecture, etc. — have been retained, in the conviction that Sullivan's literary style is imbued with the tone and color of the spoken word, which would be distorted by dogmatic theories of consistency.   ISABELLA ATHEY

Acknowledgments

The publishers and editor wish to acknowledge their indebtedness,
for material, assistance and advice, to the following persons:
Mr. George Grant Elmslie, executor of Sullivan's literary estate,
whose wholehearted cooperation made this publication
possible; Mr. and Mrs. Hugh Morrison, of Hanover, N. H.; the
staff of the Burnham Library of Architecture, The Art Institute of
Chicago, especially Miss Etheldred Abbot and Mrs. T. M. Hofmeester, Jr.
(particular thanks are due for generous loan of manuscripts); the
staff of the Avery Library, Columbia University, especially Mr.
Talbot Hamlin and Mrs. Corinne Spencer; all other persons who
have kindly aided in obtaining documents and illustrative material.

Biographical Note

1856   Born, September 3, Boston, Massachusetts.

1860–70   Attended local grammar school; most of his summers were spent with maternal grandparents upon their farm at South Reading.

1870   Entered the English High School, Boston, where the teaching of Moses Woolson made a lasting impression. Sullivan's immediate family moved to Chicago.

1872–73   Attended architectural courses at M.I.T.; left without finishing. Obtained drafting work in the offices of Furness and Hewitt, Philadelphia (where an uncle lived). The "depression" of that time induced Sullivan to move on to Chicago, where he was employed by William LeBaron Jenney.

1874   To Europe, for study at the Beaux-Arts. Arrived in Paris via Liverpool and London, and in 6 weeks prepared for the *Ecole* entrance examinations. After passing brilliantly, Sullivan spent approximately two years in the *atelier libre* of Vaudremer. He visited Italy, where particularly the works of Michelangelo moved him profoundly. In Paris, Sullivan lived most of the time in rooms at the corner of rue Monsieur le Prince and rue Racine (building still standing).

1876–79   Return to Chicago and a succession of drafting positions, until put in charge of Dankmar Adler's office.

1881   Partnership: Adler and Sullivan. During the next 12 years, this was one of the most active architectural firms in Chicago (for instance, the Auditorium, 1887-89); between 1880 and 1895 Sullivan designed more than 100 buildings.

1893   Transportation Building, World's Columbian Exposition, Chicago (the only building to receive foreign recognition, a medal from the French government). Crucial consequences for architectural development in the U.S.A. and for Sullivan's career.

1895   Dissolution of the partnership.

1895–
1924   Practice alone. Very little data can be given for this period; Sullivan's straitened circumstances are reflected by the auction of his property in 1906. For many years office space was retained in the Auditorium Tower (No. 1600); most of his writing was done at the Cliff Dwellers, a club in which Sullivan held life membership. The personal interest of friends and colleagues was responsible for the revision of *Kindergarten Chats* (1918) with book publication in mind but not achieved, the writing of the *Autobiography* and the drawings for *A System of Architectural Ornament*.

1924   Died, April 14, in a hotel room, in Chicago.

Bibliography of Writings by Louis H. Sullivan

"Characteristics and Tendencies of American Architecture"

A paper read before the second annual convention of the Western Association of Architects, St. Louis, 1885; published in *Builders' Weekly Reporter* (London), some time in 1885; no references available.

"Inspiration"

A prose poem read before the third annual convention of the Western Association of Architects, Chicago, November 1886; published in brochure by the Inland Architect Press, Chicago, 1886. (Part 1 of "Nature and the Poet" series.)

"What is the Just Subordination, in Architectural Design, of Details to Mass?"

A symposium at a meeting of the Illinois Association of Architects, Chicago, April 1887, with talks by Louis H. Sullivan, L. D. Cleveland, O. J. Pierce and with a summary by Sullivan; published in *Inland Architect & News Record,* vol. 9, no. 5, pp. 51-54, April 1887, and in *Building Budget,* vol. 3, no. 3, pp. 62-63, April 1887.

"Ornamentation of the Auditorium"

A paper quoted in part in *Industrial Chicago,* vol. 2, pp. 490-491.

"Ornament in Architecture"

Published in *Engineering Magazine,* August 1892, vol. 3, no. 5, pp. 633-644.

"Emotional Architecture as Compared with Intellectual: A Study in Objective and Subjective"

A paper read before the 28th annual convention of the American Institute of Architects, New York, October 1894; the title has always been listed with "Classical" in place of "Intellectual," the result of a misprint overlooked by the author; published in *Inland Architect & News Record,* vol. 24, no. 4, pp. 32-34, November 1894. Under a different title ("Objective and Subjective, A Study in Emotional as Compared with Intellectual") and with certain textual variations, this essay was published as a brochure by the Inland Architect Press, Chicago, 1895.

"The Tall Office Building Artistically Considered"

Published in *Lippincott's* vol. 57, pp. 403-409, March 1896; *Inland Architect & News Record* vol. 27, no. 4, pp. 32-34, May 1896; republished, with slight changes, in the "Architectural Discussion" department of *The Craftsman,* vol. 8, pp. 453-458, July 1905, under the title "Form and Function Artistically Considered." In January 1922, *Western Architect,* vol. 31, no. 1, pp. 3-11, republished the essay under the original title with the notation: "Mr. Sullivan himself states that he has nothing to add nor to subtract from his early statement."

"An Unaffected School of Modern Architecture: Will It Come?"

Published in *Artist* (New York), vol. 24, pp. XXXIII-IV, January 1899.

An address before the Chicago Architectural Club, the Art Institute, Chicago, May 1899. Unpublished (MS in Burnham Library).

"The Modern Phase of Architecture"

A short address, apparently delivered in Cleveland (n. d.); published in *Inland Architect & News Record*, vol. 33, no. 5, June 1899.

"The Master"

Part 2 of "Nature and the Poet" series, begun 1880-90, completed July 1, 1899. Unpublished (MS in Burnham Library).

"The Young Man in Architecture"

A paper read before the Architectural League of America, June 1900; published in *The Brickbuilder*, vol. 9; no. 6, pp. 115-119, June 1900; *Western Architect*, vol. 34, no. 1, pp. 4-10, January 1925; *Twice a Year*, no. 2, Spring-Summer 1939.

"Reality in the Architectural Art"

Published in *Interstate Architect & Builder*, vol. 2, no. 25, pp. 6-7, August 1900.

Kindergarten Chats

Published in *Interstate Architect & Builder*, vol. 2, no. 52-vol. 3, no. 51 (52 issues from February 16, 1901-February 8, 1902); in book form, edited by Claude F. Bragdon, by the Scarab Fraternity Press, Lawrence, Kansas, 1934. See Appendix E for chronology of manuscripts, revision, etc.

"Education"

A paper read before the annual convention of the Architectural League of America, Toronto, 1902. First published here (MS in Burnham Library).

"Sympathy—a Romanza"

Part 3 of "Nature and the Poet" series. Written about 1904, unpublished (MS in Burnham Library).

"Natural Thinking: A Study in Democracy"

A paper read before the Chicago Architectural Club, February 1905. Unpublished (MS in Burnham Library).

"The Possibility of a New Architectural Style"

A reply to an article by Frederick Stymetz Lamb on "Modern Use of the Gothic," *The Craftsman*, vol. 8, pp. 336-338, June 1905.

"What is Architecture: A Study in the American People of Today"

Published in *American Contractor*, vol. 27, no. 1, pp. 48-54, January 1906, and reprinted in the May, June, July issues of *The Craftsman*, 1906, vol. 10, no. 2, pp. 145-149; no. 3, pp. 352-358; no. 4, pp. 507-513. The *Akademie der Künste*, Berlin, published in connection with an exhibition, *Ausstellung Neuer Amerikanischer Baukunst*, January 1926, "Was ist Architektur," with a foreword by Irving K. Pond. Selections of the essay, "interpreted" by William Gray Purcell, were published in *Northwest Architect*, vol. 8, no. 1, October-November 1940, and a reprint of this version was published July 1944, (details unavailable).

Democracy: A Man Search

A book in 44 chapters, of ca. 180,000 words; first draft completed July 1, 1907; revision completed April 18, 1908. Unpublished (holograph pencilled manuscript in the Avery

Library, Columbia University; typed manuscript in the Burnham Library). Excerpts appeared in *Twice a Year*, no. 5-6, Fall-Winter, 1940 — Spring-Summer 1941, pp. 17-28.

"Is Our Art a Betrayal rather than an Expression of American Life?"

Published in *The Craftsman*, vol. 15, no. 4, pp. 402-404, January 1909.

Letter replying to an article by Gutzon Borglum, *The Craftsman*, vol. 17, no. 3, December 1909.

"Suggestions in Artistic Brickwork"

Foreword to a pamphlet entitled *Artistic Brick*, published by the Hydraulic-Press Brick Company, St. Louis, undated (ca. 1910) pp. 5-13.

"Wherefore the Poet?"

Published in *Poetry*, vol. 7, pp. 305-307, March 1916.

"Development of Construction"

A paper read before the Illinois Chapter of the A. I. A.; published in *The Economist* (Chicago), vol. 55, no. 26, p. 1252, and vol. 56, no. 1, pp. 39-40, June and July, 1916.

The Autobiography of an Idea

Published serially in *Journal of the American Institute of Architects*, June 1922-August 1923. Published in book form by the Press of the A. I. A., 1924; reprinted by W. W. Norton & Co. in "White Oak Library Series," 1934.

A System of Architectural Ornament According with a Philosophy of Man's Powers

A series of 19 plates drawn during the period January 1922-May 1922 and published in folio by the Press of the A. I. A., 1924 (Original drawings in Burnham Library).

"The Chicago Tribune Competition"

Published in *Architectural Record*, vol. 53, no. 2, pp. 151-157, February 1923.

"Concerning the Imperial Hotel, Tokyo"

Published in *Architectural Record*, vol. 53, no. 4, pp. 333-352, April 1923; in H. Th. Wijdeveld: *The Life Work of the American Architect, Frank Lloyd Wright*, (1925), pp. 124-131.

"Reflections on the Tokyo Disaster"

Published in *Architectural Record*, vol. 55, no. 2, pp. 113-117, February 1924; *ibid*, pp. 101-123.

(This list has been based upon the bibliography in Hugh Morrison's *Louis Sullivan: Prophet of Modern Architecture;* some additions and slight modifications have been made by the editor.)

A complete general bibliography of books and articles on Sullivan, and a list of Sullivan buildings, is available in the volume by Hugh Morrison (Museum of Modern Art and W. W. Norton & Co., 1935), to which very little can be added.

In April 1946 the American Institute of Architects conferred its Gold Medal posthumously upon Sullivan (see Appendix D); in September 1946, commemorating Sullivan's ninetieth anniversary, a plaque was placed upon the house where he was born, now 42 Bennet Street, Boston (see *Journal of the American Institute of Architects*, vol. 6, no. 5, November 1946).

The first exhibition devoted to Sullivan, "The Genius of Louis Sullivan," was arranged by the Institute of Modern Art, Boston, Massachusetts; after being shown at that museum, March 4-April 19, 1947, it will have an extensive itinerary.

Contents

List of Illustrations

13.

Foreword

The following work appeared in serial form in the Interstate Architect[1] of Cleveland, Ohio, during the year 1901.

It was originally written for young architects. In its present form it has been sufficiently recast to broaden and extend its appeal to all those who may be interested in the nature of Architecture as a creative art.

The work is free of technicalities, is couched in easy dialogue form and its doctrine should be intelligible to all: for it is based on the realities of every-day life and is essentially democratic in its ——[2] of our common natural powers.

The plot, if such it may be called, is very simple, namely, a graduate of one of our architectural schools comes to the author for a post-graduate course. Interest therefore centers in the ——[2] unfolding in the pupil of those natural, spontaneous powers which had been submerged and ignored during his academic training.

The central purpose of the work is to liberate the mind from serfdom to tradition, and to exhibit man's natural powers in their creative capabilities when expanding in the open-air-of-the-spirit-of-responsible-freedom; in other words, in the true spirit of democracy. From which it follows that the operation of the historic feudal mind and the advancing democratic mind are placed in sharp contrast. The appeal therefore is to the broad intelligence of the public mind seeking not only a knowledge and understanding of architecture as a plastic art, but, as well, a clear view of its social basis as an art of expression.

The present world-tragedy will, at its ending, call for a new valuation of human power, a new and clarified social view and vista, a new illumination of the basic nature of democracy as contrasted with its merely political aspect.

It is in the hope that this work may contribute its share toward such clarification that the author has consented to its publication in book form.

The ideas underlying the work are simple and elementary; hence the title "Kindergarten Chats."   Louis H. Sullivan, *The Cliff Dwellers. Chicago, July 10, 1918.*

1. *The Interstate Architect and Builder;* Feb. 16, 1901-Feb. 8, 1902. Sullivan's letters in Appendix A refer to the series of articles.   2. Illegible word.

I. A Building with a Tower

Now what is this? What building I mean?

It is a structure that looks out upon the fair spread of Lake Michigan.

Has the Lake then a fare spread?

It has indeed — for the judicious to feast the eyes upon and to delight in; but, strange to say, like many another choice thing, it is caviare to the general.

To what general?

To the general apathy.

Is it true that Chicago people do not delight in this superb Lake?

No, not strictly true, but truer than it should be. It is a wonderful body of water — changeable as the days, moody and whimsical as a human being, but always impressive, in its broad stretch of varying, shifting color, its turbulence, its serenity, its smile and its frown. I have watched it for many a year, and never has it been the same on any two days.

Yes, but what about the building?

Not very much.

Isn't it high art?

Yes, 390-feet-high art — I am told.

Then the tower is very high art indeed?

You reason logically. By the way, speaking of the tower, it is said there was, originally, a difference of opinion as between the owner and the architect, that bid fair to become acute. It seems the owner wished one tower, the architect insisted upon four of them. [Fig. 1]

Indeed, that is interesting if true.

It may or may not be true, but in any event it is interesting, for, if you will examine with a little care, you will note how cleverly the architect has contrived to have his way.

You choose to be facetious at the expense of the architect.

Well, turn about is fair play. Is he not facetious at your expense and mine, at the expense of the owner, and of John Doe and Richard Roe — and, incidentally, of the Lake?

Yes, it looks a little that way. But is there not some even higher art, up yonder? What is the gilded thing upon the apex? It is the work of a sculptor, is it not?

An eminent sculptor, they say.

It seems to be a lady. But what is the lady doing up above the earth so high — like a diamond in the sky? Twinkle, twinkle, little star, how I wonder what you are! What is the lady doing?

Can't you see? She turns this way and that way, round and about, east and west, south and north — seeking ever to espy her features in an invisible mirror which ever eludes her pursuit.

Oh, she is a vain lady then?

No, she is but a lady-vane. You see her at the bath: Behold the water gushing merrily from the fountain in her hand. And in the other hand, with arm outstretched, she waves a caduceus, a real caduceus, a most real caduceus — the kind so well and favarobly known in the West.

But what does the figure symbolize anyway?

You mean, perhaps, what does the figure symbolize any old way. I do not precisely know, but I have heard that it represents Temperance lightening the load of Labor — or something of the sort. Still, you can't always tell what is going on in the mental depths of these "artistic fellers," sometimes they cannot tell themselves. It may be this is a case in point.

Then their ways are not our ways?

Tut, tut! Don't be pharisaical. Besides, by ways, you mean or should mean, highways, and his ways are her ways, hence her ways are his ways, and her ways are high ways, airy ways, fairy ways.

Would she not look more modern clad in some kind of suit? More "Chicagoey," so to say.

She is already acquiring a soot that is characteristically Chicagoan, and it bespeaks our civic pride, our refinement, our love of the beautiful, our "awakened public consciousness," as they say. Here we dote on everything that tends to charm, elevate and inspire. It is our nature, our gift, we cannot help it. But it does seem that we are verging toward puritanism in our austere insistence; we are, perhaps, going too far.

Surely you don't mean to imply —

Yes, I do. You think the contrary. But what you seem to see is but a mirage that disquiets your faculties. It is inconceivable that we would tolerate a state of affairs corresponding to your illusion. We have, here, too much enlightenment, too fine a sense of ultimate economy, and, in addition, too much self-respect. What you see is, in reality, but a most gratifying assurance of industry, thrift, public spirit and a high order of civilization.

Well, it all looks pretty barbarous to me, though I suppose you are right. But what about the building?

But, strange to say, we have an architecture here that is tending in the same or an opposite direction, and is evolving from itself evidences of what we may or may not become. It is very interesting; but when you look at it you must suffer no mirage,

1. Montgomery Ward (now Tower) Building, Chicago *(Chicago Architectural Photograph. Co.)*

2. Illinois Central Station, Chicago *(Courtesy, Illinois Central System)*

3. Marshall Field Store, Chicago *(Chicago Architectural Photograph. Co.)*

4. Marshall Field Wholesale Warehouse, Chicago *(Chicago Historical Society)*

you must see things just as they are or are not. In this way your thoughts will take on the clarity of our local atmosphere and you will have a correct start in your studies. For all depends on starting right, as the gunner said to the shell.

That's lucid enough — but what about this particular building? That's what I'm interested in.

Yes, so are the owners and the tax-gatherers. What part of the building do you mean?

Why, the rest of the building, to be sure.

The architect did not give the building any rest, but as to the remainder of the structure — it seems an ill-compounded salad, with a rather rancid New-Yorky flavor.

I can't see the connection between a building and a salad.

But I can see the connection between a salad and a building, for I know how buildings are made — as a rule.

Then, if your discourse is a salad, you are not using much oil. What do you think of the building by and large?

By and large, it cost much money.

That's pure vinegar, isn't it? Your salad is too peppery and too sour. You might omit the tabasco, use a milder vinegar, and add oil, it seems to me. It would improve the flavor quite a little, to my thinking.

II. Pathology

Persiflage is very well in its way, but don't you think you were unduly jocose, not to say severe, in discussing the building we looked at? I have been thinking about it for the past week and I can hardly agree with your point of view.

Exactly. All of which means, in plain English, that you believe you have been thinking — and that you do not at all know, or even suspect where my viewpoint is located. Nor does it signify much, at the present moment, whether you do or do not. The building under observation, or discussion, if you will, is but a mild type of a weird race of structures that mildew the land; and which we two are to study as a scientist would study a pest of any kind, that is to say, with a view to a remedy.

The particular building which was under consideration is, perhaps, considered from one viewpoint, merely a youthful befuddlement: from another, a striking illustration of the inability of an untrained mind to perceive and grasp a rare opportunity. Again change the view a little and it becomes an instructive example of that futility which goes with the misapplication of money. Again a little change in view, and we perceive the impotence of money when not impelled by carefully selected brains. But enough of this building. The broad question or phenomenon we are about to investigate is pathologic in its immediate aspect and even more deeply so in its spirit. It is a sad fact, but a hard fact, that American building is demoralized, and the architect not only mentally unhinged from his art, but socially and economically out of joint with his times. It is a curious condition that we see; a tangled skein that it will require patience and perseverance to unravel. The way is plain to me — how to make it plain to you is quite another matter. Yet the facts are there and we must look them squarely in the face.

So, willy-nilly, to perceive health, we must look through and beyond disease; to locate sanity, we must wander through the jungle, the swamps, the marshes and the arid places of confusion worse confounded. We must hold a steady course — guided by the sun in the daytime and the stars at night. There is no help for it; we are choking in miasm; we must find the way out to a pure air, or perish. We are rotting — we must purify; we are wasting in a profound torpor; we are growing senile before our time; we are like unto a wormy windfall. Alas! alack the day! to what depths have we descended! Into what a putrid mush have our minds deliquesced! Were we really born in sorrow? Was our infancy a bane? Is there no health in us? Or is there a vital and a saving grace, a force, a power that will regenerate? From the ugly worm shall there come a beauteous creature of the air? From this compost shall there grow and bloom the rose?

These are grave questions, my young friend, and hourly they become more grave. Whether we are going to the devil, or the devil is coming to us, I leave to the casuist. The times are surely pregnant — but what the new birth is to be, Heaven only knows.

So let us wander through the house wherein the mad will vote us mad. The soonest over, soonest done.

Really you are encouraging. The prospect is delightful, the outlook most attractive. Worms and bugs, marshes and jungles, madmen and lunatics, miasms and deliquescence, and things and lots of other things. Charming. I accept with pleasure. Let us sally gaily, blithely, forth. Cheer up, my friend, the worst is yet to come.

And so it is. You are precisely the young, "well-educated," self-confident and unsuspecting hopeful I assumed you to be when you came to me. Cheerfulness such as yours has been fatal, to others; but it is a good thing in a way, provided you don't hang yourself with it. So gird your loins, and strengthen your stomach. You may not feel so gay later on. You are like a sailor who has never been to sea. A life on the raging deep is all very well when you are used to it, but in the meanwhile? If you really believe you can wade into morbid psychology, up to the neck, without getting squeamish and creaky, and a bit uncertain as to the whereabouts of your own ego — well, try it — I'll keep from drowning, anyway.

You are exeeding kind, most gracious master.

And you are a flippant, but not wholly unattractive, young person. Our first building viewed is simply absent-minded, inarticulate and semi-demi-something-or-other. Let us draw near to the more vicious cases — those which, whether of ferocious or of milder aspect, are more deeply saturated with the virus that is threatening our social life, and urging its decay. We will, in so doing, unearth some strange responsibilities, some unsuspected metamorphoses — in short, a few plain and much-needed facts. This done — then will we seek to exalt the valleys, make the crooked straight, and the rough places plane.

III.   A Terminal Station

My son, here is the place — perhaps a unique spot on earth — holy in iniquity, where, to go in you go out, and to go out you go in; where to go up you go down, and to go down — you go up. All in all it seems to me the choicest fruit yet culled from that broad branch of the tree of knowledge, known as the public-be-damned style. In this instance the outward aspect of the style takes on the semblance of architecture, much as a speaking-tube conducts the voice. Let us regard it curiously. Its lucidity of thought is like unto the Stygian murk. Still it is characteristically, too characteristically, an American work; there can, alas, be no doubt of it. And, the study of our contemporaneous architecture, its origins, inspirations, animus, growth, trend and destiny constituting a part of our inquiry, the general and personal responsibilities and accountabilities resident behind its distorted and mendacious screens of brick and stone constituting a correlated part, let us pause before this object, this subject, this it; let us pause, and wonder. I say, it, because it is neuter. The masculine implies, in mental terms, that which is virile, forceful, direct, clear and straightforward, that which grasps and retains in thought; the feminine: intuitive sympathy, tact, suavity and grace — the qualities that soothe, elevate, ennoble and refine. But this it! This droll and fantastical parody upon logic; this finical mass of difficulties; this web of contradictions; this blatant fallacy; this repellent and indurated mess; this canker on the tongue of natural speech [Fig. 2]

Why does not the Lake engulf it? Why does not the fire from Heaven consume it? Is there no sane tribunal on earth? It must be that the Lake is too busy, and the Lord of Heaven is too busy; and that the people below are too busy — too busy to think, too patient to care, too nonchalant to trouble, too sordid to see, and too ignorant to smile. That must be why, in this instance, as in many another, the people are successfully flouted and damned, and not the building. When the great big American public runs its great big head into a great big noose, and the noose begins to tighten —

Please don't talk politics, Mr. Professor, I am not posted. Tell me, rather, something about the architecture of the structure, its exterior treatment, its style. I don't see what all this going in and out has to do with aesthetics.

I have already told you what its style is, and the exterior is merely a half-hearted, half-witted reflex of a vicious plan. It is but a local symptom of the constitutional affection.

And what is the affection, if I may ask? I don't seem to grasp your vocabulary. I don't know what you are driving at; I don't follow your reasoning — if there be any reasoning; I am quite at sea.

Yes, I remember. But don't let these little waves disturb you, for we are far as yet from the broad swell of the open sea. Disease is a departure, more or less great, from the normal health; and the disease, in this case, is implied in the name I have given to the style. Moreover, I did not start to talk politics to you, but sociology, which is quite another matter. Having received the conventional college and fine-art education of your day, it is a matter of course that you were not taught to observe what was going on in the great world in which your school was engulfed and sealed up tight, and in which school in consequence your own mind in turn was carefully and hermetically closed by your so-called teachers, after they had put into it whatever product of the past they thought it should contain. And thus, like any other sample of canned goods, you remain quietly on the shelf where you were put. Naturally you did not know, nor do you now know, what a man of unfettered observation and fair average intelligence might soon have learned to know and fully grasp, namely: *that every building you see is the image of a man whom you do not see.* That the man is the reality, the building its offspring. That the bricks, stones, steel and what-not came into place in response to an impulse; and the cause at work behind that impulse was mental, not physical: That the impulse came from a *man.* Now if the mind of that man has departed from the normal and is more or less perverted, more or less degenerate, so will the building, which is its image, be more or less pervert or degenerate.

I have told you that we must of necessity seek sanity by observing and noting the symptoms of insanity; that we must needs study disease, to discern the functions of health — because examples of the normal, healthful working of the corporate mind in the corporeal body of architecture are specifically so rare, in our so-called art, degeneracy of function and aspect so widespread, that we must, in self-preservation, searchingly look through the affected building to the affected mind, its parent; and, through the affected mind, to the affected social fabric of which it is a minute fibre.

In other words, if we would know why certain things are as they are in our disheartening architecture, we must look to the people; for our buildings, as a whole, are but a huge screen behind which are our people as a whole — even though specifically the buildings are individual images of those to whom, as a class, the public has delegated and entrusted its power to build.

Therefore, by this light, the critical study of architecture becomes not merely the direct study of an art — for that is but a minor phase of a great phenomenon — but, *in extenso,* a study of the social conditions producing it; the study of a newly-shaping type of civilization. By this light the study of architecture becomes naturally and logically a branch of social science; and we must bend our facilities to this bow if we would reach the mark.

Every building tells its story, tells it plainly. With what startling clearness it speaks to the attentive ear, how palpable its visage to the open eye, it may take you some little time to perceive. But it is all there, waiting for you; just as every great truth has waited through the centuries for the man with eyes to see.

But I can never learn to do this. I feel that it requires the eye of a poet.

Never fear. We are all poets. You do not see things now; but a little later on *things will begin to see you and beckon to you;* and then you will marvel greatly — but you will understand. So, when I tell you that this wretchedly tormented structure, this alleged railway station, is in the public-be-damned style, is degenerate and corrupt, I repeat to you only what the building says to me.

Yes, I understand.

Do you!

Well, perhaps not fully — but an inkling.

Bravo! If you possess even so much as an inkling you are richer than some eminent architects I know. And so if perforce we must study disease let us study it systematically. I cannot indicate to you at once the precise nature of that constitutional social disturbance of which our architecture is symptomatic; but little by little I will reveal to you the hidden causes and make clear and palpable to you the aspects and the nature of the malady.

Don't make it too sudden.

I couldn't if I would. It's an entirely new subject. The exposition will take time.

IV.   The Garden

Your suggestion that a building is a screen behind which a man is hiding is decidedly interesting and novel. It is really startling to reflect that every building one sees implies a definite personal responsibility and accountability on the part of someone not seen, probably the architect — although you have not said so. It puts architectural criticism in a decidedly new light; and I am anxious to see what you are going to do with it. I can feel, in a general way, that you intend to dissolve my old habits of thought; but just how, is not at all clear; in fact, it looks like an uphill undertaking. You will probably knock away all my props; but what in the world are you going to give me in the place of them? I feel uncomfortably interested, so far, and that is about all I can say. Still, in this theory of responsibility and accountability I feel a sense of personal insecurity — you might get after my future work, some day, and then, where would I be? I wish you would follow it up right away; so I can get my bearings as quickly as possible. Won't you?

Not now. Besides, personal responsibility and accountability is not a theory, but a latent fact. You are not prepared or fitted, by prior training, to follow, at once, so deep, abstruse and devious an investigation. I say deep and abstruse, not because I believe it, especially; rather the contrary — I think it all plain as a pikestaff. But it is somewhat the fashion, in modern thought, to make simple things complicated, to artificialize natural things, and to envelop all in a web of words and recherché reasons; to assume, too much, that man lives in a world apart, and that the little thing he calls his brain is independent of the universe; and to assume that the thing he calls liberty is a special sort of license-tag that enables him to go without a muzzle. Therefore, for a while, we may use the jargon of the day in the manner of the day, until such time as we may come to a fuller, simpler and more direct understanding of what simple words and simple things truly signify.

The "good gray poet"[1] says: "Nature neither hastens nor delays." So let us neither hasten nor delay, but go forward little by little, step by step. I shall not seek to instruct you or reconstruct you. I shall seek, only, to persuade the faculties which nature gave you at birth, and which, now, are partly shriveled, to revivify, to send out new roots, to grow, to expand, and to bring forth as nature intended.

You are to be, for me, the neglected but fallow field, under the broad sky of

1. A well-worn copy of Whitman was in Sullivan's library.

humanity: to be plowed, to turn under the weeds and bring up the subsoil; and then, harrowed for a while, to give it tilth. I will plant therein the seeds of many thoughts; but they must germinate in the fertile darkness of your own soul, under the beneficent influence of the compelling sun that shines for all, and sends the rain upon the just as upon the unjust. But I will also be the good gardener. And, when these tiny seeds put forth into the light their tender shoots and leaves, each after its kind, I will care for them, and water them with the water of life, drawn from nature's well-spring.

Thus shall you grow, and put forth branch and bud. The fragrance of your blooming shall be my reward, the fruit thereof shall be yours.

Is it not Canon Hole[2] who says: "He who would have beautiful roses in his garden, must have beautiful roses in his heart: he must love them well and always"? So, the flowers of your field, in so far as I am gardener, shall come from my heart where they reside in much good will; and my eye and hand shall attend merely to the cultivating, the weeding, the fungous blight, the noxious insect of the air, and the harmful worm below.

And so shall your garden grow; from the rich soil of the humanities it will rise up and unfold in beauty in the pure air of the spirit.

So shall your thoughts take up the sap of strong and generous impulse, and grow and branch, and run and climb and spread, blooming and fruiting, each after its kind, each flowing toward the fulfillment of its normal and complete desire. Some will so grow as to hug the earth in modest beauty; others will rise, through sunshine and storm, through drought and winter's snows year after year, to tower in the sky; and the birds of the air will nest therein and bring forth their young.

Such is the garden of the heart: so oft neglected and despised when fallow.

Verily, there needs a gardener, and many gardens.

And such is youth — receptive as a soil of virgin mold: The ever-renewed humus of untold ages of the past: the wondrous, mysterious and prophetic past filled with glimpses of smiling sunshine and storms of bitter tears. Into its depths I will look with you, my friend, as soon as you shall have truly grasped, and held, and owned, one flitting, vital moment of the present.

So let us go our way, slowly and surely, step after leisurely step.

No strenuous folly shall be ours; no kill-joy haste; no fretful, peevish grasping after life, that brings the bitter chaff of moral death.

The French have a saying: "Time will not consecrate that in which she has been ignored." Bear this admonition ever in mind for it is deeply true.

And so, while I say we will neither hasten nor delay, let us not delay. All of which is summed up in the proverbs:

> Haste makes waste.
> Delays are dangerous.
> He who hesitates is lost.
> Be bold yet prudent.

2. Samuel Reynolds Hole (Dean of Rochester Cathedral), author of *A Book about Roses, How to Grow and Show Them*: first published 1869, it went into many editions. Sullivan was an enthusiastic rose-grower, and had nearly a hundred varieties at his place in Ocean Springs, Mississippi.

V. An Hotel

I wonder if you know, Professor, what this particular building is.

You do well to say particular — for it is made of particles. Substantives and adjectives are lacking — verbs, especially, are lacking. It is all thes, ands, ifs, buts: it is all connectives, that connect nothing; qualificatives, that qualify nothing; prepositions, that prepose nothing; conjunctives, that conjoin nothing; exclamations, that exclaim nothing. It is all inflection, where there is nothing inflected; conjugation where there is not a verb; declension, without the noun. Then there are thrown in, for makeweights, bits of grammar, pronunciation, rhetoric, prosody, orthoepy, syllabication, etymology, punctuation, etc., but no syntax — surely no syntax. It is "perfectly fine"; "awfully lovely"; it's "just grand" — and all about what? Nothing! It's the young miss in architecture; in short, it is the Imperial Hotel. [Fig. 3]

What an idea! The Imperial Hotel is in New York, and we are in Chicago.

And so we are! How curious! Then it must be the Imperial's long-lost child.

No. I happen to know it's a department store, and not at all a hotel — never was a hotel. So you are on the wrong track.

Not at all. I say it's a hotel. You may think it a department store, if you will.

But I know positively that it is a department store, and so that ends the discussion.

On the contrary, it begins one.

But look at the lower windows. You see the merchandise displayed, do you not?

I look at the building and I see other merchandise displayed, which might, perhaps, hearken back to an architectural department store. But that, for the moment, is neither here nor there. I tell you it's a hotel — or even an hotel, if you prefer.

You speak in riddles, and in plain contradiction of the facts.

My young friend, you do not speak by the card. Look at the building with your own eyes. Surely, if it were a department store, all masonry would be reduced to a minimum, and there would be an expanse of glass for light and display. If you doubt it, there are several department store buildings hereabout that will serve to illustrate my meaning. So, you see, you are proven in error by the testimony of the structure itself. Therefore, if the building be anything nameable, it is, as I have said, a hotel.

Oh, no! I see where you are misled. It is a department store, surely enough, but there are offices above.

No, my young friend, there are not offices above, that is an illusion; you are misinformed. The structure is a hotel. It is not even a department store with offices, combined, as you would have me believe. It is a hotel; the lower two stories of which have, probably, been rented to some merchant.

What nonsense! I tell you, emphatically, that there are offices in the building. I have been in some of them and so I know. Why do you persist in denying a self-evident proposition?

On the contrary, I am maintaining a self-evident proposition. Were it an office building, it would suggest that function. There would be that regular and equable spacing of windows, that general suggestion of business and business housing, which would be unmistakable. There are a number of well-arranged office structures hereabout, and not one of them has this somnolent, irresolute disposition of its masses.

This, manifestly, is a building to sleep in, to rest in, perhaps to eat in. It suggests the drowsy, not the busy, god.

Well —

Well?

I begin to see a light. Yes, I begin to see a light — not altogether a pleasant light, either.

My young friend, a sudden light hurts the unaccustomed eyes. But as the light grows stronger, and the eye, gradually, clearer and steadier, you will see eventually what I see: A vanishing illusion called a building, and a dawning reality — the positive substance — a smirking imposition.

If I have taken the trouble to discuss this structure with you, it is not, be assured, for its own account, for that is too trivial, but because it stands, for our purpose, as the type of a large class of structures, fortunately, for us, more rampant in the East than in the West, which represent what I might denominate the current jargon of architecture: the incapacity of the insufficiently educated, the unleavened, the half-baked, to express in simple well-chosen language the casual, current experiences of life.

This particular building is, to be sure, not characteristic of the West. It lacks, utterly, western frankness, directness — crudity if you will. It is merely a weak-rooted cutting from the eastern hot house; and it languishes in the open air. An expert gardener would not have done so foolish a thing.

To be sure, in mere money outlay, it cost dollars enough, and for that very reason, if for no other, its finality seems cheap-John in motif. For of what use is money alone without a chastened guiding spirit? It merely serves, uncontrolled, to make its owner ridiculous and pitiful.

To say, then, that this building is canting and hypocritical, is to couch our definition in mildest terms.

Against the malice of such structures I would forfend your untrained, untried judgment, your too-confiding, cocksure nature. For such structures are treacherous of spirit. They are the Judases: they betray their Lord for pieces of silver.

VI.   An Oasis

Let us pause, my son, at this oasis in our desert. Let us rest awhile beneath its cool and satisfying calm, and drink a little at this wayside spring.

For, when we fret amid the barren wastes of meanness and of littleness of soul, wherefrom arise strident, harsh and paltry sounds, a rich, sombre chord of manliness, as this is, comes the more awelcome since we have, as yet, afar to go, 'cross many weary stretches.

You mean, I suppose, that here is a good piece of architecture for me to look at — and I quite agree with you.

No; I mean, here is a *man* for you to look at. A man that walks on two legs instead of four, has active muscles, heart, lungs and other viscera; a man that lives and breathes, that has red blood; a real man, a manly man; a virile force — broad, vigorous and with a whelm of energy — an entire male. [Fig. 4]

I mean that stone and mortar, here, spring into life, and are no more material and sordid things, but, as it were, become the very diapason of a mind rich-stored with harmony.

I mean that —

I see; you mean that it's simple, dignified and massive.

I mean, just now, that you are assive, priggified and a simpleton.

But I see defects in it —

And I see your eye has a mote in it. In Heaven's name, what defects are you justified in seeing in so fine a work? Do you put yourself in the scales with a mountain? Will you estop the wind? Would you hold back a tree from growing?

But, truly, has it not defects?

Forsooth it has. And so has the bark of an ancient tree; and so has the bark of an ancient dog, if you will: but the faithfulness is there, the breath of life is there, an elemental urge is there, a benign friendliness is there. Would you peck at the features of the moon, and ignore her gracious light that makes a path for you in the forest? Go to, my young friend, go to!

Then I was right in calling it massive, dignified and simple?

You used three big words, and, in so doing, made three empty sounds.

Ah, I see, you are provoked because I interrupted you while you were speaking to me.

Evidently I was not speaking to you.

To whom then?

I thought aloud. You happened to be present.

Why do you say that?

Because you heard nothing.

Ah, now I begin —

You are a wise young man, in your day and generation, and, in token of your progress, we will resume amiable relations.

But tell me truly, why do you give such high praise to this building when you have so rebuked others? I must confess that, in my ignorance, viciousness, baseness, and all that, as you would probably say, I don't see anything so wonderful about it — certainly nothing calling for hysteria. On the other hand, I take it for granted that you know whereof you speak. But why do you show this partiality? It seems to me a work that almost anyone with a good head and reasonable taste could have produced — where is the wonder?

The wonder is that it exists in fact, and not in talk. We hear much of greatness, we see little of it. It is for this little, this little-much that I give thanks. I have meted justice to the other buildings, in their iniquity; I would give justice to this one, in its justice. Where I find inhumanities, I scourge — where I find humanity, I bless. Where I find vanity, I prick, and where I find corruption, I will use the knife. As you say, the structure is massive, dignified and simple. But it is much more, unless you make each word as deep as a well, and as full. It is so much more that I have called it an oasis.

Four-square and brown, it stands, in physical fact, a monument to trade, to the organized commercial spirit, to the power and progress of the age, to the strength and resource of individuality and force of character; spiritually, it stands as the index of a mind, large enough, courageous enough to cope with these things, master them, absorb them and give them forth again, impressed with the stamp of large and forceful personality; artistically, it stands as the oration of one who knows well how to choose his words, who has somewhat to say and says it — and says it as the outpouring of a copious, direct, large and simple mind.

Therefore have I called it, in a world of barren pettiness, a male; for it sings the song of procreant power, as the others have squealed of miscegenation. So, here, with you beside me, "singing in the wilderness," a lonely song, I would place a modest wreath upon the monument of him who stood alone, an august figure in his art, and now, across the bridge invisible made vital by these stones, breathes forth a strain of noble poesy.

My dear sir, pardon me —

It is well to feel that way now and then, for it helps to bring the mind again to its center when it has suffered aberration. Buildings such as this, and there are not many of them, stand as landmarks, as promontories, to the navigator. They show when and where architecture has taken on its outburst of form as a grand passion — amid a host of stage-struck-wobbling mockeries. This is "good for the body and good for the soul"; "it filters and fibres the blood." It refreshes and strengthens, because it is elemental, bespeaks the largeness and the bounty of nature, the manliness of man.

But really, in seeking to do justice to buildings, have you not forgotten to do justice to me? You began to speak of this building in a lofty strain — way over my head. And then, because I could not at once follow, you said unkind things. First you assume that I know nothing of the architectural art, and then, of a sudden, you assume that I know everything of it. Now is this not as palpable an injustice as it is a palpable error?

It is not an injustice because I wish you well, and would do well by you — and because it serves as a means to an end. It is an error, certainly, in a sense, but not of the kind you suppose. As a matter of fact, I should bear constantly in mind the slipshod education you have received, the superficiality of it, and how woefully it handicaps you; I should bear in mind that you know, not merely nothing of the architectural art, but, worse than that, that your knowledge is an obnoxious minus quantity; and I should ever bear in mind, also, that this is not your fault, so much as it is your misfortune.

But can you not teach me the real Art?

I don't know. I will try. Realities are images very difficult to awaken in a mind nurtured in an atmosphere of unreality and falsehood. Personally, I would rather, any day, try to teach architecture to a clod-hopper than to the over-cultivated man. One may have a heart, the other may not. With the one, I can be patient; it is difficult to be patient with the other — his opportunities have been so much the greater; his vanity is what eats his heart out. But you are young; and while there is youth there is still hope, for there is still heart. So we shall see what we shall see. Be of good cheer.

VII. The Key

So far, we have dealt, chiefly, with the physiognomy of each building: its external aspect considered as a revelation of character and taken as a key in our hands wherewith first to unlock a somewhat rusty door, called architect, and thereafter to note what lies in the open world beyond him. In other words, to observe, at our convenience, in how far, if we choose to put it that way, the architect represents or misrepresents society at large; what his plain duty is, if any; what society has an equitable right to demand and expect of him, if anything; what is the nature of that particular trust, if there be such a trust, which society places in his hand — the talent of old — and to what extent he takes on definition as faithful or false to that trust.

In a democracy, and by the light of democratic institutions, such an inquiry is bound, if logically conducted, to terminate in one of two conclusions: the one, vital and optimistic, the other cynical.

The materials for such an investigation are completely at hand. The character of our architecture has defined itself unmistakably, and the time is ripe to reckon with it. You have come into your architectural career at a most critical period, a period in which the forces that make for growth or decay are in strenuous but delicate balance. Whichever way our architecture goes, so will our country go; or, if you prefer, whichever way our country goes, so will go our architecture; it is the same proposition stated in different ways. We are at that dramatic moment in our national life wherein we tremble evenly between decay and evolution, and our architecture, with strange fidelity, reflects this equipoise. That the forces of decadence predominate in quantity there can be no doubt; that the recreative forces now balance them by virtue of quality, and may eventually overpower them, is a matter of conjecture. That the bulk of our architecture is rotten to the core, is a statement which does not admit of one solitary doubt. That there is in our national life, in the genius of our people, a fruitful germ, and that there are a handful who perceive this, is likewise beyond question. All this and more, I shall strive to make clear to you as we go on.

Building materials do not come into their places, in a structure, of their own initiative, or by accident. The tree does not quit the forest of its own accord, nor does the stone split itself from the mother-ledge, and leave the place of its quarry to go to number so and so, such a street. At the moment the tree in its forest starts and quivers at the first stroke of the axe, at the moment the first blow is struck on the rock that has slumbered through the ages, at that moment the human element makes its entrance into that absorbing drama we call architecture, and the dénouement is ever as various, as strange, as involved, as is human character.

I might go on for hours, tracing step by step, breath by breath, span by span, the simple elements of earth touched by many hands, and by the power of steam, slowly converging and shaping in orderly sequence, in time and place, toward so and so street — there to make a beginning and an ending of a beautiful or an untoward building. And you might say: How curious, how dramatic, how pictorial, how full of human interest: And you would end in an entertaining but inadequate view. For such a statement would be akin to that of the novelist, the romancer, the playwright — dealing with picturesque externals, parading surface causes, ignoring hidden ones. For the true cause of a building is not external, but internal. It lies, proximately, in the mind of one man, and that man the architect. If that mind is normal, the building will be normal; if the mind is awry, the building will be awry. Indeed, whatever the mind is, the building will be its image, regardless of materials, regardless of labor, regardless of cost.

But my aim is not that of romancer, or rosewater critic. I wish to show you realities in all their ugliness, and then to show you other realities, in all their beauty. Or, if you prefer, first I would dissolve for you this wretched illusion called American architecture, and then cause to awaken in your mind the reality of a beautiful, a sane, a logical, a human, living art of your day; an art of and for democracy, an art of and for the American people of your own time.

This may not prove an easy task; but the charm of your youth, the brightness of a possible future, will stimulate me throughout its undertaking.

So, while I must go slowly, carefully, methodically, you must be all eyes and ears, quick to observe, absorb and retain.

Try never to forget, from now on, that everything, each thing, you see and hear, has a double meaning: first, its objective or outward meaning or aspect; second, its subjective or inner meaning and significance. Remember the word, significance, it stands for that which we seek.

Nature, in its visible, objective forms, impinges on the eyes its aspects of beauty of form and color: Here are the elements of earth and air shaped by the delicate hand of time; but the subtle charm of these externals would be incomplete did they not further signify, and suggest, an internal, a subjective, a creative impulse of origin divine.

So the materials of a building are but the elements of earth removed from the matrix of nature, and reorganized and reshaped by force; by force mechanical, muscular, mental, emotional, moral and spiritual. If these elements are to be robbed of divinity, let them at least become truly human.

All the varied elements of human nature and its surroundings concur in a special fashion in the individual, and form what we call character. Character is that — in the technical language of mechanics — which we would style the resultant of all the forces at work in an individual man, and it predetermines the amount and the direction of his energy.

This resultant is by no means a straight line, but rather it varies with the individual, from the extremes of crookedness and sinuosity toward the mean of a relatively simple curve.

The simpler the sweep of this imaginary curve, the greater the simplicity and strength of character — the more nearly do they parallel the elemental forces and movements of nature.

Still, however wandering may be its course, this resultant eventually, like a great river, debouches at some definite spot and there it delivers its output.

To explore a river and know it thoroughly, we may begin at the thousands of widely separated well-springs which flow away in rivulets that conjoin to make its branches, and follow these as they conjoin to make its trunk, and this trunk, on, to its delta; or, we may begin at the delta or estuary, and follow up the trunk, the branches, the branchlets, until we shall have sought out the minutest headwaters.

Character is a large word, full of significance; no metaphoric river can more than hint at its meaning. Character is not confined to the individual, it defines, also, the municipality, the state, the nation; and, inversely, it trends toward the minutest qualities and quantities that we can ponder.

When we would search out its ever-subdividing, ramifying branches, we become lost at last in a maze of attenuated complexities. When we follow the branches toward the main stream, we float agreeably toward simplification.

And so shall our course lie: up-stream, against the current, down-stream with it. We will broadly trace physical appearances to their moral causes, and moral or social impulses to their manifestations in brick and stone.

We will seek and find the architect through the meaning of his executed work, not through his words, gestures, or suavities.

Likewise we shall search out an architecture based upon a normal, a real architect — even if he be a figure of speech.

In so doing, we shall confine ourselves to the simple, the natural, the reasonable, the very practical and human.

You shall see and judge for yourself, which comes the nearer to your heart and mind, the decadent lie that is now abroad — a rampant anarchy and social evil — or the wholesome truth toward the threshold of whose abode I will guide you — the threshold of that hidden, modest temple that we call the heart, that heart whose pulse is human but whose impulse is divine.

VIII. Values

How will you contrive to make your subjective my objective? How will you shape up something tangible for me? How will I get a footing in the fog?

In many ways. For the present let us take a single illustration — that of values.

Everbody knows, or thinks he does, what value means. Crudely it is expressed in Dollars and Cents: we say, such a thing is worth so many Dollars; and there, usually, the matter rests. Also, we regard other things as of value, and these values we recognize in medals, diplomas, eulogiums or monuments. To an heroic fireman we give a medal, and thus we express the value, to the community, of his act of devotion. To the memory of a great poet we set up a monument; to this man, we give fame; to that one, reverence; to the other, love. And so it goes, through the range of values and compensations. Theoretically it is fine. In practice it is not always so fine, for some men have been crucified, others burned at the stake, for wishing well to their fellows.

Still, taking it all in all, there is a general sense in the community that there are certain values which money cannot and does not measure; certain services rendered, of which money is not the impelling cause, or the mechanism of exchange, or the standard of estimate. And it is tacitly felt and recognized that such services are of great and positive value to the community: that they add to its wealth, if wealth be taken in its broad, comprehensive sense.

In its scantest sense, the value of a great painting might be computed on the cost of the canvas, the paint, and a reasonable every-day allowance for the manual labor of applying the paints to the canvas. Yet everybody knows that this is not so. Everybody knows and feels that the great painter has imparted to the paints a value that they did not before possess. That he has transferred to them something of himself, and something of the world. That he has made subjective what was before objective.

This subjectivity is his art. By virtue of it he has sublimated the material.

This added value we call genius, talent, skill, as the case may be.

Eventually this added subjective value comes under the measure of the standard of all current values — money — but, too often, only when the author of it, the giver of it, the would-be benefactor of his race, has passed under the scrutiny of that final measurer and equalizer of all mankind — the sod.

So with the poet and his poems made of printers' ink and paper.

So the musician and his score.

So with the sculptor and his marble block.

So with the soul-inspiring orator, who breathes in the common, physical air and gives it forth, a new, an awakening message to Man.

And so all real values are subjective: all objective values are unreal; they dissolve, under analysis, into subjective value after subjective value, and the residuum, if ever we reach it, is not what man made but what nature gave: and what nature gives is never objective — it resolves itself step by step, remove after remove, into the infinite creative mind.

Now, shall a building be held to differ from these other things, my list of which is meagre, to be sure? Shall this manifest rule hold for other things, and not hold for buildings? By virtue of what wrinkle in the popular mind are buildings to be held exempt? To say the least, is it not strange? There certainly is no doubt concerning the physical fact of such exemption: witness the buildings, witness the people.

Any good builder can tell you the value of a building in Dollars and Cents. He will figure up the cost of materials and the cost of labor, and the salary and incidental account — and give you the total. He has done his duty, you accept his statement and take it for granted that the matter is closed: and why not? — you have it in Dollars!

Now comes the critic and says: "Here, let me see those Dollar marks and let me see the building: let me take your figures, and confront the building with them. Yes, very good: this is the value of material of every kind, and labor of every kind, but where is the architect? I see no entry, except his fee. I put your cost in one scale of my balance, and the building in the other, but see — the beam is not level — something is lacking either in your accounting or in the building. Who is straddling the scales — who is pressing with his foot? It is a man. I find no man in your account, I find only a name; but I feel the man, I know he is there. Your accounts do not balance the building. Your values must be revalued — your method is crude; it is unwisely selfish. You see no further than the end of your nose. If your nose were longer, you would see that much further away from yourself. Have you paid your architect for destroying? Has he added, and you do not know it? Do you balance architecture with a sneer, on your accounting? What is your own value? How much are you worth a pound avoirdupois? Oh, you have a value, have you? The question is impertinent, is it? What is your value outside of your bank account? Who values you, and why? What are you good for, when you are sifted down, and your externals removed? What is your worth? What have you ever done? What can you do? Who are you? What are you? Why are you on earth? Do you think if you were an architect you would be more, or less, valuable than you are? If so, why? What are you? What is an architect? What is a building? What is a Dollar? Answer me these things and let me weigh your answer in the scale I hold in my hand — a scale in which I ask only that you balance one little milligram of humanity."

Are these questions fair, or are they not? Are they in order, or are they not? Are they practical, or are they not? Are they economical, or are they not? Are they social, or are they not? Are they democratic, or are they not?

You may think about these things at your leisure. The buildings are there, for good or for ill — they cannot run away; they cannot conveniently avoid investigation. And, if the building is there, the architect is there with it; he cannot escape either. Little by little we will ferret him out. There is no hurry.

Very good. But tell me: When you say; The value of a building, do you really lay more stress on the subjective value than on the Dollar value?

On both. For human nature determines that subjective value, sooner or later, becomes money value; and the lack of it, sooner or later, money loss. The subjective value is far the higher, by far the more permanent; but money value is inseparable from the affairs of life; to ignore it would be moonshine.

IX.   A Roman Temple   (1)

Seldom, my son, is a building gifted with so romantic, so strange a history as is this one before which we now stand. On this account I have led you here. For, as I shall presently discover to you, a gem — unsuspected — has fallen among us, from the overflowing treasury of our noble art, and rests, all unvalued, here, among the heedless throng, in the very heart of this great Chicago, so renowned as the center of a vast contiguous territory. Strangely as this statement may jar upon your super-sensibilities — you who have been cradled in the culture of older and wiser parts of our land, and have brought with you here the very nectar of the sweet flower of learning — it is yet nevertheless so true an utterance that but a little time will fully prove its verity.

It seems that not so long ago, in fact I might say recently, a group of ancient Romans by some miracle of cadaverous introspection, became resurrect and incarnate as of yore, in the very proper flesh itself.

Following the trend of modern emigration they, in due time, reached our country's shore, and, westward wending, over mountains, through deep valleys, crossing many streams and many fertile prairies, made their way to Northern Illinois, where, settling in the country immediately adjacent to Chicago's western limb and quite close to the propinquity thereof, they made, of this wanderer's abode, their new, their chosen home.

To its citizens, in due time, and in consonance with the traditions of their own sunny land, the cradle of melody, they unwound and unraveled the mysteries of that organic art, which is theirs by right of birth and by just inheritance.

Speedily they amassed wealth thereby; and soon waxing richer and richer, they determined, in thankfulness of heart, and in grateful recognition of the providence of their guardian deity — Simia by name — who had so generously prospered them, to give, each, of his hoarded means a part, wherewith, as a people, to erect a temple to his glory, his honor and his power.

Indeed, in the very heart of this great modern city, amid its strenuous sights and sounds and odors, they resolved to rear a temple to their pagan god: a fane in whose silentious hall this solemn austere deity might brood and rule in fateful isolation, and in the splendor of a fatidic serenity.

Among their number was, it seems, a master-builder of lofty mind and high resolve; a man full many a cubit high in mental stature: and in his hands they placed the making of the god's great home, charging him with weighty words and mystic ceremonies.

Among them, too, were master-craftsmen, hewers of stone and workers of bronze, and many cunning artisans of divers sorts.

So gathered they together, filled with a certain high resolve.

And so the temple was created by its own people; blood of their blood, flesh of their flesh, bone of their bone, and gold of their gold; the work of their sturdy muscles and of their militant spirits, according truly with immutable laws.

So stands it now.

How fortunate, how godsped are we, to be here on this their ceremonial day, and at the very solemn hour that draws their rite unto its close. We may not enter. Surely we may not profane. For such holy precinct shall be doubly sacred to us in our reverence for this unison of old and new. So let us here abide awhile, until such time — their ceremony having reached its ordained ending, and its just and solemn closure — that they come forth, clad in toga, sandals, and their bound-up brows radiant as of yore.

It is no common boon to see a Roman temple and its Roman throng consent to make a western holiday.

So be not over-anxious, but await, with patient eye, and heart attuned responsive
to this harmony of twenty centuries agone —

What in the world you are talking about I don't know. I have let you go on, thinking you were maudlin; or that, perhaps, it was some more subjectivity. But come. Let
me lead you away. You are ill. Your eye wanders. This is no Roman temple built
by a motley crowd of organ-grinders — spook-creatures of your fertile brain — it's
a bank; just a plain, ordinary, every-day American bank, full of cold hard cash and
other cold things. I know all about it, I read all about it in the papers. I saw it built
and I know the president. And, as to the nectar of some flower or other that you say
I brought here, that's only a little less Greek to me than the bank is Roman. [Fig. 5]

Stay! Young man! If I dream, these money-people dream! How did they get into
the temple? Was their architect a dreamer too? Have I the trance, or has he the
trance, or have they it? Have we a trance, or have they all and we all lost our bearings? Who is sane, and who is walking on the earth, they or I, you or I, they or you?
Methinks the world is topsy-turvy when such eerie things occur. Who is who? And
what is what? Where are the axes of the earth? Which way does it turn? Where
hides the path we seek? Where lurks elusively the tiny spark of sanity?

But the president of the bank is a smart man. He wouldn't have had a bank like
this if it hadn't been the right thing to have. A good business man doesn't do such
things; it wouldn't be plain, hard common sense if he did. You are away off this
time.

How did the hard common-sense man come to think of a Roman temple? How did
common sense manage to get in its deadly work?

Why, easy enough. His architect made a picture of what *he thought* was a Roman
temple, and showed it to the banker, telling him, on the side, that Roman temples
were rather the go now for banks, and the banker bit. That's plain enough, isn't it?

Yes, but it's queer; singularly queer; very curiously abstruse. Still, it's lucid, and
clear as it is a pert.

It *is* lucid? Well, if *you* say it's lucid, after your headache, I'm going home. Perhaps *I'm* a bit off.

Yes, it is lucid now; for the banker in selecting, became, in a measure, the architect. Wise people hold that to select an architect wisely is the next thing to building
wisely. To select unwisely, therefore, is to share in the ultimate folly, as we see, and
goes to show what folly is still shyly hiding here and there.

Well, that may be so, but what are you going to do about it?

I am going to insist that the banker wear a toga, sandals, and conduct his business
in the venerated Latin tongue — oral and written.

Then you don't like Roman temples?

With the ancient Romans I should say they were rather apropos. But I do not
relish Roman-temple banks; and the common-sense-Roman-temple bank particularly
disagrees with me.

Well, I suppose they can make just as much money in any old kind of a bank;
although I guess his royal highness thinks this is real style, eh?

My young friend! Truly I deprecate your freedom of speech; yet your activity of
thought has a certain spice, of which, I trust, time may temper the pungency.

37. *A Roman Temple* (1)

Well, it is to laugh, anyway!

Yes, I fear it is. But what a woeful come-down from my dream. What a singular débâcle of a vision, old in story, rich in wonder, of a people proud in conquest, wise in laws — what a deep descent to this frenetic pigeon-house you call a bank.

Yes, but you didn't say so in the beginning.

I was dreaming — and you woke me.

X.   A Roman Temple   (2)

Even after what you have said, I really don't see why, as a matter of common privilege, a man shouldn't make an imitation Roman temple if he wishes to do so. Isn't it, after all is said and done, a question of temperamental selection, of scholarship, of individual taste?

I don't either, if he will make it in his own back yard. If it is for his own private use, gratification or amusement, I see no objection. But, when he puts it on the people's highway, and labels it modern American architecture, there are those who will cry humbug, and, what is worse, will prove it. Furthermore, the true architectural art, that art toward which I would lead you, rests, not upon scholarship, but upon human powers; and, therefore, it is to be tested, not by the fruits of scholarship, but by the touch-stone of humanity. Taste is one of the weaker words in our language. It means a little less than something, a little more than nothing; certainly it conveys no suggestion of potency. It savors of accomplishment, in the fashionable sense, not of power to accomplish in the creative sense. It expresses a familiarity with what is *au courant* among persons of so-called culture, of so-called good form. It is essentially a second-hand word, and can have no place in the working vocabulary of those who demand thought and action at first hand. To say that a thing is tasty or tasteful is, practically, to say nothing at all. But, the word humbug is only a little less strong than the word fraud; and to say of the imitation Roman temple that it is a specious imposition is to put the charge mildly. We make a great to-do when a bank officer diverts some of its funds to his own use — we call that misappropriation, defalcation, abuse of confidence, betrayal of trust, and all sorts of harsh names, and we put him in the penitentiary if he is not clever enough to keep out of it. But when a man betrays a trust that the people at large have placed in his hands — a specific trust that is expressed in the word architect, we call his weakness taste, scholarship, temperamental selection, and all sorts of euphemistic names. In reality there is no valid moral distinction to be made between the men. It is the capacity correctly to weigh the values at stake that is at fault. What is everybody's business has become nobody's business; and this incapacity, this indifference, it is the function of the critic to rectify; otherwise architecture, as a fine art, goes to the bargain counter, and the people become merely shoppers; and so, through bargain and sale, values must tend ever downward, and the buyers ever grow more sordid, until, all settle at last into the mire of democracy gone wrong, and the people learn, at last, to their cost and chagrin, what it means to have leaders who betray them. For such is the course of democracy — either downward or upward. The stability and the value of democracy depend, when the last word is said, upon the fidelity of those to whom the people delegate their powers.

Well, that begins to sound like business. I thought, at first, that your point of view was personal, but I begin to understand that it is not; it is broader. So, I take it, you hold that the modern imitation of a Roman temple is not a good thing under any circumstances?

Certainly it is not; especially in America. Scholarship has its uses, its most excellent uses. But when scholarship becomes a fixed habit of mind, that very habit unquestionably enfeebles creative power. It is well that we should know what the Roman temple was in fact, as nearly as we, through archaeological inquiry, can arrive at it. But the deepest reach of our scholarship will reveal only this: that the Roman temple was a part of Roman life — not of American life; that it beat with the Roman pulse, was in touch with Roman activities; and that it waned with Roman glory — it died a Roman death. The Roman temple can no more exist in fact on Monroe Street, Chicago, U. S. A., than can Roman civilization exist there. Such a structure must of necessity be a simulacrum, a ghost.

Of course you and I know well enough that the reason why the bank building is an imitation Roman temple is because it is easy and cheap to make that sort of thing — but the people at large do not know it. They do not know how easy it is for the architect to turn to a book of plates, pick out what he wants, and pass it on to a draughtsman who will chew this particular architectural cud for a stipend. They do not know that when it is done, and is lauded, by its alleged architect, as in the Roman style, that, in reality, it is in the hand-me-down style. When done it's cheap, and it is as slovenly as it is cheap. Such things are false enough when they are done in the spirit of highest, most careful, most industrious scholarship. But as for this bargain-Friday performance, this commercial smear, what is to be said otherwise than in terms befitting so crumpled and soiled a by-product.

I begin to surmise that you don't quite like the imitation Roman temple. In fact, you have almost said so, in a roundabout way.

Furthermore, if the pseudo-Roman temple were good for any one thing American, it must, *ipso facto*, be good for anything and everything American, because American means American, and expresses the genius of the people. But Roman does not mean American, never did mean American, never can mean American. Roman was Roman; American is, and is to be, American. The architect should know this without our teaching, and I suspect that he does know it very well in his unmercenary moments. The public would know it instinctively if they were not continually bamboozled and wheedled by architects and thus bereft of their sense of fitness; and so could become free to regard the archtect in any other light than his self-made one of peddler of fashions.

Now where does the responsibility justly lie? Who is to be censured in this particular case? Is it to be the banker who pays for the building and feels no further concern unless it be a pride in his expenditure and a pleasurable blush as he preens his sense of public spirit? Or is it to be the public who delegate the power and the function to build and let it go at that? Or is it to be the architect? Who is creating a false impression, who is holding up a misguiding standard, who is demoralizing popular education — the banker, the public, or the architect?

Who is wound about with left-handed notions of what the architectural art is in reality?

Is architecture a plaything, or is it a great force — a revelation of human character and an inspiration? Is it a remnant, or is it a whole cloth from which we are to make for us new garments? Is it human, now, or is it post-human? Has it a foundation, or has it none? Is it a part of human utterance, is it a phase of universal speech, or is it dumb? Is the art I advocate to be built upon the sands of books, upon the shoals of taste and scholarship, or is it to be founded upon the rock of Character?

What I say to you is either witless or significant. To discern which it may be, we must lock horns with our conditions — we must either throw or be thrown. So, open your eyes that you may see with the clarity of the spirit that which is of the spirit. To half close your eyes is to belittle the creative power of man. Touch not with feeble finger the exuberant pulse of democracy. And do not throw a noble art into the sewer.

But let me tell you now that, to grasp masterfully, you must first feel the surge of psychic power; to realize your responsibilities you must first truly know them.

To know your art you must broaden your sympathies, not constrict them; you must nurture your mind, not forsake it.

Strive then, so that, when your time comes, you may not be a misfit in your day and generation.[1]

XI.   A Department Store

This time, it is evident, my son, that we are looking at a department store. No one can mistake it for a hotel, an office building, a railway station, or a bank — and yet it is not trigged out in the guise of a Roman temple. Its purpose is clearly set forth in its general aspect and the form follows the function in a simple, straightforward way. The structure is a logical, though somewhat bald, statement of its purpose, and an unmistakable though not wholly gratifying index of the business conducted within its walls. This is a great deal to say of any building at any time; it is high praise in these days of architectural distraction. Its directness of statement is its chief virtue. Its comparative freedom from verbiage causes it in a manner to approach eloquence of form. Its architect evidently proceeded — if he proceeded in any manner approaching consciousness — by a process of elimination. He left his favorite "architecture,"

1. A letter to the editor concerning this article was the first, and apparently the only, evidence of public reaction printed in the periodical. This communication and Sullivan's reply are to be found in Appendix B.

for the time being, in his portfolios — which is a clever thing to do. He used the eraser on his mind instead of on his paper, which is another clever thing to do. He looked a little before he leaped, which is cleverest of all. Such things, such acts, such relatively sane mental processes are refreshing and uncommon. If they are accidental, let us welcome the accident. I make my bow and my compliments.

It seems to me you are piling it on pretty thick. It's a nice plain simple building, I admit; but I don't like that ornament up there by the —

No matter about that ornament up there by —. We are a long way from discussing ornament — if ever we discuss it. Ornament, when creative, spontaneous, is a perfume. It is, to change the figure, the smile of a sentiment, the last line in the sonnet. But we are not now discussing sentiment, we are considering common sense.

But, granted that, I don't like the proportions of some of the upper stories, do you?

No matter about the proportions of some of the upper stories. We are not discussing proportion. But I may say, in passing, proportion is a result not a cause. It may be imprisoned for a while in academic ratios, in rules of thumb; it does not reside in them of its free will. It has its becoming in much more delicate origins: it is a thing, not made, but begotten. It is a creature of the open. It is shy; it fears the bookish man. So, no more of proportion for the time. Let us stick to our text, which is to be: Function and Form.

In its simplest applicable terms this dictum means merely a right start and a right finish. The architect has here shown sufficient common sense to start right. If he has not shown the higher common sense to realize that he was on the right track and of remaining on it until the last word was said, why that is another story, and does not immediately concern us.

But I do want to know all about it, right now. You say, in effect, he started right in the main thing, but fizzled out in details and proportions — minor matters, as you call them. Now I don't think they are minor matters at all. I like good detail and fine proportions; I demand them in a façade; but you shut me up every time I try to talk about them.

Steady, boy, steady. Details later on.

I can't bandy words with you; you have too many. But, tell me: How can a man be right and wrong at the same time? I heard you say, once, that like begets like. Now, how can a right start beget a wrong or partly wrong finish — as in this case? Can't I just as well argue that a false ending in detail necessarily implies a false beginning in mass?

You can if you wish, but you will make a mess of it.

Then how does it come?

Very simply. Most men in our profession are small-minded: that is, they lack the power of generalization, of abstraction. They lack the gift, the power to analyze that which is fugitive, the living, or to synthesize their common sense with steadiness and resolution. Indeed they intermittently forego their common sense in yielding to the exigencies of "art" — as you see. Now a small-minded man gets hold, occasionally, on a partial truth, a fragmentary truth, so to speak; but, because he lacks active sympathy with that partial truth, he lacks thereby the power to abstract from it the germ of a broader, a general, truth, or to analyze out of it those hundred and one truths which the simplest state of feeling contains. Now most men, and, specifically, most architects, are of this class; a defective education lies hidden at the root of their failing power. Hence for them a comprehensive law does not exist; and hence such a building as this one. It has many relatives of all shades of consanguinity.

Now, when I say, by implication, that the architect of this building is small-minded, I do not mean to speak unkindly — because of the redeeming presence of so much common sense. It would, perhaps, be less ungracious to say that he is not sufficiently broad-minded, not as full-minded as he might be, and, as I trust, he may become. Where there is a leaven of common sense much is to be hoped for.

Moreover, as you used the word start, you partly distorted my original meaning. If you are to use words, be reasonably sure you understand their values, their form, texture, color; their literal, their figurative meanings, their inborn tendency to shift. Words are alive. Drive them carefully — as you would herd sheep, or handle spirited horses; else they will slip away, or run away, or stampede. You do not now know words well enough to treat them honestly, nor do you know them well enough to treat them craftily. You are not clever enough as yet to be disingenuous with words; but I warn you that ultra-shiftiness, super-cunning, is the basis of fallacy. In truth, it is the basis of much poetry. A single word may mean a thousand things to a thousand men, according to the context they invariably supply. Once you become partly familiar with words and their habits, you will not pay much attention to what others write or say — you will listen, rather, to what they are thinking.

Well, that's a good joke: You started to tell me something about architecture, in which I am concerned, and you made it effective enough, as far as you went; but, in so doing, you wandered into a turgid discourse on words — with which I am not concerned. I cite it therefore as a case in point: You started right and you ended wrong. What under the sun have words to do with architecture?

Your question reveals the uncanny nature of your unknowledge. I hear the owls hoot in the gloaming.

No! You really mean it?

It would so seem.

Then tell me all about it all, I will listen with both ears.

Sometime.

XII. Function and Form   (1)

You were going to tell me more about language, and you —

No, I was not. I began to tell you something about function and form, when you interrupted; and that is what I am to do now.

That is so; we didn't finish, did we?

We can never finish. We may talk for long, and get only a start; but it will be a right start, I believe. We may, perhaps, see where the end lies, but it will be and remain like a star in the sky, unreachable and of unknown distance; or it will be like life itself, elusive to the last — even in death; or it will be like a phantom beacon on a phantom stormy sea; or as a voice, calling, afar in the woods; or, like the shadow of a cloud upon a cloud, it will glide, diaphanous and imponderable, floating in the still air of the spirit.

What's that you are talking about?

The interrelation of function and form. It has no beginning, no ending. It is immeasurably small, immeasurably vast; inscrutably mobile, infinitely serene; intimately complex yet simple.

But you surely told me to listen, not to the words, but to the thought. How can I follow, if you are always thinking away ahead of the words? You seem to take delight in it.

That is true. I will specify: Now, it stands to reason that a thing looks like what it is, and, vice versa, it is what it looks like. I will stop here, to make exception of certain little straight, brown canker-worms that I have picked from rose-bushes. They looked like little brown, dead twigs at first. But speaking generally, outward appearances resemble inner purposes. For instances: the form, oak-tree, resembles and expresses the purpose or function, oak; the form, pine-tree, resembles and indicates the function, pine; the form, horse, resembles and is the logical output of the function, horse; the form, spider, resembles and is the tangible evidence of the function, spider. So the form, wave, looks like the function, wave; the form, cloud, speaks to us of the function, cloud; the form, rain, indicates the function, rain; the form, bird, tells us of the function, bird; the form, eagle, is the function, eagle,-made visible; the form, beak of that eagle, the function, beak of that eagle. And so does the form, rose-bush, authenticate its function, rose-bush; the form, rose-branch, tells of the function, rose-branch; the form, rose-bud, speaks for the function, rose-bud; the form, full-blown rose, recites the poem, full-blown rose. And so does the form, man, stand for the function, man; the form, John Doe, means the function, John Doe; the form, smile, makes us aware of the function, smile; so, when I say: a man named John Doe smiles, — we have a little series of functions and forms which are inseparably related, and yet they seem very casual to us. If I say, John Doe speaks and stretches out his hand, as he smiles, I add a little to the sum of the functions and the forms, but I do not affect their validity or their continuity. If I say, he speaks ungrammatically and with a lisp, I merely modify a little the form your own impressions are taking as you listen; if I say, that, as he smiled, and stretched out his hand, and began speaking, with a lisp and ungrammatically, his lip trembled and a tear formed in his eye, — are not function and form moving in their rhythm, are you not moving in your rhythm while you listen, am I not moving in my rhythm as I speak? If I add that, as he spoke, he sank into a chair, his hat fell from his relaxing fingers, his face blanched, his eyelids drooped, his head turned a little, have I done more than add to your impression and my sympathy? I have not in reality added or detached; I have not made or unmade; I speak, you listen — John Doe lived. He did not know anything or care anything about form or function; but he lived them both; he disbursed them both as he went along through life. He lived and he died. You and I live and we shall die. But John Doe lived the life of John Doe, not of

John Smith: that was his function and such were his forms. And so the form, Roman architecture, means, if it means anything at all, the function Roman; the form, American architecture, will mean, if it ever succeeds in meaning anything, American life; the form, John-Doe architecture, should there be such an architecture, must mean nothing, if it means not John Doe. I do not lie when I tell you John Doe lisped, you do not lie when you listen, he did not lie when he lisped; then why all this lying architecture? Why does John-Doe architecture pretend it is John-Smith architecture? Are we a nation of liars? I think not. That we architects are a sect, a cult of prevaricators, is another matter. And so, in man-made things, the form, literature, means nothing more or less than the function, literature; the form, music, the function, music; the form, knife, the function, knife; the form, axe, the function, axe; the form, engine, the function, engine. And again, in nature, the form, water, the function, water; the form, rivulet, the function, rivulet; the form, river, the function, river; the form, lake, the function, lake; the form, reeds, the function, reeds; the forms, fly above the water and bass below the water — their related functions; and so the fisherman in the boat; and so on, and on, and on, and on — unceasingly, endlessly, constantly, eternally — through the range of the physical world — visual, microscopic, and telescopic, the world of the senses, the world of the intellect, the world of the heart, the world of the soul: the physical world of man we believe we know, and the borderland of that world we know not — that world of the silent, immeasurable, creative spirit, of whose infinite function all these things are but the varied manifestations in form, in form more or less tangible, more or less imponderable — a borderland delicate as the dawn of life, grim as fate, human as the smile of a friend — a universe wherein all is function, all is form: a frightful phantasm, driving the mind to despair, or, as we will, a glorious revelation of that power which holds us in an invisible, a benign, a relentless — a wondrous hand.

My goodness! What a light that throws on the bank!

What bank?

You know.

Bank me no banks — that has neither form nor function here — but listen: Like sees and begets its like. That which exists in spirit ever seeks and finds its physical counterpart in form, its visible image; an uncouth thought, an uncouth form; a monstrous thought, a monstrous form; a thought in decadence, a form in decadence; a living thought, a living form. Light means light — a shadow means eclipse. How many shadows do men cast! How many live in shadows! How many walk in darkness! How many struggle in their night! How many wander, all forlorn, in the verge of Death's deep valley! How many are mired in the black pit! How many drag others thereunto! Great is the light that shines. Profound the shadow that Man casts upon his own spirit! Opaque and moribund that man who gives forth, not a light, but a shadow in his daily walk. A dense, material, moving phantom, he, who stands before the sun and puts his art in obscuration! Stand out of my light! Stand out of our light! I say! Platoons of dead men! This is the day when strikes the hour upon high noon, within a cloudless sky! Avast the sun! Avaunt, the clay that doth eclipse it! Shall the hour sound, and no man answer cheerily its call? Shall the sun shine and no flower bloom in gladness? Shall the joyous heavens find no answer to their smile, but sullen turbid stares? It cannot be, it shall not be: for of the wilderness I'll make a song of spring that shall dispel its gloomy wintry skies and icy snows, and make awake to sweet rejuvenance the lark, the soaring, singing lark that doth abide within the hearts — of all the young!

That's fine! Although it looked pretty dark at one time, especially for the claymen. Do you often have these fits? If you do, telephone me so that I can get around in time to hear the next one. By the way, what has become of function and form in the shuffle?

I dreamed again. But this time I awake to that of which I dreamed — the charming reality of your own proper person, your wit and your ways. My dream was its own function; the words, its audible form.

Is there then form in everything?

Form in everything and anything, everywhere and at every instant. According to their nature, their function, some forms are definite, some indefinite; some are nebulous, others concrete and sharp; some symmetrical, others purely rhythmical. Some are abstract, others material. Some appeal to the eye, some to the ear, some to the touch, some to the sense of smell, some to any one or all or any combination of these. But all, without fail, stand for relationships between the immaterial and the material, between the subjective and the objective — between the Infinite Spirit and the finite mind. Through our sense we know substantially all that we may know. The imagination, inituition, reason, are but exalted forms of the physical senses, as we call them. For Man there is nothing but the physical; what he calls his spirituality is but the most exalted reach of his animalism. Little by little, Man, through his senses, divines the Infinite. His highest thoughts, his most delicate yearnings arise, through an imperceptible birth and growth, from the material sense of touch. From hunger arose the cravings of his soul. From urgent passions have the sweetest vows of his heart arisen. From savage instincts came the force and powers of his mind. All is growth, all is decadence. Functions are born of functions, and in turn, give birth or death to others. Forms emerge from forms, and others arise or descend from these. All are related, interwoven, intermeshed, interconnected, interblended. They exosmose and endosmose. They sway and swirl and mix and drift interminably. They shape, they reform, they dissipate. They respond, correspond, attract, repel, coalesce, disappear, reappear, merge and emerge: slowly or swiftly, gently or with cataclysmic force — from chaos into chaos, from death into life, from life into death, from rest into motion, from motion into rest, from darkness into light, from light into darkness, from sorrow into joy, from joy into sorrow, from purity into foulness, from foulness into purity, from growth into decadence, from decadence into growth. All is form, all is function — ceaselessly unfolding and infolding — and the heart of Man unfolds and infolds with them: Man, the one spectator before whom this drama spreads its appalling, its inspiring harmony of drift and splendor, as the centuries toll and toll the flight of broad-pinioned Time, soaring, from eternity to eternity: while the mite sucks the juices of the petal, and the ant industriously wanders here and there and here and there again, the song-bird twitters on the bough, the violet gives her perfume sweetly forth in innocence. All is function, all is form, but the fragrance of them is rhythm, the language of them is rhythm: for rhythm is the very wedding-march and ceremonial that quickens into song the unison of form and function, or the dirge of their farewell, as they move apart, and pass into the silent watches of that wondrous night we call the past. So goes the story on its endless way.

XIII.   Function and Form   (2)

It seems to me that I could have gotten a clearer idea of your recent harangue on function and form, if you had used half as many words. Still, I think I catch your meaning after a fashion. The gist of it is, I take it, behind every form we see there is a vital something or other which we do not see, yet which makes itself visible to us in that very form. In other words, in a state of nature the form exists *because* of the function, and this something behind the form is neither more nor less than a manifestation of what you call the infinite creative spirit, and what I call God. And, allowing for our differences in education, training, and life associations, so that we may try to see the same thing in the same way, what you want me to understand and hold to is, that, just as every form contains its function, and exists by virtue of it, so every function finds or is engaged in finding its form. And, furthermore, while this is true of the every-day things we see about us in nature and in the reflection of nature we call human life, it is just as true, because it is a universal law, of everything that the mind can take hold of.

You are "arriving," as we say.

Well, I suppose of course there is some application of this to architecture?

Well rather. It applies to everything else, why not to architecture?

But there must be a definite application of the theory. What is the application?

Can't you figure it out?

I suppose if we call every building a form —

You strain my nerves — but go on.

I suppose if we call a building a form, then there should be a function, a purpose, a reason for each building, a definite explainable relation between the form, the development of each building, and the causes that bring it into that particular shape; and that the building, to be good architecture, must, first of all, clearly correspond with its function, must be its image, as you would say.

Don't say good architecture, say, merely, architecture; I will know what you mean.

And that, if a building is properly designed, one should be able with a little attention, to read *through* that building to the *reason* for that building.

Go on.

Well, that's all right for the logical part of it; but where does the artistic side come in?

No matter about the artistic side of it. Go on with your story.

But —

Never mind the buts.

Well then, I suppose if the law is true of the building as a whole, it must hold true of its parts.

That's right.

Consequently each part must so clearly express its function that the function can be read through the part.

Very good. But you might add that if the work is to be organic the function of the part must have the same *quality* as the function of the whole; and the parts, of themselves and by themselves, must have the quality of the mass; must partake of its identity.

What do you mean by organic?

I will tell you, later on.

Then if I am on the right track, I'm going to try to keep on it. It's rather fun to do your own thinking, isn't it?

Yes, it is: and rather good for the health and the happiness. Keep on, and some day you will get the blood to your brain. If the surge is not too sudden, you may yet become a useful citizen.

I overlook your sneer, because I am interested in what I, myself, am saying. I would observe in passing, however, that you are not any too considerate. But, to go on: If it is true of the parts in a larger sense, then it must be equally true of the details, and in the same sense, isn't it?

In a similar sense, yes.

Why do you say similar?

Because I mean similar. The details are not the same as the parts and the mass; they cannot be. But they can be and should be similar to the parts and to the mass.

Isn't that splitting hairs?

If there were more of such hair-splitting it would be well for our architecture.

Why so? I don't understand.

Because its significance reverts to the *organic quality* which I mentioned to you. There is no limit to the subdivisibility of *organic thinking*.

And what is the difference between logical thinking and organic thinking?

A world of difference. But we haven't come to that yet.

Then, I infer, I can go on and consider my detail as of itself a mass, if I will, and proceed with the regular and systematic subdivision of function with form, as before, and I will always have a similarity, an organic quality — if I can guess what you mean — descending from the mass down to the minutest subdivision of detail. That's interesting, isn't it? The subdivisions and details will descend from the mass like children, grandchildren and great-grandchildren, and yet, they will be, all, of the same family.

That's the first enlivening word I've heard you say.

Well, it's catching, you know. I begin to get an inkling now of what you meant by the "voice, calling, afar in the woods." Perhaps, too, some of the little seeds are coming up and will need watering by and by.

Yes, yes. Very good as far as you go. But I wish to warn you that a man might follow the program you have laid down, to the very last detail of details, and yet have, if that were his make-up, a very dry, a very pedantic, a very prosaic result.

47. *Function and Form* (2)

He might produce a completely logical result, so-called, and yet an utterly repellent one — a cold, a vacuous negation of living architecture — a veritable pessimism.

How so?

Simply because logic, scholarship, or taste, or all of them combined, cannot make organic architecture. They may make logical, scholarly or "tasty" buildings, and that is all. And such structures are either dry, chilling or futile.

Well then, tell me *now*, in anticipation, what characterizes a real architect?

First of all a poetic imagination; second, a broad sympathy, humane character, common sense and a thoroughly disciplined mind; third, a perfected technique; and, finally, an abundant and gracious gift of expression.

Then you don't value logic.

It has its excellent uses.

But cannot everything be reduced to the syllogism?

So the text books would seem to claim; yet I should not wish to see a rose reduced to syllogism; I fear the result would be mostly syllogism and that poetry would "vanish with the rose." Formal logic cannot successfully deal with the creative process, for the creating function is vital, as its name implies, whereas the syllogism is an abstraction, fascinating as a form of the function, so-called pure reason; yet, when subordinate to inspiration, it has a just and high value. I say there is a logic over and above book-logic, namely, the subconscious energy we call imagination. Nevertheless, formal logic has its purpose and its place.

Then you do prize logic?

I surely do. It is a power of the intellect; but it has its limitations. It must not play the tyrant.

By the way; you were to explain the word organic.

You have a memory — which shows that you are following and, still better, anticipating my argument. I had for the moment overlooked the item. But we will take it up next time, when we may discuss it leisurely.

I think this is great sport.

So do I.

XIV.   Growth and Decay

In seeking now a reasonably solid grasp on the value of the word, organic, we should at the beginning fix in mind the values of the correlated words, organism, structure, function, growth, development, form. All of these words imply the initiating pressure of a living force and a resultant structure or mechanism whereby such invisible force is made manifest and operative. The pressure, we call Function: the resultant, Form. Hence the law of function and form discernible throughout nature.

I have already cautioned you against the fugacious nature of words, their peculiar tendency to transformation in meaning while they retain the same outward form.

This is because the form of a word is not, itself, truly organic; it is arbitrary, and has very little inherent capacity for change in response to a change in significance — especially if the change be a subtle one. Beyond the mechanical changes that the grammarians call declensions, conjugations, compoundings, affixes, suffixes, etc., words, when written, can be modified or developed in significance only, or nearly so, by association with other words — when they are in rhythmical, organized motion. In speech, the word is rendered more plastic: hence the value of oratory. Statically words have little significance, as you may assure yourself by consulting any dictionary; but, when once they are treated dynamically and pictorially, their power to convey thought increases enormously; still, let it always be understood that the powers are not in the words so much as in the mind and heart of him who uses them as his instrument. The thought, the feeling, the beauty is not so much in the words as in what the words suggest, or are caused to suggest, to the mind of the reader, the hearer; and this power of suggestion, of evoking responsive imagination, is the power of the artist, the poet: he who surcharges words.

Some time ago you asked what connection there might be between words and architecture. There is this immediate and important connection — that architecture, for the past several centuries, has suffered from a growing accretion of words: it is now in fact so overgrown and stifled with words that the reality has been lost to view. Words and phrases have usurped the place of function and form. Finally phrase-making has come to be an accepted substitute for architecture-making.

Now, as we two together are seeking the sense of *things,* as we are searching out *realities,* let us pronounce now, once for all, that the architecture we seek is to be a reality in function and form and that that reality shall unfold within the progressing clarity of our view.

The architecture that we see today bespeaks lost organic quality. Like a man once strong but now decrepit, it no longer functions normally. Hence its form has become abnormal. It no longer speaks in tones of ringing eloquence as of yore — it now cries out to the attentive ear with an appalling, inarticulate cry, now muffled, now piercing, but ever the wail of disorganization, the sigh of dissolution. Its features have a pallid leer, a rictus. Its eye is lustreless, its ear is dulled, its vitals atrophied. So moves it wearily on its crutch of scholarship — groping through spectacles of words.

The architecture *we seek* shall be as a man active, alert, supple, strong, sane. A generative man. A man having five senses all awake; eyes that fully see, ears that are attuned to every sound; a man living in his present, knowing and feeling the vibrancy of that ever-moving moment, with heart to draw it in and mind to put it out: that incessant, that portentous birth, that fertile moment which we call Today! As a man who knows his day, who loves his day, who knows and loves the exercise of life, who rightly values strength and kindliness, whose feet are on the earth, whose brain is keyed to the ceaseless song of his kind: who sees the past with kindly eye, who sees the future in a kindling vision: as a man who wills to create: So shall our art be. For to live, wholly to live, is the manifest consummation of existence.

NOTE: This chapter was considerably shortened in revision.

XV. Thought

I am quite a little impressed by what you say concerning our search for realities rather than mere words. It sounds straightforward and penetrating in one sense and illuminating in another. It seems to direct the faculties straight ahead of one, to focus them on something definite, something that I feel sure must exist and must be true. Still, for all that, we must use words, must we not?

Not necessarily. You need words only when you are to communicate with others by that special method called written or spoken language. Music, painting, sculpture, architecture are manifestly wordless forms of communication; so is gesture, so is facial expression. Words, however, are sometimes useful in explaining these and other things; in fact, explanation is one of the chiefest uses of words, if not the most important. By means of words we try to make clear to others our feelings, thoughts, intentions, recollections, and a great number of other things — in short, our mental or emotional attitude at any time on any subject, and for these purposes words are pretty well adapted, especially where purely human relations are concerned. But there is a vast domain lying just beyond the reach of words; and, to express our impressions of it, our insight into it — our contact with that which lies beyond man — the fine arts enter and carry on a form of language, of expression, of communication, of explanation, that lies beyond words. Now architecture as at present practised is a crude pretense at art. But, believe me, it is truly a fine art when its capabilities are once understood, when its true nature is once known, when its plasticity, its power for eloquence, its dramatic, its lyric resources, its fluency of expression are once grasped by the mind and the heart. No form of expression can excel it in force, beauty, delicacy, subtlety and versatility when in sympathetic hands. Take my word for it now, my young friend, and I will try to explain it to you later when you shall have come to understand, through your own inward experiences and the growth of your moral nature, what real thinking and real feeling mean — that there is no state of feeling that may not find its true image in the real, the plastic, the poetic architectural art, that art which I am forced to call the New Architecture.

But in passing I may say that real thinking is better done without words than with them, and creative thinking *must* be done without words. When the mind is actively and vitally at work, for its own creative uses, it has no time for word-building: words are too clumsy: you have no time to select and group them. Hence you must think in terms of *images*, of pictures, of states of feeling, of rhythm. The well-trained, well-organized, well-disciplined mind works with remarkable rapidity and with luminous intensity; it will body forth combinations, *in mass*, so complex, so far-reaching that you could not write them down in years. Writing is but the slow, snail-like creeping of words, climbing, laboriously, over a little structure that *resembles* the thought: meanwhile the mind has gone on and on, here and yonder and back and out and back again. Thought is the most rapid agency in the universe. It can travel to Sirius and return in an instant. Nothing is too small for it to grasp, nothing too great. It can go in and out of itself — now objective, now subjective. It can fasten itself most tenaciously on a fact, on an idea; or sublimate and attenuate itself with etheral space. It will flow like water; it may become as stable as stone. You must familiarize yourself, my boy, with some of the possibilities of that extraordinary agent we call thought. Learn its uses and how to use it. Your test will always be — results; for real thinking brings real results. Thinking is an art, a science of magnificent possibilities. It is like an army with banners, where the horses cry ha! ha! at the sound of the trumpets. After a while you will instinctively learn to know whether a given man is thinking or mooning. It's a great art, my lad, remember this, it's an inspiring art. I mean the real, fluent, active thinking, not the dull stammering and mumbling of the mind: I mean the mind awake.

Words, after all, are but a momentary utterance of thought. They may be, in that utterance, as beautiful as the song of a bird we hear, but they are not the bird: for the bird is flown, and sings elsewhere another song in the forest, ere the first has become a memory with us. Of all the songs sung in the forest how many do we hear? And the forest sings its own song: how many of us hear it? And the song is of the forest, it is not the forest. So, let your thoughts be at times like the songs we hear not, the song of the singer in the solitudes. Therefore I would take your mind away from words, and bend it to thinking.

Thinking is a philosophy. Many people believe that when they are reading in a book they are of necessity thinking; that when they listen to someone's discourse they are thinking; but it does not necessarily follow. The best that reading and listening can do is to *stimulate* you to think your own thoughts, but, nine times out of ten, you are thinking the other man's thought, not your own. What occurs is like an echo, a reflection; it is not the real thing. Reading is chiefly useful in that it informs you of what the other man is thinking, it puts you in touch with the currents of thought among your fellows, or among those of the past. But you must carefully and watchfully discriminate between pseudo-thinking and real thinking. Pseudo-thinking is always imitative, real thinking is always creative. It cannot be otherwise. You cannot create unless you think, and you cannot truly think without creating in thought. Judge our present architecture by this standard and you will be amazed at its poverty of thought, its falsity in expression, its absence of manhood. Moreover, real thinking is always in the *present tense*. You cannot think *in* the past, you can only think *of* the past. You cannot think *in* the future, you can think only *of* the future. By great power of imagination you may think of the past and of the future *almost* in terms of the present: the one is the function of the historian, the other that of the prophet. But *reality* is of, in, by and for the present, and the present only. Bear this strictly in mind, it is highly important, it must lie at the very root of your new education, for it is with the present only that you are in physical, vital contact, and I have told you that real thought, vital thought, is born of the physical senses. It is in the present, only, that you *really live,* therefore it is in the present, only, that you can *really think*. And in this sense you think organically. Pseudo-thinking is inorganic. The one is living, the other dead. The present is the *organic moment,* the *living moment*. The past and the future do not exist: the one is dead, the other unborn. The present is that twinkling of an eye that separates death from life, as time moves on: but thought is quicker than the twinkling of an eye.

Bear this all closely in mind, my lad. Do not for a moment suppose that it is hair-splitting. I want you to get at the vital essence of things, and this is vital, it is momentous, it is profoundly significant, for it is of *the search after life* — that search on which the mind of the world has been concentrated, with indefatigable intensity, since the beginning of man as a thinking being. The first thing upon which you must bend your mind is, to learn to think seriously, accurately, methodically, persistently, thoroughly and fearlessly. Never doubt the powers of your own mind, for they are there, waiting for you to discover them, to know them, to use them. You will not learn in the printed books how to think this way, but you will find it in the great open book of the life about you. It is all there waiting for you to discover it, to know it, and to use it. Have no fear, and have no doubt. I tell you it is so. It is only the conventional teacher of architecture who could tell you that you are a dullard by birth and an imbecile by predestination. I tell you you were born all right and that you have powers of which you are not aware: every lad has, and might develop them if his parents did not ask him every five minutes how much he is "getting," and if he can't get a "raise" next week. Money-grubbing will defeat any kind of education.

So, first, learn to think, then, learn to act. Learn to think as an architect should think, then act as an honest architect should act. When you think organically you will act organically. Just so soon as your thoughts begin to take on an organic quality, your buildings will begin to take on an organic quality, and thereafter they will grow and develop together. But they will not do this until you have so begun — no, never until then. But do not be ashamed to begin in a small way. Everything begins in a small way. Make sure, only, that it is the right way. Seek to learn something of your own nature — your aptitudes, your powers, your limitations. Strive to increase the powers, to remove the limitations. You cannot hope to know your own powers until you test them with the force of will and the backing of character to overcome obstacles. It is almost folly to talk of the limitations of the mind: leave that to the idlers. I tell you that the limitations of your mind are much farther off than you suppose. I would not waste a moment on you did I not profoundly believe it. The so-called average mind has vastly greater powers, immeasurably greater possibilities of development than is generally supposed. But we need teachers — we need teachers of the right sort. The popular notions on this subject are grotesquely untoward, woefully inadequate. The main thing is to catch the mind young enough, start it right, and train it right. The power of the individual mind is great. It is sheer fiddle-faddle to think otherwise. Those who doubt it are those who have not taken the trouble and will not take the trouble to inquire of the nearest child of tender years. Go to, the subject exasperates me, for I have eyes to see. Think for a moment, think what would be the power and the glory of a people if the individual minds were properly trained, instead of all this disastrous waste and malpractice. Would it not reverse some of the cherished notions of the political economists? But enough of this.

I will start you right, and start you carefully: after that it will be your business to keep right. I will give you the landmarks and the blazings in that country which I have explored alone: but it is the land of promise — and I return to tell you of it, and to point the way.

So don't trouble much about words for the present. They will come into useful play when you shall have thoughts that naturally seek expression in words. But do

5. Chicago National Bank, Chicago *(Chicago Architectural Photograph. Co.)*

6. Design for a Bicentennial Memorial for Detroit

7. Columbia University Library, New York

8. An example of the period. . . . . .

not misunderstand me. I would not for a moment underrate the study of language, on the contrary, I highly cherish it; I mean only that for the present you are to turn all your faculties toward realities and let the words go. Think your thoughts in terms of your own nature, of your own surroundings, of your own art. Seek toward this end: That architecture, its organic forms, its inorganic materials, may respond to your will, to your persuasion, and become the plastic medium whereby you shall express not word-thoughts but building-thoughts, and the function then will flow to the minutest details of form in orderly sequence, as surely as the sap flows to the tip of the slenderest tendril of a vine — to the tips of the uttermost leaves of the giant forest tree.

But you cannot do this in a day, in a week, in a year. It must be for you a life-work, a long, steady, continuous infolding and unfolding — just as the tree grows and expands year after year. For, as I have quoted to you, "Time will not conse-crate that in which she has been ignored" — that so runs the French saying. And to realize a little of what the saying means, "Nature neither hastens nor delays," think on the one hand of the lightning-flash, of the speed of thought, and, on the other, of the gradual elevation of a continent, of the revolution of the sun about the earth [sic].

You have set me a terrible task. I feel discouraged from attempting it.

Nothing of the sort. The more you think, the more you will delight in thinking; the more you contemplate, the more you will delight in contemplation; the more you act, the more you will delight in action. Little by little I will suggest to you how to think and how to express your thoughts. Meanwhile bear in mind that you are not to think merely *on occasions,* as a sort of ceremonial, but daily, hourly, all the time — it must become your fixed and natural habit of mind. So will your think-ing steadily grow in power, clearness, flexibility and grace; and you will ever there-after feel what the spirit of independence and self-control truly means.

XVI. Imagination

In our last talk you hinted a little of the power of imagination. What do you believe imagination to be? I have thought about it, in a vague way, but I don't seem to get anywhere. It is a word commonly enough used, but no two people seem to use it alike or understand it alike. It seems to me a something — a reality, you would probably call it — that disappears when you reach for it; and the only satisfaction I can get is in the use of the word itself, which I affect to believe I understand, and yet I am sure I do not. When I leave this anchorage I am adrift. What is it, anyway?

Really, you make me smile. I don't know what imagination is any more than I know what electricity is. Imagination is the very soul itself, so intangible is it. And yet it is near, direct, simple. We don't know what it is, but we do know certain of its activities. Imagination is a phase of life, and if you will tell me what life is, I will tell you what imagination is. You might as well even ask me if life and death are the same thing, and, if not, which is the real thing. I might hold that life is all; that death does not exist, that it is a name we give to a change, that it is a word, a symbol. And, if I were of different temperament, I might urge that life is merely a word, a mirage, a phantom, an illusion; that the deep-down reality is death — immeasurable quiescence. Or, if I were of still another temperament, I might say that life and death are both illusions, unreal as ourselves; that there is but one inscrutable reality.

So, with imagination, you may say anything about it that suits your own imagination; I may say anything about it that suits my imagination; for it is the personal imagination only that can grasp imagination, as it is the spirit only that can grasp spirit, only the physical that can grasp the physical — only the heart that can reach the heart. If you are deficient in imagination you will not understand imagination; if you are defective in sensibility you cannot know the physical; if you have no heart you can never know the world of the heart. For, as like begets like, so only like can understand like. Understanding and words are often far apart, they have but little in common. Understanding is of the heart, words are man's inventions; understanding is subjective, visible words are objective — else why should oral discourse affect us more intimately than the written page, else why does the spoken word go so quickly to the heart, and the written word so often lose itself on the way there, as it wanders through the alleys of the mind?

Now, I can at best tell you only what may be transmitted by the spoken word, but *if your imagination does not grasp and receive what I mean, I fail.* I cannot convey to you in words the bloom on a fruit — you must see it to know it. I cannot depict to you in words the melody of a bird's song — you must hear it to know it. I may have seen the bloom and heard the song, but I cannot convey their reality to you. I can only suggest. To know them you must hear and see for yourself. By your living power you must absorb them.

All we know of imagination is what we, through the power of our own imaginations, may infer from its manifestations. These manifestations, to be sure, are highly varied and complex. There are in fact as many imaginations as there are men, women and children on the face of the earth. It goes without our saying that these individual imaginations vary in kind and degree and also have marked common resemblances. But it is the variations that are the more suggestive and instructive, for you will find that *the imagination of each person is that person:* it is the key to his character: it determines what that person will receive and what that person will reject. Incidentally, you cannot put one foot in front of the other unless your imagination has prepared the way — much less can you construct a poem.

So, again, when you ask me what is imagination, I might reply, Yankeewise, by asking you, what is a plant? You say a plant is a vegetable? Well, what is a vegetable? You proceed to describe more and more minutely, and I to question more and more closely. Finally you are at a loss to say whether a plant may or may not be an animal. Yet we well know that there are hundreds of thousands of plants, each with its pecularities of structure and form and function; and not only thousands of kinds, but thousands upon thousands of individuals of each particular kind; and that each of these individuals has its pecularities, its specific life, its identity. For such is the subdivisibility of nature; and it is within the power of analysis measurably to follow this delicate flow of function into specific form. So are there thousands upon thousands of imaginations, each vital and peculiar; yours is one of these, mine is one, but they are not wholly alike, they cannot be, for identity prevails throughout nature to the minutest limits of observation. You may arrange and classify these imaginations if you wish; but classification is largely an arbitrary process, done for convenience, for ease of reference and use.

And by all of this I am trying to get you out of your school rut where everything was classified and tabulated, and tagged for you, and bring you out into a large, fluent conception of the continuity of nature, the indissoluble continuity of all that surrounds you, of all that is within you, of all that is without you — of the world of the spirit and the world of the physical. If you grasp this and the relation of your own faculties to it: that the mind, the heart, the soul have no delimitation, no boundary, no barrier, you will have a hint of the universal aspect of the imagination, of its fluency, its quality, its range, its visibility.

So you see, my young friend, by your simple question you have opened up a world. And when I hinted to you of the possible power of the individual mind, and of the power and glory of a people whose individual minds were so trained, I was not speaking in what might be called a flight of fancy, but with a close and practical sense of realities.

So, while we may say that the imagination, in some of its aspects, seems superhuman, in others it is most beautifully human. If it implies the power to receive, it also implies the power to give. If it is as simple as a drop of dew, it is also as complex as a drop of dew. However furtive and shy it may be, still it is domestic of habit. It is steadied, controlled and made amenable by the other faculties. If it is a wanderer, so it ever returns. It knows where its home is: it needs you as much as you need it. It goes where you send it, and returns laden with airy nothings. It is your other self — your best friend when you know it and it knows you. It will go anywhere after anything; but beware lest it beguile you, for it is a tricky, mischievous thing when you are not looking. You must train it carefully for its work as you would train a retriever, for, whatever else imagination may be, it is a magnificent retriever. They say that imagination is a great painter of pictures, and a famous maker of images, a most skillful and ingenious craftsman. If this be so, then house and feed him well and lavish gifts upon him. They say, too, that he is a great constructor and reconstructor. That may be, too, but I tell you that he is also a great destroyer. They say that children are imaginative. That is truest and most beautiful of all. Let us remain children as we grow old: For I tell you if you kill the child in man you kill the man in man. No truer saying was ever said than this: The child is father to the man. So recall to your heart your childhood, which is looking at you with a wistful eye and not so far away.

XVII. A Doric Column

I am absorbed in what you said in your last talk. I feel the reach and force of it. But can you not give me a specific instance of imagination?

I can perhaps do better in giving you a specific instance of *lack* of imagination.

It seems that once upon a time the people of the good city of Detroit conceived a plan to celebrate the two hundredth anniversary of the discovery of the site of that interesting town, by the erection of a noble and suitable memorial. [Fig. 6]

Forthwith they appointed the usual committee. Forthwith the committee proceeded to sit and to think — or to deliberate, as they might say — which same is a shade more deadly than thinking. They thought of an architect, far in the East like a morning star. They summoned him. He came — he pondered; then the committee pondered; then they all brooded together — in conference, as it is said. They, the committee, asked him, the architect, to think of a memorial that should be expressive, fitting, appropriate, and "proper": and behold! the morning star dreamed of a Doric Column — *"the largest in the world."* The architect states in his published report that this Doric column is to commemorate the "bicentenary of the *discovery* and *foundation* of the *city* of Detroit." Save the mark! How can a "city" be "discovered" and "founded" at the same time. You or I in our innocence might think that two hundred years ago there was discovered a wilderness wherein Detroit subsequently arose. And further on in the report we are told that from the top of the column is to spring a "great flame of natural gas, *so characteristic of the West,* and impossible elsewhere" — as though there were not "natural gas" enough in this Doric column itself, without calling in the facetious aid of natural adjuncts, and as though there were not "natural gas" in the East. Then the architect modestly closes his report by saying that his Doric column will "rank with the famous monuments of all time." Had he added, in parentheses, that it would be famous among the "rank" monuments of all time, I would cheerfully agree with him. That so large a report should have accompanied so large a column, as the "idea" was detonated, seems only natural.

Then the committee figured on cost and ways and means. And when you think of dollars and ways and means you have to think in dead earnest.

You may perhaps incline a little to infer from my remarks that I do not approve, and, indeed, I do not. And why? Because it would seem to a man up a tree that the architek, here, was not on familiar terms with the rudiments of imagination: a most distressing form of illiteracy, in an "artist." Indeed, imagination alone is that distinguishing quality which marks apart an architect from that which vulgar persons call an architek.

In the beginning, I say, was the architek — without form, and void, and darkness was upon it. And the Inscrutable Creative Spirit moving through the darkness said: Let there be light — and *Imagination* was that light. And the Great Spirit found it good, and he separated the light from the darkness.

And thus, in reverse, when an architect parts company with imagination he becomes at once an architek — whether he be originally of low or of high degree matters not a whit.

So you may infer, indeed I urge it, that an honest imagination is henceforth, in your philosophy, to be held inseparable, in his province, from the title, architect.

No, I do not like humbug in general, and I particularly abhor wanton, expensive humbug: where the lavish use of money is relied upon to hide the peccant inanity. Hence I do not like this particular "Doric" humbug, even if it be not specifically the largest of its kind in the world.

All of which perhaps seems reasonably clear, but I will make it clearer:

I will hazard a surmise that this particular architek never made his bed of boughs in the sombre gloom of the primeval forest; never saw the gleam of opalescent eyes across the waning fire-light; never heard the curdling cry of the screech-owl over-head: nor the distinct wolfish bark — now faint, now louder, always hungry, ever passionately mournful; now the low, sudden moan of the forest, in night's stillest, breathless hour, as an aged giant hemlock sank heavily to earth; nor saw the dawn break, pale and white through the filmy branches, interlaced, of pine and tamarack and their stately brethren, clustered upright and close in mute communion; nor heard the belch of a fired musket bellow and roar and roll along the edge of a slum-bering woodland lake — now fainting around its capes and bays, now swelling aloud and dying again, reaching around and turning back in reverberation upon reverbera-tion along the upright wall of woods, and breaking and flying to and fro across the startled waters in a wild harangue of echoes, slowly blending, subsiding and melting into the air and into the forest slowly away, until, after long and long, stillness reigns again, and solitude — engulfing and resolving the strange, harsh dissonance; nor climbed through tangle and over fallen trunks, nor cushioned his foot on the mold of what was once a proud thing of the forest, nor smelled the faint sweet odor, oh, so faint, so delicate, of the deep woods, standing in sombre array with trunks ever more serried, ever growing grayer and darker as they close and deepen in obscurity — while the straight long paths ever open and close to the huntsman, he of keen foot and nimble eye, as he moves like a wraith through the sylvan depths; nor crossed the black chilling waters of turbulent winding streams, as they foam over boulder and snag, rushing and tinkling through yellow froth, or gleam in smooth, silent or gently singing cascades, anon to rush and turn, always cold, always black; nor saw the furtive deer, startled, vanish like a sprite; nor heard the mournful cry of the loon, solitary, vigilant, wary, afar on the bosom of the lake; nor heard the storm break, in terror sweeping through the tossing forest herd, with blue, blinding flash and ponderous crack and rumble and snapping, and the downpour, and the swash and and swish and sodden soak; nor saw the bright blue sky over the beaver meadows; nor crossed great rivers; nor toiled, patient and hungry over hills, through deep ravines, following when he could the red man's trail; nor paddled, silent and steadily, up the rivers — up and up, deeper and deeper into the far-spread forests; nor came at times upon a great lake so vast that the eye could not cross it, angry and fierce in storm, placid and beaming in fair weather, shining and sparkling in the sunshine, in the crystalline air, blue and lovely under the pellucid vault of blue above, far-stretching and serene and solitary — so deep, so dark, so placid under the young moon, under the gleaming, glinting stars —

But the men who set foot first on the spot where Detroit now stands beside the narrow strait: they — saw these things, heard these things, lived these things, died these things, and many more. They — thought not of Greek columns, they thought of the wilderness, they thought of hunger, of disease, of death, of foe upon foe, hardship after hardship, misery piled upon misery, conquest wrested after conquest. Hardily they faced toil and danger. Struggle was theirs. Heroism was theirs. The solitude of a continent was theirs. The faith of the fanatic was theirs. Heroism, and devotion, and patience, and fortitude were the stars in their night, the breaking dawn of whose second century of after-narrative we are to "celebrate" in unblushing puerility. Verily they might say, in their nameless graves: We ask not even for bread but ye give us a stone.

What souls have we when such deeds knock and cannot enter. The door is closed, the keeper of the house is fled. Two hundred years have come and gone upon the spot where once the forest stood in grandeur.

XVIII. Attention

Do you know, I became so interested in your story of the forest that I forgot all about the blamed Doric Column. Oh, that was great — in the forest. I wish I were there. You must have lived in the forest or you couldn't describe it so — didn't you? Let me tell you, that awakened the old cave-man in me. And architecture put out of the door. You *were* in the forest, weren't you? Don't say no and shatter my romance.

No matter about that now: Let's get to business.

Yes, but I understand loons are very difficult to hit — even with a rifle. You can't get near them. And they dive like a flash. How do you get near enough to make a shot?

Never mind. You are loon enough for me for the present. I'm trying to get near enough to hit you with an idea, but the best I have done, so far, is to raise a few feathers. Still, you're not going to get away from me — for I am a hunter of men. And the said men are "scarier" than any loon. The wild moose in his native fastness is a pet poodle in comparison. Man can sniff a new idea afar off, if the breeze blows toward him, and away he goes through the covert, or under ground, or under the nearest patch of brush, or up a tree, Man, mentally, is the most *farouche,* most timid of animals. I know him well: that is to say, I do not know him at all. He is un-understandable, he combines in himself all the characteristics of all the animals, of all the birds, all the reptiles, all the fishes, all the insects and all the plants.

Yes, yes — but —

I know; I know. You would rather hunt than study, and I can't blame you overmuch. But the trick is to hunt *and* study. If you learn to do that you will learn nearly all of the secret. Now, here have I been talking architecture directly and indirectly to you for quite a while, and at best you have given a perfunctory grunt or two by way of response; but the moment I talk of the forest, or of a wild creature, you are all on fire; which goes to show that you are nearer to nature than I am, that the primitive man and the primitive forces awaken in you at one touch of Nature's wand. Now I know in my heart that the architectural art I am seeking to reveal to you is like the loon, like the forest, like all things in unhampered nature; but its pursuit is of the *spirit:* not of the rifle, nor of the book. I am puzzled how to make it clear to you — for it is clear in fact. I fancy I have grown sophisticated, with my generation, and have lost the art of simple statement.

Oh, don't let that worry you, pa. I'll fall into your pit some day. There are other ways of catching game besides shooting. And then, you are not so modest as you would have me assume. You are laying for me, I know it. I can sniff you in the air — which I am pretty sure is right now blowing my way. But I'm not scared, I'm just a bit curious.

Well, let's see: What were we talking about?

Oh, I don't know. Whatever it was, you would make a sermon of it for the good of my soul.

And if I tell you about the loon?

Now you're shooting!

And if I tell you about yourself?

Oh, I don't know.

Well, the loon pays attention to what concerns him and you are to do the same, for *attention* is of the essence of our powers;[1] it is that which draws other things *toward* us, it is that which, if we have lived with it, brings the experiences of our lives ready to our hand. If things but make *impression* enough on you, you will not forget them; and thus, as you go through life, your store of experiences becomes greater, richer, more and more available. But to this end you must *cultivate* attention — the art of *seeing,* the art of *listening.* You needn't trouble about memory, that will take care of itself; but you must learn to *live* in the true sense. To pay attention is to live, and to live is to pay attention; and, bear in mind most of all, that your spiritual nature is but a higher faculty of seeing and listening — a finer, nobler way of paying attention. Thus must you learn to live in the *fullest* sense.

So many people are half-dead. They go their way in a kind of dull somnolence. Show them a Dollar, they brighten up; talk sense, they yawn. If you make a statement, they half-hear it: if they are garrulous they don't hear at all but wait inertly for you to end, that they may talk — a stream of meaningless speech which turns and turns in an orbit of etceteras. And so they go, here and there, like rag-pickers, and poke around among the scraps, fag-ends, and waste-paper. And through the mist they call life, they wander, formless and dim. This class is sprinkled through all the social strata from top to bottom — it is confined to none. It is the empty class — the pessimists. For them life has no color, it is all grays, and they, like grays —

For heaven's sake what has all that to do with architecture?

It has everything to do with the New Architecture, something to do with the old;

1. In this paragraph, and throughout those passages in *Kindergarten Chats* and other writings dealing with education, there is reflected the profound influence on Sullivan of his teacher at the English High School in Boston, Moses Woolson: see *The Autobiography of an Idea,* Ch. IX.

so don't interrupt me with your chatter. For them life has no urge, no current — it is a sluggish stream filled with sewage.

But this isn't precisely what I wished to talk about. I had rather talk of cheerful things, of bright and sunny things, tinkling with laughter, and jogging along in innocent mirth. But that isn't just what I wished to talk about either.

Well, what is it then?

Can't you guess?

Well, was it about —

Say, why don't you tell me how to get near that loon!

I was intending to take you for an outing in the country, but I shall have to postpone it now until you quiet down. You are a youthful wild-man-of-the-woods, I fear.

Oh, come! Let's go to the country.

No. Discipline is part of my program. You must stick to your lessons until they begin to stick to you.

Oh, I know all you've said. It's in the back of my head somewhere: I'm a good listener.

It may be so, but you'll have to be a better one before I let go of you.

Why, governor! I can tell you all you've said — pretty nearly every word. Listen —

I haven't time. I want to talk, myself. Besides this isn't what I wished to say either. By the way, speaking of loons —

Yes?

There is another class of people —

Oh, pshaw!

Who are shy, furtive and solitary. They have mental furniture, but wish to sit in it themselves — alone in a certain prim, horse-hair splendor, with the shades carefully drawn down. If one approaches them, they retire, they dive below the surface of themselves, they withdraw, definitely, as it were, into the depths of solitary waters. And yet they are not wild creatures, they are exquisitely tame creatures. The world concerns them only as a harsh intrusion — likewise their fellows: for all with them is self, withdrawn, timorous, chary, suspicious, miserly of their hoarded store of tidy bits of mental porcelain put away here and there in carefully remembered secret drawers.

Well, what about it? They don't interest me.

They do me, for they are all attention — to themselves.

And you wish me, I suppose, to be all attention to others?

No. But when you accumulate, accumulate abundantly, absorb totalities, not fragments. Grasp the largeness of things, not the petty isolated aspects. Lay hold upon the warm significance of realities, not the mere cold currency passing from hand to hand. Seize upon the drift, the color, the intensity, the what-you-may-call-it of the moving, teeming life about you, not merely upon its broken facts of definition, and follow, follow, follow every path, every trail that leads toward emotional and spiritual riches — paths hidden alike to the heedless and the over-sure — and then, when you give, give of your abundance: And this it is to live.

If you receive not, you cannot give. And to receive of life you must be awake to it. Shut the heart and you close the open door of sympathy upon yourself, and in the doing exclude the light of the world. It is sympathy that leads, sympathy that draws us on with an invisible hand — beckoning, persuading, illuminating all things with her smile. She knows the heart's desire, she divines a simple longing: for she is that longing, going ever outward through the doors of sense, and she seeks until she finds, until she finds her mate, then together they return to you and enter — and ye three are one. Of such is sympathy, the liveliest tenant of the heart. So what I call *attention* becomes what you call *interest;* so what you call an *impression* becomes what I call an *answer.* So, living becomes action; seeing and listening, functions of life: and all by virtue of the gentle force we call sympathy: sympathy the receiver, the giver — sympathy: I — you — the poet.

XIX. Responsibility: The Public

If now, my son, we pause for a little, to make a survey of our field — a bird's-eye view, a cloud-view if you will, that shall give us some just notion of its length, breadth and topography — the striking, the characteristic element of our human nature coming nearest and receding farthest in the view is that almost universally prevalent disregard of the American people for those things, those thoughts, those feelings, aptitudes and demands that do not immediately concern the immediate Dollar. To be sure, as in overlooking a forest we might declare it pine, although hemlocks, spruces, and many an other tree might in fact be found scattered through it, so, in this instance, the statement is to hold in its sweeping generality of view, and does not, for the purposes of our rough sketch and broad overlay of color, need specific qualification.

To one who realizes vividly the immensity of our land, and whose sympathies are wide enough, inclusive enough, to comprehend and entertain the vital reality that we are a people of one-hundred-odd millions held in common weal or woe by the most elastic tie that ever, in the course of history, has drawn a great people in a flexible bond: the subtle ideal of self-government, the altruistic conception of a fundamental right to the pursuit of happiness — the very soul and function of freedom — to such a one it must likewise be apparent that, in a large measure, the sense of liberty has not drawn even with it the companion sense of responsibility; like an ill-mated team of horses, one of which pulls while the other balks. This curious spectacle, enlarged in view from my little simile, and broadened over the people in the length and breadth of the land, cannot do otherwise than fill the thoughtful mind with deep regret and serious apprehension, and, at times, blot out the sunshine of our hopes with its heavy cloud-drift of pessimism and foreboding, deepening the general fair tone of color with sombre shades of gray and darkening gray.

Deeply must such a nature be impressed by a view, continental in its scope, of a great people unconscious and careless of its actual greatness, and grasping, with contracted vision and feverish nervosity, for the shadow they believe to be real. For this shadow they pursue with an idolatrous obsession; and the fair sunlight of their land and their institutions, which gives them daily strength and a path so to grope in, is held commonplace and valueless.

This sun, so much in obscuration nowadays, is the luminous spirit of Democracy. That orb, whose superb refulgence shall dispel the heavy night of autocracy, is, indeed, a new sun under the sun; but its day is not cloudless; would that it were!

The fact that we are so really great a potential democracy, is one which, stupendous though it be, seems to impress us chiefly in its aspects of geographical spread, physical force, and material national power, rather than in its spiritual potency and glory as the liberating and the vitalizing impulse of the soul of the people and of the individual man.

Profoundly does the heart cry out in yearning that this light of life might shine forth in all its splendor upon upturned radiant faces, upon eyes that might see the clear blue vault of our national sky, and the ample air of health and promise over them; and that this pig-like rooting and grunting and sniffing for the hidden Dollar might cease, if for but one clear-cut luminous moment at a time.

There is a far too wide-spread, too general feeling in the mass, and too acute an accentuation of it in the individual, that this deeply and seemingly surely-founded social fabric exists solely for personal profit and exploitation; and that, once his taxes paid, or evaded, and his voting done or left undone, he, the individual, has rendered quid pro quo; that his responsibilities to his fellows, to his country, to himself are at an end — and that he may move on in his narrow groove of self-interest without detriment to his fellows, to himself, or to his country.

But this view is rudely false as a theory and a practice. I can see that you, young as you are, already have the taint of it in your blood and brain, and the knowledge of this fills me with a certain heaviness. For in this inverted view lie the beginnings of decay and the origins of that anaemic diathesis manifest enough in other ways but peculiarly so in our buildings — false, gloomy and pessimistic as a forest of leafless trees in which the sap no longer freely runs.

It is useless to say that these symptoms are of the signs and sins of youth. It is not so. They are the warnings of premature maturity; the symptoms, slight, but significant, of disturbance of function. If these buildings of ours were merely the uncouth expression of a national rowdyism, I might have said so to you at once and spared myself the task of analyzing their characteristics. But they are too sophisticated for that. There is in them hardly a line that does not show on the part of the architect an overweening desire for approbation, and the vanity of a stricken mind. It would be laughable and indeed most unscientific to call this architecture *naïf;* for there is in it nothing of the direct, simple, homely method that speaks of native method. On the contrary, it is hysterical. It signifies the morbid brain, not the fallow. It is selfish, cynically expedient, and far adrift from the moorings of sanity. Instead of responding to the vigor of the best that is in our national life, it reflects the banal, the intemperate.

Nothing more clearly reflects the status and the tendencies of a people than the character of its buildings. They are emanations of the people; they visualize for us the soul of our people. They are as an open book. And by this sign the tendency today is disquieting.

Now, a people clearly is accountable, willy-nilly, for all of its acts. It cannot logically accept responsibility for one class of acts and deny responsibility for others; for a people is an aggregated individual, to be held in the balance of fate morally responsible for *all* of his acts.

It is trite but none-the-less true to say that the national life is but the reflex of multitudinous individual lives; that Democracy varies in its states of health accordingly and likewise in the rhythm of its growth and development. Individual neglect, indifference, inattention thus become, in the aggregate, national. If the individual is not impressible by things, qualities, relations of a certain kind, that unimpressibility becomes by force of numbers a national trait. If the individual denies or ignores his responsibility, how shall he protest when others do so? Thus, national characteristics accurately reflect the preponderance of individual characteristics; and thus our national politics, our municipal politics and our architecture are precisely what we are willing they should be.

Our national adolescence is passed and gone. We are entering manhood and we must recognize and face its responsibilities, or pay the penalty. A prudent man takes his bearings carefully. So should a prudent people — entering, as are we now, over the threshold of a new era that is to liberate moral forces of a power and insistence hitherto unknown though not unsuspected; a century that is destined to bring forth unique outbursts, explosions, catastrophes and the cataclysms of new birth.

But how is a people to take its bearings unless the individual reckons with himself? And when I say the individual I mean *you!* I mean myself! I mean the specific, localized sense of the individual.

To discuss architecture as a specific art is interesting enough in a way. But to discuss architecture as the projected life of a people is another story. That is a serious business. It removes architectural thought from a petty domain — the world of the book-worm — and places it where it belongs, an inseparable part of the history of civilization. Our architecture reflects us, as truly as a mirror, even if we consider it apart from us. But that is not my way. I don't want you to look at it in books or photographs. I want you to see it *in situ* with all its intimacy of surroundings, uses and associations. I want you to see it growing, breathing, living, however morbidly, and with however much of hectic flush, turgid opulence and internal decay. I want you to see it just as you may see, if you will, your own people and your own nation function, grow and take on form about you.

Architecture has been made a plaything long enough: I am tired of the farce, weary of the melodrama, sick unto death of the masquerade.

Let us therefore place the art on an intelligible basis. Let us test it, and reveal it for gold or dross, by the sure touchstone of healthful human nature. Let us test it by the solvent of reason, by the crucible of common sense, by the sure test of the spirit of democracy. Let us ignore the books, the schools, and go forth into the broad open world where real things are. Let us there study the living organism, the real thing, in health and illness. Let us do this with minds wide-open.

It is clear that the people, the public as a whole, are responsible for the architecture we see. Inattention, not indifference, is the root of the trouble — we will consider the trunk and branches in due time. But the responsibility does not end here, however surely it begins here. This is its general aspect only. We will push the investigation until we begin to see definitions — until this word, responsibility, becomes a living thing; until the word, democracy, becomes a living thing; until we see, beyond doubt, that our architecture must become a living force.

XX. Responsibility: The Architect; The Schools

It would seem that inattention, in the many, implies either that the faculties of the individual have not been aroused and trained, or that a lethargy has supervened. The attentive mind does not voluntarily become inactive; it is by nature lively; and, while it may grow accustomed to move more freely in one direction than in all others, it does not lose its common receptivity unless there be an inhibitive cause.

"Brains," are prevalent; the exercise of far-reaching thought is rare. Capacity to receive large impressions is notably so.

It might seem as though it were easier to receive than to give — on the assumption that it costs nothing. But this is not so. To receive, especially to receive the higher, finer, broader impressions of life, of nature, of humanity, implies as fine if not finer powers than giving. One cannot, in any event, give until he has received.

It affects one curiously, therefore, to view a people or an individual so engrossed as are we in the minute liberties — the legal liberties; so cautious and guarded in legal infraction — yet heedless of the larger liberties, the larger powers — not to say the larger obligations.

Intelligence we have, but it is mainly of the kind we enthusiastically call smart, shrewd, keen, clever, cunning, shifty. It has no background. It has no foundation whatever, except in a raging materialism. It is useful and dangerous, heedless and incongruous in its reversion to the primitive.

Time will answer these activities and inactivities in its own way. They concern us here chiefly in this aspect: that the intelligent people, having delegated to a certain class called architects their need and power to build, never ask of them thereafter an enlightened accounting; never ask for that which in business affairs they are so ready to demand, to wit: a balance sheet. Has it ever occurred to you how such a trial balance would look? Well, it has to me. I am looking at it now; it covers the length and breadth of the land; it shows some extraordinary entries — for instance:

Does the intelligent public say to its architects: We have trusted your intelligent profession: how have you administered the trust? We are an aspiring democracy; is your aspiring art equally democratic? The intelligent public does nothing of the kind. It asks for nothing, except in the immediate business of Dollars and Cents. The larger business, the larger trust, it ignores as inconsequential. Nor, in effect, does the *individual* ask more. An assurance that the "style" is Louis XIV, Francis 1st, Italian of this or that period, Greek, Roman, Gothic or what not, balances his inquiry, and he is satisfied that the transaction is legitimate.

But you and I are not so easily disposed of. We have unwelcome inquiries to make; searching questions to ask; we insist upon an accounting. For you are I: are we not of the intelligent public; are we not also smart, shrewd, keen, clever, cunning, shifty? And are we not, further, of the body politic, economic, and social? Are we not also individuals, freemen, free-lances? If democracy is worth anything, we want to know *what* it is worth; and why we find *no such entry* in the balance sheet. We are stockholders, as it were, in that Great Corporation we call our Country. That is why we are to look into the books; not the books that you were used to in your school, and that cultured people cherish because they satisfy the intelligence, but the books that record modern facts, actual transactions, current phenomena. We will put an inquiring finger here and there, and ask what *this* means; and moreover we will follow back each item through the ledger, the journal, the day book, etc., and through all the cross accounts until we run it down, until we find out all about it. For we in our way are expert accountants, careful auditors — they cannot fool us by any double set of books. The open set already suggests a secret set. We mean business; not Dollars and Cents business solely, but real, democratic business, and the true purposes of the art of architecture in this land. We need to know why the intelligent public, the intelligent individuals, the intelligent architects are jointly and severally so lacking in intelligence. We wish to know just why and where and when they need more intelligence. We have been told as stockholders that the most interesting part of the books is the oustide: and this is as near to the contents as a small stockholder usually gets; but we will take care of all that. When we are through we may conclude that a new set of books must be opened, many old accounts written off, and new ones entered. But sufficient for the day is the bookkeeping thereof — we will bear it all in mind as we go along.

It is perhaps not to be wondered at that architects believe themselves justifiably unaccountable in the sense I hint at, if, perchance, they give the matter a thought. Why should they not, you say. That *why* is precisely what we are going to look into: There is an answer to the why.

If a certain man is given a certain as-it-were education as a beginning, and a certain subsequent technical training, we naturally wish to examine their value and to inquire *to what use he puts them*. And, if his workmanship prove defective, if he show weird inclinations, palm off strange substitutes, imitations, and laud these while rather intelligently deprecating us, we want to know how and why he has come to prefer this form of evasion. If we give him a gem and he returns us paste, if, in a larger way, we give him, theoretically, the blessings of national freedom, of geographic grandeur, of boundless energy, of optimism and of somewhat childlike faith in our intelligence, trusting to his skill and fidelity to shape them to our uses, and in return we receive heirlooms; if, in the improbable case we ask that he create — and he disinters — we must know why. Should we say we are Americans and he reply: The more fools we, and we agree with him; should we, on the other hand, insist that we are what we are, and he beguiles us — we must know the reason.

We ask for style — he gives us fashion. We ask for youth — he give us old age. We ask for fitting common sense — he gives us inanity. And all these things we are apt to accept as matters of course.

Now why is the intelligent architect a grave-digger — does quasi-culture lead to this? Why is he a ghoul — is this what scholarship means? Why is he a fashion-monger — is this what is meant by taste? Why is he a plagiarist — is this what books lead to? Why is he a denier — is this the flower and fruit of optimism? Why is he constantly quoting — is not free speech for use?

Where there is an effect there is as surely a cause — we all know that. We see this effect, this phenomenon, this attitude. The cause may seem obscure, but it is not. It is a little one, such a little one: He, this architect, went to school. So it were better if all the architectural schools were at the bottom of the sea. They have no discernible function on land — other than to make mischief.

Anyone who will take the trouble to investigate the architectural schools will shortly discover that, as institutions of learning, so-called, they are bankrupt, if, by solvency we assume what makes for the good of the people. Not only are they useless to our democratic aspirations, they are actively pernicious, and their theory of operation is a fraud on the commonwealth which supports them. Their teachings are one long continuous imbecility. They are undemocratic to the core of their dried-up medievalism, although a democracy pays their bills and houses and feeds them in a land of freedom. They are essentially parasitic — sucking the juices of healthy tissues and breeding more parasites.

If an institution whatsoever were to receive healthy lads, and after four years of "care," return them mentally and physically crippled, broken-winded, weak-hearted and infected, there would be a hue and cry. And why? Because we could easily see, easily understand. It would speak at once to the heart, to the intelligence. It would be everybody's business; it would create popular clamor. But, when precisely such young men are taken in by an institution, so-called of learning, a so-called school of architecture, and, in four years, are turned out of it mentally dislocated, with vision obscured, hearts atrophied and perverted sensibilities — who cares! And why? Because it is not so easily seen. The social consequences are not obvious. It is nobody's business — but ours.

These institutions declare with a certain craft of speech that they train the young to become architects; and they allow it to be inferred that by this they mean architects fitted by a proper mental and moral training, a complete equipment of head, heart, and hand, to deal with the realities of American life, of American democracy, to grasp and retain its potencies, and to express and sublimate its characteristics in the building which they will create for it. If this be so, then, certainly, judging by their practice, their actual, devitalizing methods, architecture and feeblemindedness are surely synonymous terms in the lexicon of these schools.

But my dear sir, you forget that I am a graduate of one of these very schools.

I have not forgotten it for one moment. Indeed, the fact that under your fair exterior I saw shriveled faculties, led me to take up with you and see what could be done. I have scarcely said a word to you from the beginning of our talks, with the exception of a few fine-spun philosophizings, that you should not have been able to say to me, or to anyone else, had you been properly and righteously watched, warded and trained at your school, instead of being filled with architectural piffle. And even what little I have said, and it is or should be elementary in any true theory of the architectural art, you have received in a semi-obscurity of mind. And this, as I have told you before, is not your fault, for anyone can see that you are naturally bright and apt; it is your misfortune. I tell you, if ever we are to have a real architecture, not this infernal make-believe, this stupid scholasticism, we must have life, not death, in our architectural schools, or else abandon them utterly. I tell you the cry of the hour, the yearning of the hour is for life! The need of the hour is for men! The appalling lack of the hour is true education: education that will make men — men to the heart! I am tired of man-shadows, and I detest these schools as they are now conducted, because they make shadow-men.

Thus does the responsibility for our buildings trace itself, in part, a step farther — but this is not the end of the story.

XXI. The Professor

I think the way you have handled the schools is uncalled for; without warrant, in my estimation, and seemingly done only to please yourself. Of what use can it be to you or to me to slaughter in this fashion? I see no sense in it; I don't believe there is anything to be gained by it. If you wish to show how clever you are, that is one thing; but I believe the labor, the life-work of all well-meaning people, mis-guided though they may be, should be treated with consideration. What good does this perpetual hammering do, except to wound my feelings, and to slur the feelings of those whom I had learned to love and respect. I don't like it. It's all right to have the gift of gab, but why use it in a spirit of conscious power? I don't think it's dignified and I don't think it's humane. You are striking at the very root of what I have been brought up to revere. Now why is this? I have too much sense to be-lieve you are talking at random. At the same time, what you say both soothes and irritates me; it stimulates one moment, and depresses the next. I see no outcome. I see only a chaos of hope and despair. Why is all this? You have undermined me, and you will merely make of me, in turn, a savage, as far as I can see. I don't like it; I wish to get my bearings again and learn whether I belong to myself or not. All that you have said thus far is elusive, full of certainty and uncertainty, begin-ning nowhere and ending nowhere. At one moment I think it luminous and full of brain, at another mere gush and piffle, as you are so fond of saying of others. I am in revolt, my stomach is turning, my soul is rebelling; where are you drifting to anyway?

Doubtless you believe all that now, and your irritation is an excellent symptom; it shows that a ferment is going on; that your thinking faculties are awakening from their long torpor. This delights me greatly, for when one is profoundly irritated, something important is going on; a ferment of some kind, whatever it may be, is at work. It is Nature's way, and possibly something may come of it in your case, who knows! I used to have such attacks when I was a youngster. But, my truculent friend, when you have reached a certain age, have done some sustained thinking, have taken the glorious art of architecture one whit as deeply to your heart as I have, fought for it as you would fight not for yourself but for your "ladie faire," have grasped a fraction of its possibilities, have thought with care of your country, your people, have fathomed the surface of the mind of man, have fluttered near the surface of that infinite mind in which we can see our own fleeting reflections, when you have drunk but one quaff from the crystal well-spring of creative, of divine art, have felt one soft breath of the gently blowing zephyr of reality — of the infinite poesy of nature — have caught one strain of the sweet song of the seasons, you will disdain the fetid schools as I do, if by that time they be not changed from the lethargy of their indifference, the squalor of their inattention. But who knows! The shell may crack some day. Do you really suppose that I would speak to you out of hand? Go to; you are young and over-sure, and over-chivalrous.

Yes, but why so pitiless?

Because the condition is inhuman.

Yes, yes; but you have excused the public in a measure, have excused the architects in a measure; is there not a word to be said for the schools? I have some affection for my alma mater. I cherish the recollection of those years, happy enough it seemed to me, with their associations, their triumphs, failures and companionships. What you say may be true, for all I know, but it sounds bitter, biting. It's like throwing vitriol in my face. Is there no word to say?

There is. I sympathize with your feelings because I had them at one time, only mine were rather more involved than yours; for I was left to struggle and fight alone; to get my bearings in the wilderness as best I could, to go by the sun, the stars, the mossy side of trees, through dense forests, over deserts, over precipitous hills, across tangled ravines, across free-running rivers, through rain and fog and fair weather, through swamp and marsh, through tangle and brush — lonely at night, hungering, solitary, a wanderer, a seeker, a hoper. But you — you have a friend to lead you by the hand! I am that friend! I have gone before! I know what hardship means, and it means all things that make a man. How can you love if you have not love in your heart? How can you sacrifice if you have not sacrifice in your heart? How can you prevail if you have not "I will" in your heart? For the heart is all in all — the beginning and the end of man. Don't talk to me of brain. I tell you heart is all in all. Heart means devotion, courage, consecration, tenacity, inflexibility, determination: the heart will make any sacrifice, the brain will make no substantial sacrifice; the heart is generous, the brain is selfish.

As to your schools, I treat them usually with silence, so weak are they, and let it go at that. It is when I think of you in such connection that I wax wroth. For you stand, in my eye, for all the youth of our land. And the youth of a land is the hope of that land. Woe to a land that cherishes not its youths. That land is doomed.

But you don't mean to say —

No, no. That is another matter. Some day, watch the night give birth to dawn and you may perhaps know how I feel when I look on you. But, as to the schools — a plague upon them — this much may be said, and to the point you make: Silly as they are, empirical as they are, still they are as it were the blind. But who made them the blind? Their predecessors! The professor had his professor, and that professor his, and before him that professor his, and on and on backwards in a thin, singlefoot line, to the pettifoggers of the Middle Ages, the men who knew nought

9. "When the lintel is placed upon the two piers, architecture springs into being." (Stonehenge)

10. "Some man at some time . . . conceived and carried out the idea of wilfully placing stones to span over something or other." (Tiryns, Greece)

11. Sullivan at Ocean Springs, Mississippi

of reality and cared less. These old-timers hated the light, they hated Nature that makes the light, they hated freedom, they worshipped rule and precept, they loved in their cadaverous way the schoolroom and distrusted the world. Yet, in justice, let me say a word for your professor: To break his bondage is not easy for him; for scholasticism becomes a habit of mind so fixed as to become an addiction, and is eventually believed to be a virtue. Moreover, the said professor is, by force of tradition and custom, shut out from the world's activities. They are to him non-essentials. In other words, he would weigh the world outside of himself in the balance of his conventions and, finding it wanting, would declare its aspirations nil. He is steeped in the formularies and the disdains of intellectual aristocracy, and, through the easy process of denial, Democracy, for him, does not exist.

But, verily, these are times when the old values must all be revalued. When they must be weighed and judged in the balance with Democracy, and, if found wanting in that balance, they must go. These are the times when all the old measures must be remeasured by the standard measure of altruism, and, if found short, must be rejected. Such are the times, such is the trend of the age, such the inexorable drift. So shape your thought accordingly — no matter what you may think you see for the moment, Democracy will prevail as surely as you and I are now talking here together. It is in the soil, it is in the air, it is in the genius of our people, it is a primordial world-aspiration; nothing can stay its urge. Don't forget this for a moment, no matter what you see or think you see to the contrary, for all such signs are factitious, they do not touch the core of the people. This is a shaping democracy and it will abide a democracy. Trust your country, my lad — no matter about the schools. Do exactly what they warn you not to do, and you will be apt to come nearest to your people. I cannot tell you just now how titanic a struggle is going on in our own land between aspirant Democracy and the inherited obsession of feudalism, but time and energy, and optimism and personality will work this all out. You may take your hand in it when the time ripens. Go ahead as though it were settled, for it will be settled. The forces you now think dominant are not really dominant, they are symptoms, transitory symptoms that will be shaken off when the time comes. Therefore, arrange your architecture for Democracy, not for feudalism. Gird up your heart!

There is a ferment in the soil, rest assured of that. Your professor does not know what to do with ferments. So is there a leaven in our people, but your professor knows of no such leaven: he, who should himself leaven, knows of leavens only by hearsay.

So have I really spared your schools, my son, the outpour of my dissent, and have let fall but a few drops of wrath from the vial which is over-full. Let them alone: they have that pride which goeth before destruction, and the haughty spirit which goeth before a fall.

So goes on our investigation of responsibilities.

XXII. The Tulip

My wound is not yet healed. You have condoned the schools after a fashion, but in a way that does not cheer. You have a thought, a feeling, in reserve. I can sense it. You have not clinched matters in your usual style. You have a secret rancor — what is it?

Not very much. A little thought, a very little one. You have heard, perhaps, that in growing tulips to make new varieties, the raiser does not propagate them from the root, or from cuttings, or from subdivisions of the root, or from buddings, or from the leaf, or from suckers or off-shoots, for all such methods tend to *perpetuate* a variety. So, seeking a new variety, he plants seeds naturally or artifically fertilized as he wishes. They come up, are pricked out and cared for. When they are strong enough to bear it, they are set in open beds. Year after year they bloom, a common grayish blossom — showing reversion to the early tulip type. And so they live along, a dull and stupid brood, without apparent promise, until suddenly, of a blooming time, one of them "breaks," as they say, into a gorgeous, stately flower, and lo! — a new variety, a tulip of tulips, its gardener's joy and recompense, a new thing of beauty born of untoward surroundings into a needy world.

And so it chills me when I think of this, as now and then I do, and as especially I did while talking to you of the schools, that in the beds of the ill-favored whom we perforce call teachers there is not, here and there, among them, one who bursts his bonds and adds a glory to the race. How often have I yearned for such a breaking-tulip. Why in this putative flower-bed that one watches year by year, does there come forever the same unwelcome blooming? For are they not men, however poor in seeming promise? And may not a man perhaps burst his bonds asunder? May not his spirit, hidden though it be, break forth, and show such form and color of manliness that we shall say: Here is a new flower, a man-flower, come to us from the father of flowers. But no; after five, six, seven years if there be no "break," the seedling tulip never breaks. There is a moment in our lives when we burst our bonds or fail to burst them.

And have we not all heard of the ugly duckling; and of Cinderella? But those are fairy tales; and, it seems, are to remain fairy tales. Why is there so little of the sweetness and the joy and the beauty of the fairy tale in our real life, so little of its magic? Fairy tales are of the very bloom of the heart. Why does not the heart bloom every day? Why is this ethereal charm found only in children's tales? Why the Sleeping Beauty, why Prince Charming? Why do we call these things childish? Why are we ashamed of the best, the truest, the sweetest, the loftiest in us? Why do we relegate these things to children? Why are we the reverse of tulips? Why do we flower so wondrously in childhood, and then, as the years pass, turn dull and inglorious? Are men and women less than tulips?

Well, *that* is beautiful. And if by any chance I acquire tulip seeds, you shall surely grow them for me. You should have been a gardener of men.

Maybe. But were I "gardener of the skies," no fairer orb should glow there than shines the star of youth below. But to return to our muttons — I mean our profes-

NOTE: This chapter was considerably shortened in revision.

sors. It may be rather their misfortune than their fault that they seem appointed, in our bashful social scheme, to transmit the strain and stain of feudalism. Contrariwise, Democracy liberates nothing if it liberates not the mind. I hold it against a man that he prefers not to free his mind; that he chooses the habitual, rather than that self-government, that initiative, which is the perpetuating force of a free people. I know that few men care to face the truth; not because it is the truth, but because they fear the truth may prove too large. All of which is timid and unlovely. It ill becomes us: for Democracy is large and true. So must we be. So are we in many ways.

I am glad to hear you say that last. It heartens me a bit.

XXIII.   An Office Building

Well, say, Papa when we talked of coming to New York did you ever imagine we would strike anything quite so rich as this? Talking of breaks, and speaking incidentally of responsibilties, this is a wild weird one! What do you call it in the vernacular, anyway? It has a name, I suppose; everything has a name. Adam started that. But what is it anyway — this lean, long, lanky bawd, this brazen thing turned loose on the streets? What, in or out the dictionary, do you call it, anyway?

Saint John the Divine[1], perhaps?

Oh, no! I say, no! I draw the line at sacrilege.

I draw the line at nothing. All values are zero to me.

Bah! You are starting wickedly. To be sure, there isn't anything divine about it; it seems more like a temple of Mammon.

Well — St. John or Mammon; it's all one in New York; and I am not sure that they are two elsewhere.

Still, there is, I think a "saint" somewhere in the name, if not in the building.

Probably the one who fell dead: it gives me that same tired feeling.

How can you make so ribald a jest? I blame myself; I started you wrong.

Because I have two good precedents: the building itself and the Great Corsican. If they have made them, of course I can.

That's a villainous jibe, a wobbly effort for my counselor and guide. Your native wit is on vacation. Still, I admit that the structure has a seeming locomotor ataxia of its own; five jumps or jerks or slides of four stories, per jerk, and a hop and a skip at the top of my thumb; a sort of course-I-can-can, debilitated joke of its own, and like my own, by way of a finality. It's funny enough, in its way, isn't it?

Worse than that; much worse. While we are punning: what did the Great Corsican say; Scratch a Tartar and you get an emetic? Now if we scratch this Saint

1. First stone laid in 1892; the Romanesque design was later changed to Gothic.

Tartar will we find a Saint Emetic; or, if we scratch the saint shall we find an architek? And if we scratch the architek, what then?

You might find an architecticus emeticus, perhaps, if there be, and I'm sure there is such a thing, outside of the dictionaries, but you won't find any architecture — that's dead sure in this case. Still, for all that, I find your joke coarse and repulsive.

Admitted. But so is the building. Mine may be a minstrel joke, but the structure, likewise, is a rude blatancy in the "minstrelsy" of our art. But there is another phase of it to which I wish to call your immediate and helpful attention: this copious un-swallowing and expectoration of undigested architecture makes me, in turn, ill at the stomach — and that is no joke at all.

You choose to be brutal again.

The building is so all the time.

But it is the work of an eminent architect, I am told.

Then they both are "eminently" unsavory.

Have you no regard for a fellow-practitioner?

None. I have regard only for our art. Moreover, this architect, this "eminent" architect, save the word, has shown no regard for you or for me or for any other passer-by. Why then should I regard him? Why should I regard other than as brutal a man who poses openly thus to me while declaiming like a stump orator to others. That sort of thing won't go with us. It may "work" with the public at large, but we are not the public at large, we are the public sharpened to a point; and with this point we will prod until we let some of the wind out of the bag. The time has come when we must press these matters home. Why should I spare this eminent man? Has he a license to commit a public nuisance? Does eminence necessarily imply irresponsibility? Is he to be eminently immune? Am I to say thank you when filth is thrown in my face? Indecent exposure of person is forbidden both by the social and the statute law: why then this indecent exposure of a building! Is there no law wherewith to reach such perversion? If not, let us make at once a lynch law of our own to fit the case, and dispense justice in a primitive way. If he won't accept re-sponsibility to society at large of his own accord, why we'll hold him responsible to us personally whether or no — for he outrages me personally. So I pass the law and we will act on it at once, to wit: Oyez! The greater the eminence the greater the accountability. The impudence of this building is precisely in proportion to its size, cost, truculence and pessimism: truly an ugly work: a kind of insolence which is, *sui generis,* a part of New York. By what right does this eminent hoodlum, this bully, make a building that must stand here for generations a monument to the unholy passions of our civilization? Shall he escape censure? Shall he hide behind his eminence? I think not! I am looking into the books. I want you to know the why and the wherefore. I want you to know why it is that this building and others of its class — there are scores of them — make lower New York an architectural pest-house and a mad-house. I wish to inquire why New York with all its wealth, and, therefore, its great power to build, has not the best, as it should have, but, on the exact contrary, the most decadent, the most bumptious architecture in the country. I wish to ferret out the reason. That there is a fundamental crookedness of attitude is evident. Indeed it is something worse than that! It is akin to rapine. No chivalry, no scruple there!

This barbarian structure serves us as a type: and, that done, we may dismiss its individual vulgarity and turn to the class it represents. The buildings of this class, singly and in chorus, proclaim the negation of our art. They seem to strut and glory in it. They stand for an extraordinary egotism: the low ebb of strength. They flout manhood and the decencies that manhood must respect for itself in its respect for others. Sordid folly can go no further; nor can the systematic spurning of ideals that are worth the living for. They constitute a vast denial. These buildings, as they increase in number and uproar, make this city poorer and emptier, morally and spiritually; they drag it into the mire of materialism. This is not American civilization, it is Gomorrah. This is not Democracy, it is madness. It is the growl of a glutton hunt for the Dollar, a yelp with no thought for aught else under the sun or over the earth. It is decadence in its most convincing form: so truly does this architecture reflect the causes which have brought it into being. Such structures are *profoundly anti-social;* and, as such, they must be reckoned with. An architect who acknowledges no obligation to society at large, who gives no heed to the just claims of posterity, is not an architect in my sense of the word — he is an outlaw! And so these buildings are not architecture, but outlawry.

Aren't you laying it on pretty strong?

Not half strong enough. I know the situation. I know what it means. I know how to translate it into English. It means grandiose and selfish irresponsibility in an extreme sense. It means megalomania — delirium.

It means pretty stupid architecture, sure enough.

It means tainted architecture. It means a virus implanted for generations to come, that is appalling to think of. Some day the future New Yorkers will wish to spend vast sums to pull down these screaming nightmares of its [sic] morbid early sleep, and be rid of them; and they will most heartily curse the generation of architects that made them, and the money-crazy people who not only let them be done but wished them to be done. The close student knows that these structures signify much more than they seem to; that their meaning lies much deeper than the mere superficies of architectural ignorance. They are an outward aspect, revolting enough to be sure, but merely symptomatic. The truth is that they stand in evidence of forces that are undermining American life; that are bringing about a decay out of which, if not checked, some day will sprout a revulsion. You cannot ignore the fundamental duties, the fundamental rights without at the same time, by such contumely, sowing the seeds of a bitter harvest. Time brings the reckoning day, and fate strikes, at the appointed hour. He who has ears to hear notes the first, faint rumbling of distant thunder, the first darkening of the horizon. Will the storm swell and break in fury? Who can say? Storms do not always break. The first rumblings may not signify. Sometimes a change of air absorbs and disperses the gathering tempest, sometimes it does not; but the warning is here. If this morbid architecture we are now studying stands for anything really American, stands for forces powerful enough to produce a result, it will be interesting to speculate on the outcome of the reckoning day. It will be prudent to consider if in sound education may not lie a counter-force still greater. One's temperament will enter largely into the conclusion — or the prophecy — and the more broadly one knows his country, the more hopeful he must be. But if one inclines to pessimism, he will see an horizon dark and threatening. Certainly, one most hopeful sign, in its way, is this: that with the American people at large, over the length and breadth of the land, education has become a passion; a passion growing more intense, if not better-directed, as the years unfold. And he who studies true Americanism, in the character of the people — of all the people, not a part of them — becomes thereby saner and more tranquil in his own mind — and stouter of heart. On the one hand, if social forces, broad movements, are to be interpreted in the lurid light of these momentous structures, the outlook is gloomy if it be taken in other than a local sense; on the other hand, if it be considered in its purely local and restricted sense, then New York is, conclusively, the plague-spot of American Architecture. Once you learn to look upon architecture not merely as an art more or less well, more or less badly, done, but as a social manifestation, the critical eye becomes clairvoyant, and obscure and unnoted phenomena become illumined. It is a pity that, in our studies, we have to meet and deal with so much that is depressing. Yet we have no choice; we take the conditions as we find them. To know, we must touch; and it were better not to know our art at all than not to know the aspects of the length, the breadth, the depths and the heights. It is a curious reflection that here, in this city, where we should by seeming virtue of money-power be led to expect the best, we find the worst; that, where standards should be highest, we find them lowest; that, where we should find the highest type of responsibility and honor, we find the grossest exhibition of irresponsibility and dishonor; and that eminence, once an olive crown, is here made a slur and a by-word. Yet there you are — plain as print: the structures give the evidence, you need only bring the eye with power to see, the intelligence to interpret. If you can read print, you can read this.

But I do not like to read that kind of print.

No more do I. But if you wish to read the current architecture of your country, you must go at it courageously, and not pick out merely the little bits that please you. I am going to soak you with it until you are nauseated, and your faculties turn in rebellion. I may for the moment be a hard task-master but I strive to be a thorough one. When I am through with you, you will know architecture from the ground up. You will know its virtuous reality and you will know the fake, the fraud, the humbug. I will spare nothing, I will reveal all — for your sake. I will stir the cesspool to its depths, and also the pious virtues in their shallows. The suave, dexterous, diplomatic architecture I will show you also: the kind of architecture our "cultured" people believe in because they do not believe in themselves. No, my boy, we are in this investigation seriously, and we will not stop until we have ventilated every corner. Superficiality is an every-day trait; but it is not to characterize our way. When we strike we must strike hard and deep, and search out the evil thoroughly; then may we turn to pleasanter things; then may we seek out the good. For there is much good in our people: I have faith in them.

I wish you would show me some of it; for I am thus far merely blue and disconcerted. What good does it do to turn up all this filth? You have made a bitter text of my jest. What good does it do you to keep me in a turmoil of uncertainty — to shift your base at every turn? To keep me harassed and worried, and to fill me with a loathing for architecture, instead of a love for it. You stir up nothing but rottenness and the villainies of indecency and corruption. Oh, for a breath of air! I yearn for a little touch of sunshine in all this pessimistic gloom; one glimpse of lovely art, one soothing sight, a pleasant sound. My soul is sick. Is there no turn in this long, dreary, treeless, flowerless lane? No by-path? No shady nook? Nothing to refresh and please the eye, to bathe the heart? No sense of purity? Why did ever I begin, if its consequence leads only and always to negation! If beauty recedes as we advance! If poetry departs from the earth as we advance, and humans become in our eyes merely things of dry rot or wet rot! I don't care for all this philosophizing, this inexorable analysis of morbid things, this intimate observation of ulcers and running sores. Give me something living and beautiful, something gracious, if it be but a tree or a flower; or let me look far over the waves on the sea shore, into the soft blue sky — where I shall know peace of mind, relief from this nightmare.

That suits me too, my lad. Where do you wish to go?

Anywhere.

XXIV.   Summer: The Storm   1

I think summer was made for me. I should have been a farmer, or a cowboy, or a river pilot, or a trapper. I need out-doors. But, best of all, I like to lie on my back of a summer's day, under a great old shady tree. Eh, governor? This is a pretty spot, isn't it? See the charming valley, with the cattle and the fields; and the hills around about. I am so lazy now that Nature restores to me her delights. She's a good old dame, dear Nature, isn't she? It's so good to live and loaf today — I'm glad I'm alive, I rejoice that I was born. No more architecture for me; no more of the stuffy city. This will do: Yes, it will do very well. Now I'm going to have a good snooze, and you may keep the flies away: I hereby, and now, solemnly appoint you mosquito net in chief to my most royal highness, to my very nibs. This is great. I like it. And it's hot as Tophet; and I like that too. So let me sleep. If you say one word of architecture to me, or preach one sermon, I shall smite you in my dreams; but I shan't listen, now, or then.

Well; shall I make for you a little poem?

On your life not a poem — not a poem! You put murder in my heart! I am now like Siegfried's dragon: "I lie in possession: let me sleep."

Yes; but you know what happened to the dragon.

And I know, also, what happened to Siegfried.

But my back is not turned.

Well, if you will kindly turn your back, you may recite your poem: thus will I make an end at once of poem and poet.

But listen — This is adagio:

1. The purpose of this and the following chapter is clarified in Sullivan's letter in Appendix A.

Here lies a valley in the heart of summer.
Kine in shadows
Crops in dazzling light.
Dreamy and still this air:
All songsters hushed;
Leaves stir not.
Sleeping, in her dream yon pool mirrors
a smiling cloudlet.

My, but it is gloriously hot! And I am so drowsy. The air is dreamy, the songsters are hushed, even the leaves are still. Why are you not hushed and still like them? I am so sleepy I could sleep the eternal sleep and wake up in a heaven where the wicked architects cease troubling and weary buildings are at rest. Sleeping I would dream, and dreaming, I would mirror a pool of loveliness — without a sorrow and without a blight.

Then listen — to my song:

Now am I 'neath the heavy, spreading bough.
Now wild flowers and the vine
About me sigh.
In this sweet spot,
Dreaming life's dream anew,
Near ferny bank and this tree's friendly bole
I rest.

There's a mosquito biting my ankle; and you are pricking my ear with your poetic bill. That gives me a hazy idea: In accordance with the latest findings, if you locked up a raving poet, and several mosquitoes in the same room, and then put a prosy man in the room to be bitten in turn, would the virus be transmitted? And so with the money-man, and the poverty-man, and so on? Still, this is a half-dream. My eyes are closed, and so is my mind. Your words are rather soothing and soporific. Give me another verse. The air is heavy and still — precious sleep!

Heavy is this air with breath of growing things.
Benumbed they thirst,
O'erstrained, they languish:
In sorrow they are near to break and go:
By slender thread Life holds them here.
How still the air in this keen brilliant moment;
Exquisitely like unto a breath
Death sighs in his approach;
Answering, nearby,
A zephyr yearns,
Heart-broken,
And expires;
Murmuring,
The woods sway —
In languor they respire.

Was that thunder I heard or am I dreaming? A rumble, it was, in the stillness. Hear the birds twitter. Feel the little breeze.

Sad dreams flutter in the grove —
Chirping dismally o'er hidden nests of young.
Rumbling from beyond the hills
A deep boom
Softly wakens slumbering woodland echoes:
But they turn, and sleep again.
Nerveless, the air quivers;
Quickening, in startled breeze,
Anxiously it sweeps away — toward speedy end —
Anon impaled upon the weary point of vacancy.
Now falls with double heft
The pall of silence.
Now doth our very heart forget his beat.

But it was thunder! There it is again! We are to have a storm, and I shall be cheated of my nap; and all on your account. Still, it might be fun to watch a storm. I don't care what happens when I'm in the country. Nothing can feaze me — after the poetry — after the poetry?

Do you see that bank of cloud away off yonder! Let me try my hand:

Lowering, a dark form overtops the hills.
Gloomily it rises
Muttering, gathers and prepares.
It sweeps in dark array,
Shaping in dense phalanx.

Now you go on. See the lightning! The rain will soon be here. It's going to be a wild one. There's a shelter, there. Let's get under it, or we'll be soaked. Now you go on as she comes up — fire away with the poem.

Shaping in dense phalanx,
Marching on the sun,
Its flashing armament doth crumble the dry silence
As a twig is broken.
On his blue throne the sun is overturned
And pushed aside.

Well, I should say he was. Here comes the wind. What a flash! — and hear that rattle! It's going to be a nerve-jarrer. See the rain coming! It's right upon us. Get out your words, and I'll chip in the responses:

'Mid wind and roar the large drops patter.

Darkness with a firm hand grips the land.

Slender grasses bow down.

Trees sway and toss.

In a flash the air is ripped in twain,
And torn in shreds.

Crashing into chaos, strewing the fierce wind,
Jolting from cloud to savage cloud
The maddened thunder rushes to the front.

81. *Summer: The Storm*

The ripe rain falls in torrents.

Its downpour strenuously whines,

With eager wail.

Wildly, the Earth, in glutton frenzy, drinks it up:
Rolling in flood and racket,

And delirious gray gloom.

Soaking and reeking in tumult,
Overrunning,

Reckless of plenty, and
Mad from overmuch —

While the o'erburdened storm, with wild exultant cry doth stagger to the climax of his power, and sinks, in ecstasy of death, upon his sumptuous throne.

My, but it's a terror! They say every storm has two lives. Watch it! Isn't it inspiring in its frenzy! Whew! The mist of the rain is blowing in, but let it blow. Did you ever? What a roar! Are we to finish —

Loud groans the heavy Wind,
Shouldering his load
On massive bending frame.
All clouds descend and melt.
White bolts drop and drop in misty din.
The air is full of water and of noise:

Of murmurings and protests,
Whines,
Howls,
Ecstasies,
And blazonings of light.
Now they swirl,
And sway,
Into a grayish sodden monotone.

Now doth strange music rumble,
In the caverns of the deeply leaf-bound temple
Where my soul was gone to pray.
Within the storming silence,
Its harmonies unfold in a sonorous funeral-chord,
O'erwhelmingly triumphant, in gladness and in joy.
Slowly attuning,
Solemnly arranging,
Expanding,

Upbuilding,

It swells in peroration!

Arising,
On my winged spirit,
In pomp of glorious gloom
It doth bear the Dead One,
The Great One,

> The Mighty Storm,
> 'Mid train and muffled thunders
> And soft gleams of watery light,
> Solemnly, in pride,
> O'er hill and vale,
> O'er tree and plain,
> Toward a cloudland home,
> Where stands the ancient tomb
> Of his Fathers.

Bravo! You concluded bravely! Now why doesn't it occur to you to do that in your architecture?

Oh, bother architecture! This is too interesting.

But it's the same thing.

I don't care. Let's go on with our picture. See the rainbow forming so proudly in the sky! It reminds me of old Noah and the covenant: "I will set my bow in the cloud." Let *me* begin this time:

> The pensive widowed rain,
> Drying her warm, gray tears,
> Furtively, with timorous tread,
> Doth follow.
>
> Ragged cloud-streaks swing toward the day's end.
>
> Rain-water driblets putter, here and there, from shuddering trees.
> The downcast sun pencils a new world of lengthening mellow shadows.
> Tree-tops glisten in crowns of gold.
> With arch superb,
> Heaven's bow doth span the sky:
> A smiling promise o'er the land,
> Gracefully beneficent,
> Winsome, and fair for the heart to look upon,
> Soft arch in softer skies,
> Serenely flitting sign of happiness,
> All hail to thee!
> All hail, thou beauteous bow!
> Thou bow of loveliness!
> Thou smile of graciousness!
> Emblem of purity!
> Sign of peace!

See how the light is fading, softer and softer, after the sunset; and the calm of evening is coming on; how moist, and fresh and sweet the valley looks! I am going to try my hand again:

> Refreshed and satisfied
> How peacefully the vale doth smile.
> With clear sweet countenance.
> And supple limbs
> She doth compose herself
> To meet Sleep's gentle greeting.
> Soft flits the evening swallow.

83. *Summer: The Storm*

Murmuring, Night's happy insect-music
Doth begin.
While Dusk draws o'er this lovely pair, the tenderest of veils, with
*   silent, dewy fingers —*
Moonlight vigils
O'er their dainty dreams.

Now dreams within my dreams arise!
On airy wings,
In silvery, glinting coteries,
Flitting here, and there, amid the fairy throngs of tender, wingéd
*   wights that charm my thoughts*
With their sweet,
Humming,
Laughing songs of crescent leafy
Moonlit glee!

Now happiness doth steal,
So softly,
To the heart:
Rejuvenating every wearied hope,
Tranfiguring all sorrows into joys —
That I would dream,
And dream once more
Within this hallowed rest
Until
Betimes
The Dawn
With mellow flute
Shall shepherd home all wandering
Airy fancies of the night.

And I, my son, were I to take up your beautiful and youthful discourse, your sweet and pensive mood, your airy fantasy, would turn it thus:

Arising in these dreams
And taking manful shape,
Thou
Quickenest,
Master,
O'er a land more parched than this!
O'er its spent soul, thou pourest,
Master,
In abundance, thy life-lengthening waters:
To reassure
And to make glad
Man's weary heart!

Momentous that great afternoon,
Wherein thou walkest,
In thy gathering mood!
Slowly thou shalt prepare.
Portentous thou shalt rise o'er those great hills that shut out,

From thy people,
Their true horizon!
Thy power —
Arisen from thy land,
Shall fall to it again!
Its cry hath gone to thee:
Thou shalt assuage!

Thou soul, pregnant of many souls,
Thou life, sublimed of every living thing,
Thou, sum and substance,
Form and spirit,
Last word, in a long, long tale,
Thou,
Poet!
Thou, Redeemer!
Come!

That's fine and great, and noble — but my feet are soaking wet, and the water has been trickling down my neck, and it's dark and I'm hungry, and a little heartsick and lonesome. I know a little inn in the village not far away. Let us go there and get dry, and have a good supper. I think a steak would go well, after the airy nothings we have fed on. Come, let us go on to the village. I want a good sleep tonight; and then, I'm going to stay here in the country for several days. I want to be alone. I have a few things I want to find out for myself. And, as you have business in town tomorrow, that will arrange itself nicely. Perhaps when I see you again I may tell you a thing or two, but I won't promise.

Here we are! Isn't it a charming affair, bowered in vines, with a quaint garden; lights twinkling in the windows — and all dozing in the soft pure blue of the moonlight. I think I can have a very pleasant time here all by my lonesome, for a few days.

XXV. A Letter

Dear Uncle:

Surely the country was made for me. So much so indeed that, instead of returning to the town, I send you this letter as an ambassador, to arrange a modus vivendi, while I remain here with my new love — my true love. When I awoke the next morning, after the storm, the birds were singing and you were gone: for both of which happenings I was truly grateful: grateful to the birds, for their morning song sounded chummy and bright; glad to be rid of you, because you oppress me, weary me and hold me too strictly to the lines. Now I'm going to roam in the pasture, fancy free and harness free.

I doubt not that I shall be glad enough to see you later on, when I shall have gotten all tangled up in my own half-spun lariat and need unwinding; but not now, not now. I am suffering just now from mental over-nutrition, or rather non-assimilation: and what I need most especially is not more feeding, but a little rest for my alleged thinking apparatus. And here I find it to my taste: No hurry, no worry, no one to curb and interfere. The day after the storm our snug little valley was as fresh as a morning-glory; full of color and life and pleasantness. I took long walks, on the roads, up lanes and across country, and sat in the woods, and sat on the hill-tops, and took it all in.

To say that I have been entirely happy is not quite true, although pretty nearly so. What has bothered me is that since our interview with the storm I have not felt quite the same concerning things in general and myself in particular. I can't get it through my head yet, how you came to inveigle me into taking a hand in your so-called poem, and how you managed so cleverly to get me excited about it. You had some scheme or other, I don't doubt; but I can't quite figure out what it was. But no matter, you were one too many for me that time, and I'm sure that I haven't any fault to find; only, I can't straighten it out to my satisfaction; for I want to tell you, confidentially, that I didn't sleep much that night, but made all sorts of crazy poems to all sorts of bewildering things till along toward morning, when I fell asleep, at last, only to make fantastical strings of high-sounding words in my dreams. I guess, as William said, there isn't much difference between a poet and a madman, after all; only, one is a little more "regulated" than the other. And that isn't the worst of it: I've been trying it on since. I made a little one to a weed the other day. I like weeds: they have so much "style" to them; and when I find them where they have grown free they seem most interesting and suggestive to me. I think I'm something of a weed myself: if I felt quite sure of it I wouldn't be altogether uncomplimented. And then there are so many of them, and they differ so much in shape, color and arrangement; the form follows the function so beautifully, as you would say. I don't know the names of any of them — being city-bred. They wanted me to study botany when I was a youngster, but I wouldn't have it; and now I'm sorry. I wish I knew the names of the little rascals; then, it seems to me, I could talk to them better — but that's telling — I didn't mean to let you into my secret; but it slipped away from me, so let it go. And then I made another to a gorgeous butterfly I saw poised like a fairy on a gorgeous open flower. I was sitting on the ground close by, when she came fluttering along. It began this way — for I felt small:

> *You gorgeous, perambulating art-gallery!*
> *Why do you come along,*
> *To make me feel like thirty cents;*
> *With your wings immense*
> *And your color so strong?*
> *'Tis no subject for raillery!*

The creature was so beautiful that it almost made me angry; but I soon got over that. And I went along for six verses — and the butter flew, that is the flutter blew, away, over the fence, into the neighbor's garden. The last verse is rather pretty, and went something like this, at first:

They call you Psyche, dainty soul;
I call you sweetheart, honey-seeker.
Superb of hue, this sunny day's delight,
I would not by the faintest move your tiny breast affright.
Sweets to the sweet, they say, so here's a beaker;
Oh, quaff my song, in turn, and bless the bowl!

But I did not quite like it, and so made it go this way:

They name you Psyche, dainty breath;
I call you fair honey-seeker, and my joy.
So airily, so sweetly to alight and sway,
So prettily to fill my heart with pure delights so gay:
It really makes my thoughts grow meeker and more coy,
And wiser — as my uncle saith.

I wanted to get in a rap at you, but it seemed, on reflection, rather far-fetched; and, moreover, neither of the verses said what it was in my heart to say. So I brooded awhile and tried again — this way:

Oh, quaff my song, thou Psyche, fluttering!
The bowl is not a flower — 'tis only I.
But what is in my heart, oh, quaff, 'tis all I have to give:
'Tis thus I say to you that I, too, Psyche, live.
You will not, I am sure, my verse, deny:
For in my soul the storm of yesterday is muttering.

This came nearer what I really wanted to say, but still it isn't quite it. It doesn't exactly ring the bell. If I had you to coach me and give me the pitch and the key, and the counterpoint, as they say in music, and fill in the orchestration, and beat time, and do a few other things, it would go better. But I've found out this, by myself: That it doesn't do merely to have feelings, however fervent they may be. You must have also a pretty clear idea what it is that you feel, and a still clearer idea of what you are going to do with the feelings: and this is where I fall down, and miss you, uncle. It's one thing to feel, and quite another undertaking to create. And yet you can't create if you don't feel. I might have looked through some books of verses, but I know perfectly well that I wouldn't have found anything in any book that would tell just how I felt toward that butterfly; it might tell how the other fellow felt toward something else, but that wouldn't do me any good. I want to know how I am going to express, fully and intelligently, what I feel. I remember what you said about words, and about the imagination, and about function and form, and I think you said: First catch your function; if you didn't, I say it now. So you see, I'm considerably up a stump. I wonder if I'm going to have as much trouble with my architecture as I have had in trying to make a few verses to a butterfly? For I have a dawning suspicion that making a real building, as you would call it, and making a real poem, are pretty much one and the same thing. It was all very well when you got up steam for me, so to speak, and sort of hypnotized me into oratory. That is to say, you practically suggested everything; but when I try it alone, it doesn't seem to go so smoothly, by any means. And yet something tells me that I am on the right track; and that what I need is to persevere and not get discouraged, and to pay more attention to what you say. For I am beginning to suspect that you have a pretty complete system up your sleeve somewhere. I have a number of rods in pickle for you; but when I try them on I suppose you will bluff me off as usual. Of course, I didn't send you the verses for themselves, but merely to show you the particular kind of trouble I'm having. Still, take it all in all, I'm having an exceedingly fine time here, and am learning something every day. I can now tell the difference between a cow and a horse, between a pine-tree and an oak-tree. But when a farmer told me the other day that there were ten different kinds of oaks, four different kinds of pines, and thirty or forty different kinds of other trees hereabout, it gave me a shock, a shock of dread lest you might suddenly bob up and say that each one of these blooming trees has a function and the form of each follows that function with absolute fidelity, and you would expect me to observe them and give strict attention to the differences — when they all look alike to me now; and worse than that you would probably tell me there are here some three or four hundred different kinds of plants, several hundred kinds of insects, and dozens of kinds of birds, and that each has its complete correspondence of function and form, and, worse than all, you would tell me that the ability to note such correspondences constitute the ABC of architectural knowledge. All of which I would be weak enough, I suppose, to believe. Well, I've gabbled along at a great rate. They've called me twice, for dinner, and still I scribble away without having any too clear an idea of what I've written. Isn't it Ninon de Lenclos who says: "He who would write a perfect love letter must begin without knowing what he is to say and end without knowing what he has said?" Not that this is a love letter — I wouldn't have you get that idea. Nor need you pry into my business and inquire how I came to know that Ninon said that. That is my affair. So, ta-ta, until we meet. Then I shall have a long catechism to fright you with — if I don't get interested in something else meanwhile. Look for me soon.

Devotedly yours,

P.S. I wish you were here.

XXVI. The Awakening

Well, here I am — come back like a bad penny — and a pretty brown penny at that, don't you think? I made the acquaintance of some interesting lads, up yonder, farmer-boys all of them, and we had great sport together. They put me on to ever so many things new to me — and as I kept my eyes and ears open, I have come back with so many new impressions —

You have come back quite a chatter-box; that, at least, is evident.

Well, why not? It does me good and does you no harm. Besides I have so many things to tell you that I hardly know where to begin. My thoughts have become so lively, and almost robust. But I suppose the country air, the country sights and sounds, good health and good company have much to do with that.

I should say so — there's nothing better for one's mental health. The faculties always cleanse and brighten and glow in Nature's bath. I am glad you have found it out for yourself, for what one finds out by and for himself is always impressive and sure to last. It's the old story: "Experience teaches." But the adage has been assumed perhaps to mean that it is unpleasant experience which teaches. You will find out, however, as you go along, that pleasant experiences, the wholesome, the animating ones, enrich far more abundantly than do the others. It is in our nature to be happy: the wise understand this and profit by it to the utmost, but wisdom in this respect, as in many others, often comes too late.

You believe in athletics, don't you? So do I, and I took plenty of exercise, mostly walking. I was up with the birds and to bed with the chickens, except when the moonlight nights were too fascinating, and then I did all sorts of foolish things. "A healthy mind in a healthy body" is a pretty good maxim. I believe in it. But I want to tell you, just the same, that I used to get morbid now and then while I was away. There is something about nature that gets into you pretty deep and stirs you all up and brings all sorts of strange emotions to the surface. At least it affects me that way and so I suppose it must others.

You have but little justification for so supposing. That it should be so I don't deny: but I know a great many people who are simply bored in the country. That is because they have lost natural spontaneity of feeling, the capacity to enjoy simple pleasures, and to discern the beautiful when it is before their eyes. To many people Nature suggests nothing, signifies nothing, is nothing. When the sun sets it means for them that a light must be struck. When the trees and fields are rich in summer's verdure, that means nothing — one mosquito would outbalance it all; when the trees are bare in autumn, that means nothing; when the earth is white to the horizon under winter's coverlet, that means nothing; the awakening of spring with all its fantasy of joy, of color, of youth, means nothing to them — other than colds and wet feet. They prefer to see the springtime in midwinter in the picture galleries, where, within the confines of a single frame, can be found pink sheep, pink skies, pink grass and a pink shepherdess. You pay your money and take your choice: give me the out-of-doors. It is a metaphor, infinite of interpretation, this out-of-doors.

I know it. You either see nothing, in which case you are satisfied, or, once you go beneath the mere surface you see so much that you are astonished; and then you see a little further and you become depressed; a little further and you are bewildered; a little further and you are frightened; a little further and you become passionately enamoured; a little further and you become morbid; after that I don't know what happens — it's as far as I have gone. My natural cheerfulness pulls me out all right for the time being, but I began to get a pretty vivid idea of what you mean by realities; it came home to me, as they say in the heart-to-heart talks. What frightened me most and gave me a creepy sense of what seemed to be my own unreality was that after I had looked into it awhile, Nature seemed to be more real than I. As I followed, it eluded me; and in proportion as it eluded me it became more and more real. I reached out my hand to grasp — and it vanished! I opened my heart, and it advanced; as I softened, it softened; when I wept, it melted in a blur; when I smiled, it smiled. Oh! If only I were a child! But I am already too old, young as I am! You have put the virus in my blood and I am to be unhappy within. I know it! I am in love, in awe-stricken love with Nature's spiritual beauty, with the wondrous reality of living things, with the sense of being; but it is a hopeless, hopeless enamourment; a fascination, an infatuation that avails nothing! To think that I could not make a poem to a butterfly! That so simple and beautiful a thing escaped me utterly! That the exquisite reality of life and color floating so daintily through a dainty summer day, alighting like an elfin sprite upon the sumptuous flower — to think that it would not receive the touch of my coarse hand, of my coarse mind! That the flower and the butterfly knew each other and seemed to love each other in that still moment in the balmy ambient air, but they knew not me, and I knew not them! Oh, the pity of it! Oh, the wretchedness of it for me; the hopelessness of it! But I am caught, and I shall try, I suppose, and try, and try again — and always fail! And yet something HERE tells me that I shall not wholly fail; something here, where I put my hand upon my breast. My mind says I shall fail utterly, my heart says I shall not wholly fail. Which shall I believe, my mind or my heart? Why did you let me find these things, if I am to go on forever and forever unavailingly? Why have you caused this well-spring to flow, if its waters avail not, if they are never to reach the sea, or even to form a lake or a shady pool, but are to dry up on the sands, to disappear in an arid human waste? Why did you do this? And yet I would not have it undone. No, not for all the world, for it is a world, a new world, a new-found land and I am its solitary inhabitant, its Adam. I am my Adam — the first man: but God does not walk with me in the garden. I do not hear his voice in the grove and say Here am I. So turns my mind upon itself and feeds upon itself and impoverishes itself and poisons itself in my moments of introspection, in my hours of solitude, of solitude in a crowded universe, of solitude in the midst of Nature's myriad populations, a stranger in this house of many mansions, an outcast from my world, a guest unbidden at the feast: unwelcome in a garden, unwelcome to a flower, unwelcome to a butterfly! With them but not of them! Friendless and alone! And then I awaken as it were, and I'm the same old two and sixpence — no, not quite the same, only in my moments of bravado, or is the other bravado, which is the bravado, anyway? I am changed. I shall never be the same again, and you did the mischief — why did you get me into that storm-business anyway? Why did you slay that other dragon and don the tarnhelm and by the tasted blood of the dragon know the language of the birds? Is that Siegfried myth a metaphor, or a fabulous happening? Is it an allegory, or a child's tale? Why did you cause a storm to arise and break within me, was I a valley in the heart of summer? Was there a parching valley in my heart? Was I languishing in the drought? What did the storm mean? Was it, too, a metaphor, an allegory, or was it like my butterfly, my Psyche, a reality of the spirit?

But I did not make the storm.

To be sure, you didn't, you seized it though and made it your own, and it seemed easy at the time, but I can't do it with the simplest thing I find.

You are impatient, my dear boy, and a little nervous, and overwrought and excitable. Slightly hysterical, I might say. Wouldn't you like to take a little stroll to divert your mind?

I wouldn't mind the stroll if I didn't have to see any buildings.

Then you don't wish to look at buildings today?

Indeed I do not. I want to get this tangled skein straightened out a little. I want to know where I am.

Well, my lad, take it easy. It will gradually straighten out of itself, for the skein is a living skein. Don't overtax yourself. Nature is benevolent and will help you along. Her ways are healing ways. Besides, you have probably forty or fifty years ahead of you. Don't try to do it all in a day. Let time do her share; she is a skillful worker. A good farmer does not pull up his wheat grains to see if they are growing, he waits for them to sprout. Time and the sun bring bloom to the clustered grape, ripeness to the green, hard fruit. Learn to wait. And while you are waiting, let your inner development go on as Nature meant it should.

But these things, these feelings, are new to me!

They are *not* new to you! You were born that way. These activities of the mind and heart have merely been lying dormant. They were what I call *suppressed functions*. Now they are awakening again into life and they bring a certain pain and fever with them. Your morbidity is but the shadow of a bird of passage. Be of good cheer.

XXVII.   A College Library Building

My boy, if you wish to come in touch with a building that is a butterfly and yet not a butterfly, here is an opportunity. Here you have erudition, in all its fluttering iridescence, sipping the sweets of the past. [Fig. 7]

How do you like it after your sojourn among green fields and breezy trees? You should cherish this structure. This is a show building. It is precious. It is modish. It is of the wax-works of our art. It is of the rubbing of hands of our leading man-milliner.

I don't know whether I care or not.

But you should care. You are too young to be *blasé*. Leave that to your elders who have ingested the curious sweets of learning and, peradventure, have found them bitter in result.

I don't know that I care whether they are sweet or bitter.

But you should care. Here is your paternal double — your prototype. Here is a building which, regionally, typifies your state of mind, though from differing causes. Look into it as into a warped mirror, and there see your unhappy wits reflected, redistorted and redistributed. Others are as pessimistic as you think you are, but their pessimism is relatively real, at least it results from genuine exhaustion. Yours is a bird of passage.

How do you know that?

Do you really suppose the world is now revolving in an opposite direction because you happen to have passed a few days in the country? You do not know the great earth, my tender satellite. It turns as serenely now as though you never had been born; and it will doubtless so continue.

But I'll make it turn the other way.

Bravo! That's the stuff of heroes. Fix the illusion quickly, firmly. Gird up your heart and you are girded up. Faint heart ne'er won fair lady. Faint heart never won fair anything. So gird up your heart, for there is girded up the race; for there is girded up your destiny. Who shall say you nay when your heart is large and bold. Be not afraid. The world is yours. Gird up the precious beater in your breast — your mentor, your sure guide. Cast to the wild winds all wild doubt. Embark with a sure foot on the lustrous foaming sea. Let the wild wind blow and veer, let wild storms come, and wild clouds loom and drift. What care you, my hardy mariner; storms are storms and sunny times are sunny times: waves are waves, and spray is spray. Let the good craft dash and beat, for the sea is the sea and the sailor is the sailor. Gird up your heart for changing weather. Would you have your craft of porcelain and the little waves of porcelain on a little porcelain sea? Gird up your heart, for life has every weather, every water's depth.

I cannot gird up my heart for it is sick and weak.

What! So soon!

I mean —

Ah, wait until you are *blasé* of being *blasé!* Wait until the worm, the fatal borer, shall reach your root; then will your wholesome leafage of a verity turn pallid, and fall — as has happened to this man. Look at this mirage! See the Ionic columns, the entablature, the dome and so forth. Note especially the and-so-forth, for it is the untold that counts here — the discreet silence. Some say it is eloquent; and you may say in turn that it is indeed eloquent. So are the dumb eloquent of speech; so is the exile eloquent of his country. As we gaze — we pass into the land of expatriation. This, it seems, is the library building of a great academic institution of learning how to unlearn: of learning self-forgetfulness, self-denial. Of learning not only how to forget oneself, to deny oneself, but to forget and to deny one's land. To learn how to forget, to learn how to deny life cautiously, is somewhat the fashion; and by such token this is a modish building. Men must be scarce where such neutrality prevails. Surely we are in the land of expatriation. Surely this is architectural nihilism. Surely this is a vacant seed-pod: an inversion of human faculty. The saving grace of humor is not here. The worm is at the root of the rose-tree.

NOTE: The rest of this chapter was cut.

XXVIII. Revulsion

I have had my little emotional, and intellectual, and moral and spiritual, and democratic, and feudal jag, my fidus Achates — my friend, philosopher, hocus-pocus and guide. I have been turned inside out by you, and put back in place by myself. I, no adept in philosophy, have been philosophized to the death, burdened, darkened, nauseated and made rebellious by your psychology, or perhaps I had better say, your pseudo-mysticism. For, what use there is in it I can't perceive. To be sure, I have been on the stormy sea of your verbiage and I have been thereby made ill; but now I am getting my land legs again and I turn as ever when I am normal to my first learnings and my first teachings — to the classic; to what they told me at school, and what, in my heart, I believe in spite of all your jugglery with words, with my emotions and my thoughts; and in spite of the fact that truly you have turned me out of doors. Yet I come back, I come back! You can't ignore the classic. It is too firmly fixed, too deeply rooted, too surely sanctioned by the lives and the thoughts of the best men who have gone before us. It won't do! I can't stomach it! I tell you I was born a classicist and, country or no country, butterfly or no butterfly, you or not you, my heart turns where it will turn. You cannot reason with me — and that's an end of it. I won't subject myself to your domination. I won't be your plaything. I may be the slave of tradition, for tradition has roots of power holy and deep, and reaching down and back through the generations, the centuries, the ages. But I can't stand your transplanting: I am already too old for that — too young in my age, too old in my youth. I am too far gone; my earlier education has sunk too deep. I can't give it up: I cannot! I cannot!! Don't ask me to go further. Let us drop this futile investigation which is leading me only further and further into the wilderness, into the desert, into a wholly new and unexplored Sahara of our own. My heart is drying up. Of what avail all this journey, all this hardship? I don't want any more of it. I quit! Do you understand me? I quit!! Let me go back to the fold. I am a lost sheep. I am hare-brained to have let you lead me astray. I say quit and I mean quit, a permanent quit to a philosophy which has no bottom and no top, no sides and no ends. Help, help! Come back to me, my Alma Mater! Put the ground of your sure strength once more under my feet! What are *your* scarecrows to the scarecrows I have seen with this man, this ghost, this phantom! Away, all these fantasies, these supersensibilities! Away, all these bugaboos, hobgoblins, fairies, brownies, sprites and elfins of a mind too full! Give me again my dungeon cell, I have too much of liberty! What can I do with liberty? What can any man do with liberty? Liberty is a curse for such as I — not a boon! Freedom is a curse, not a blessing! Democracy is a humbug and a wild, disordered dream, a fanatical dream which disturbs, distorts and distracts all realities for such as I: a nightmare in which plus becomes minus for me, and minus becomes plus for others. *A bas* Democracy! It is the refuge of the common, the average, the vulgar. Democracy eats with its knife. Do you mean to tell me a man can be a real man in a Democracy? A Dollar-man, yes! A cheap Dollar-man, cheap among the cheap. Look at them: all cheap, the richer the cheaper. Look at the faces: see them shudder — all sordid, all pig-eyed, all self-centered in their democratic savagery; all cave-dwellers, troglodytes, men of a modern stone-age, with dirt under their brain-claws, crafty and cruel, selfish, noxious — a poisonous mob! You talk of men! I am looking for men!! But I shall never find men under this cloud and murk of democracy. I want men who are men — men of distinction, men of quality, men of tone, men of elevation of mind and spirit, men of humanity and *savoir faire* — and you can't show them to me here. You mean well enough in your way; but while you are continually prating of realities, you, yourself are oblivious to them. Reality is with you a handy phrase, a word-picture, an apparition which your ego projects into the outer world.

But I tell you that *I see* realities. I am of the new generation. I have eyes of my own, and I tell you that there is only one thing that any pair of eyes can see with absolute certainty nowadays, and that is the DOLLAR! To deny its reality, to refuse to worship, means ruin.

What a running at the mouth!

I won't let up. You are running counter to your day and generation and to mine. You seek to impose your will: to substitute your vision — to create an apocalypse for a heedless world. Take my word for it, I am right and you are wrong. You are of the old generation, I am of the new. It makes me heartsick to see the stubborn drift of your purpose. Now *my* youth has come to supplant *yours.* You have told me much that has awakened and strengthened me; but it has made me strong only to oppose you. I *will* be myself! I *shall* think what I choose and *do* what I choose! I shall gird up my heart, but it will be an up-to-date heart when I gird it. It will be a rebellious heart. Why should I differ from my day and generation? No one will pay me any Dollars for being a seer and a prophet. Seers and prophets are not now in demand; if they were, the department stores would keep them. Go to, my senescent friend! I don't want any genius in a garret, in mine. If the dear public wants genius, it can say so and come up with the wherewithal. I don't propose to anticipate any demand. I don't propose to put anything on the market that the public doesn't want and is [not] ready to pay for. My personal comfort is what *I* am looking for, and your dear democracy meanwhile doesn't seem to be disturbing itself very much about geniuses. What on earth do they care about geniuses, anyway? Democracy has nothing to do with genius, it has to do solely with the commonplace, the average, the lowest possible average, at that. I don't want to be *fined* for being a *real* architect, I don't want to be fined for being a real thinker, I don't want to be fined for being a real anything. Democracy is a rough and tumble affair, and I know it. The people don't know anything and don't want to know anything, and do you think I'm going to be fool enough to try and tell them anything they don't want to know? Not much! You know as well as I do that the Nazarene said, "Cast not pearls before swine lest they turn and rend you."[1] Now anyone not familiar with democracy might dismiss this statement as a light figure of speech, inasmuch as no one would be likely to cast pearls before swine; but I tell you the essence of it is that the damned creatures will *rend* you — not merely that they don't want your pearls, when they expected swill, but they will *rend* you because you disappointed them in their rations of offal; and such is your sweet, homespun democracy! Try them once. Try a few pearls — and look out for the teeth! So if my generation is unreal, I am going to be unreal also; for all the leading men in a democracy understand and cater to the stupidity of the

1. Here, as elsewhere, Sullivan quoted rather freely.

masses. And I have heard enough of your talk to know that my stupid masses will be the people of culture, and I will fake them to the queen's taste — none of their teeth for me! I shall, on the contrary, receive their most gracious squeaks. Truth is all right, as a bit of exquisitely delicate personal bric-a-brac; but don't try to sell truth to a false generation! You hear me! I am no philosopher, but I think I have a grain or two of American common sense. How in the world did you ever get such highflown notions about democracy? Don't you know, doesn't your common sense tell you, that democracy is merely a great *herd*, of people, getting along as peaceably as they can, but everyone goring his neighbor. I tell you democracy is a herd of cattle, a herd without a driver, without a whip. They huddle, and press, and trample in their own dung. They are a dull-eyed, patient crew; helpless and inert without a leader. Bah, with your democracy! Democracy means, merely, the liberation of numbers, the wandering and huddling of helpless units. It means disorder, filth, brutal unity, coarse appetites — a stifling crowd! *A la porte!* Your Democracy! Give me an autocrat! Give me a MAN, a real man! A man big enough and strong enough and willful enough to guide and to govern. The herd wish to be governed; they need a powerful, a dominating hand. They don't want to think: they have no vision. Give me the strong hand, the iron will, the keen intelligence, and that higher sense of humanity which can care for the herd and protect the herd against the hoof disease of its own cowardly crowding, and against the insistence of its own proletariat. Talk of your democracy! Bah, with your democracy! It takes brains to govern and guide and foresee! The very disease of which you are talking and have been talking is *democracy itself;* for democracy is, in itself, a disease. Men are *not* born equal! Some are born to rule, some to serve. It must be so, for only the hearts of the rulers are girded up. They do not value life. It is only the herd who fear death. He who can gird his heart up tight and high will thereby become a ruler; for the weak man cannot gird up his heart — he lacks the will, the abandon! Sentiment is a weakness of the heart, tenderness is a weakness — did I say so: I recall it: Sentiment is a strength of the heart, the weak know no real sentiment; and tenderness, truly, is a power of the heart — oh, a power so great! You should not have left me alone in the country, for it has defeated your object, has diverted your purpose, has given me something of the wisdom of the serpent and nothing of the gentleness of the dove. For I have seen, for myself, at my good and convenient leisure, how Nature works — how she despises the weak and exalts the strong; and how she —

What's that you say?

I say Nature favors the strong.

You are a fool, an ass. Nature favors the apt, not the strong or the weak.

I am not a fool. I tell you —

Tell me nothing! You have emptied your bile duct, now go and sleep!

But —

There won't be any but, today.

Am I not right in the main?

Yes, after a fashion.

Then everything is as I say?

I have told you: you are an ass.

XXIX. Democracy

Here comes your bad penny again!

Any worse than before?

No, I have improved. I have passed through Q for querulity, and am safely landed, now, on R for remorse.

What's it all about this time?

It's all about your infernal democracy. I told you, in the goodness of my heart, what I thought of it, and you called me an ass, for my trouble.

Well, what's wrong about that?

I have come here to find out what's right about it — I must have blown off steam without sufficient cause: hence the big R I am bringing with me.

Don't worry about a little thing like that. You were moulting: you will be all right again when your new feathers come.

I'd rather have you call me an ass again than say I am moulting: that's adding insult to injury.

No, it's adding a second truth to the first. And you perceive that I am raising you in the scale when I intimate that you are a bird. One good truth surely deserves another, you'll admit.

I'll admit anything you choose to aver, just now. I tell you I'm penitent. Won't you take me at my word?

I had rather take you at your word than in your "herd." For your word was "quit!" — "I say quit!" — don't you know?

Oh, don't tantalize me, governor!

I'm not your governor, I'm your safety valve; I let you blow off rather than burst — for which you should be duly thankful.

Then "let me not burst in ignorance," and I will thank you to the stars, I will thank you to the moon of my devotions, to the glorious sun of poesy toward whose light I aspire, that orb whose radiance you are, the light on high that shall dispel the heavy gloom of my night, that light of sympathy which illumines the whole world for such as I who walk in darkness. Let me not sink into the depths of my sea, but stretch forth your hand, and, in faith, I shall walk upon the waters as with contrite heart, my hand in an angel's hand, I might walk upon the waters of repentance, upon a moving tide from my very eyes, over the fathomless depths of my iniquity.

Stretch forth your hand and your knife — for something gnaws at my heart! My wicked spirit gnaws at the roots of my heart, and soon my leaf shall wither and fall.

Like the cuttle-fish I have murked my waters.

Like a toad I have covered my head with earth.

Like the heathen, I have furiously raged and imagined a vain thing.

Like a fire I go out in ashes. You are the "promethean heat that shall that light relume." Oh, let not the spark expire! Help me, daddy, I am in trouble. I make genuflections, obeisances, salaams, oblations; I kiss the hem of your garment. I —

You are grotesquely ridiculous.

I know it and I like it. I'd rather be a purp than a bird.

You act the part: only it is your tongue you have been wagging.

You are all of a successful poodle except the head and the tail — these are missing. What are you driving at, anyway, with these rhetorical toddlings on four aimless legs in forty and four directions?

Oh, it's my way of getting on your blind side again. A process of getting myself forgiven that I believe to be new, interesting, and of some utility — as I perceive it works.

Oh, yes: it works, of course. But what do you want?

I want light, more light. I want you to pull me out of my light and into your light concerning this matter of democracy.

Well then, come into my light: for small as it is, it is large enough for two: though, large as it is, it seems too small for one. For, after all, what do we know of the broad spectacle of democracy! We live — and we learn so little; we have eyes, and see so little; ears and scarcely hear. Why should we fail to know? Why is the keenest eye dull? Why is the most active mind as a sluggard? Why do we know and yet not know? We search, and seek, and probe, and test, and analyze, and surmise, and hope and fear, and are filled with useless longings, useless regrets; and, after all these trials, our own people, the people among whom we live and move and have our being seem as strange to us as are the Antipodeans — the denizens of far-off forests and isles. But let us garner up our hearts, and come back, little by little, upon our own land. For that which is sown in affection surely will eventuate in love; and just so surely shall we come nearer and nearer to our people. If we err, let us hope that we may err in smallest measure. If we prove right, we shall be so abundantly. Thus democracy will begin to unfold itself to us as the expression of the individual. In so far as the individual errs, democracy errs, and in so far as the individual grows and develops in the right, democracy gains thereby and grows and flourishes. *Democracy is primarily of the individual!* It is not a mere political fabric, a form of government: that is but one phase of it — an incidental phase. Democracy is a *moral* principle, a *spiritual* law, a perennial subjective reality in the realm of man's spirit. It is an aspiring power whose roots run deep into those primal forces that have caused man to arise from the elements of earth and, slowly through the ages, to assume a rectitude and poise that are of man alone. Democracy is a vast, slowly-urging impulse which little by little and more and more broadly is ever exalting man in spirit and imparting to him a definition of his true image — his true powers. Just as man was ages upon ages in learning to stand upon his feet in the physical sense; and just as this accomplishment was the work of a force persistently seeking such expression, so is there an impulse ever at work, ever tending to imbue him with the power to stand upon his feet, morally, and this force we call democracy. It is of that drift of nature which tends ever toward perfecting a type and the individuals of the type, until that impulse shall have attained to consummation. Democracy is not, as you might infer from superficial observation, merely a modern notion of a government by and for the people; it is a force, latent, and old as earth; a force for whose fulfillment the ages have been preparing the way, dissolving the obstructions one by one, and slowly making for it a pathway. It is the serene forces of nature that are most powerful; and that force which we call Democracy, lying inexpressibly deep in the spirit of man, is now as ever seeking expression. When the spirit of man first discerned One Infinite Spirit, after ages of groping, the way was opened which leads toward the discovery of man by man as a spirit. These adventures of the soul were made by a serenely contemplative people, and have become our heritage. The Nazarene — in this sense the first democrat — coming into a world crushed under the heel of absolutism, spoke eloquently to the lowly; he taught that the individual possessed his own soul. He outlined the need of self-government, the value of kindness; he preached man's unity with the divine, the immanence of the spirit. For these and other sayings in opposition to the established order, he was crucified. But his gentle, luminous doctrine has survived, because it is an utterance of nature's urge, which found, through this compassionate dreamer, a long-sought outlet through the soul.

So came the primitive truth of democracy into the world of men. Silently it has moved through the centuries, an ethereal presence for the upbuilding of the race. You may trace its various vicissitudes, obscurations, perversions, decadences and resurrections, its metamorphoses, disintegrations and reformations, in times and in lands, as it has moved among the forces, some fostering its growth, others seeking its destruction. But it is not to be denied! It grows with cumulating power, and, in our own and other lands, is seeking and will surely find its amplitude of organized consummation in a new philosophy of man. Primitive democracy, a unitary conception, impressive in its beauty of divinity in humanity, has subdivided into three separate conceptions — of government, religion and morals. This is explainable sufficiently by the record of the conflicting interests, political, sacerdotal and ethical, in the midst of which it sought to express itself or by which such expression was restrained. Yet, clearly, in our land, today, we may perceive varied currents which are dissolving these broken thoughts and are bearing them together to form a synthesis which shall define organized democracy as that high estate of man which holds in a single conception of CONDUCT, as in a spiritual solvent, the great forces of religion, morals and government. And this is the conception of Democracy that I hold.

By this light, surely, ours is the land of destiny! Here nature had prepared, through the ages, a slumbering continent, a virgin wilderness, to be the home of free men — free in their bodies, free in their souls; that the silently working calm and the power of the wilderness, the potency of the soil, of the waters and the air might permeate them physically, mentally, morally and spiritually, and lift them up to be a great people animated by a great purpose, a great force, a great beauty — the beauty and the power and the glory of democracy — the divine altitude of man's humanity.

Why then pick at little flaws, why point to petty truths, if the doing leads but to obscuration of a living principle? Rather shall we seek the broad truth, the sure truth, the basic truth of our destiny, and gauge our thoughts, our conduct and our art thereunto.

What you say reaches my heart with a convincing touch, and I am more than ever anxious to see you work out your theory of a democratic art. I am indeed come into your light, and things at last are shaping for me. But the scheme is too big for me. I could never work it out alone. You have led me, in your own way, through a lamentable art to a shaping conception of man's powers; and now, will you flood our art with its glow?

I will make the attempt.

In view of what I have said concerning function and form, it must be fairly clear to you that the spirit of democracy is a function seeking expression in organized social form. I have stated also that every function is a subdivision or phase of that energy which we have called the Infinite Creative Spirit and which we may now call the Function of all functions. In just this sense the metaphysical basis of our philosophy is gradually establishing its definition, is elaborating its inner structure and outer form.

We have been apt, and not without cause, to look upon metaphysics as a special domain of speculation having no touch with solid affairs. Now this is gruesome. For knowledge, for philosophic inquiry, if it is to have working value, must be applicable to daily needs. As a matter of fact, metaphysics and philosophy are valuable and really practical departments of thought, feeling and imagination, when once we summon courage to use them as instruments, as working tools.

Everything has a simple basis: the oak has its acorn. Our self-imposed task is thus to seek out the simple: to find broad explanations, satisfying solutions, reliable answers to those questions which affect the health and growth of that democracy under whose banner we live and hope. So we shall use our metaphysics and our philosophy in just this sense. They are to be our tools; we are to use them, they are not to burden us. For these processes mean, essentially, that in using the focusing powers of the mind, the extension of vision, the unseen becomes for us the tangible, the unusual becomes the obvious, the uncommon becomes the familiar, and the subjective becomes objective. There is no mystery: it is, all of it, a phase of man's power of observation and reflection. Not only the subjective by this process becomes objective, but, equally, the objective becomes subjective. For instance: If I say that such and such a thing is an outworking of the Infinite Creative Spirit, it may sound mysterious and inaccessible to our facilities. But if I say: It's a fine day; you say: "Why yes, it's a fine day," — and take it as a matter of course. Now as a matter of working fact, this Infinite Creative Spirit of which I speak is as much a matter of course as your fine day — if once you place your mind in a receptive mood, free from the inhibition of awe or of a factitious veneration. And so with our word, function. It sounds abstract, profound; in reality it means, only, that need, whatever it may be, which is seeking or finding fulfillment. If you put an acorn in the ground, that acorn, containing the function oak, will seek the form oak, and, in process of time, will become an oak-tree. So, if I say that a certain function, aspirant democracy, is seeking a certain form of expression, democratic architecture, and will surely find it, I am making a statement that does not differ in essence from what I said concerning the acorn. It is as simple, as natural, as matter-of-fact. Now I have no patience with those teachers who are more concerned in impressing their academic wealth upon the student than are they in exhibiting to him the simple basis of architectural phenomena and in making that basic principle clear and manageable. I am not tolerant of that aristocratic spirit which misdirects American youth in its search for knowledge — and would seek to impose upon it those formulas of learning and attitudes of mind toward learning which have descended to us from times when education was for the "gentleman" — for the few, for a class: that "education" which separates one from his people by the violence of its badge of alienation and uselessness. Yet this is what our schools of architecture are doing at this day. They are inculcating the meretricious in their pseudo-explanations of the architectural art, and, with pedantic persistency, they ignore the natural, the obvious. To be sure, you may say they teach as they have been taught. In a limited measure, that is true. Yet evasion cannot absolve them from performance; and plain performance means to teach in a thorough-going way. If they persist in teaching what is unintelligent, they cannot hope to escape an eventual accounting. The statements set forth in their school prospectuses are, many of them, sophistical. If these sophistries are due to mental laziness, because these schools *will not* seek the truth, do not want to know the truth, do not wish to have the truth pointed out to them, then are they doubly reprehensible. Now these documents are crafty in the use of phrases, specious in argument, plausible in explanation. But all the plausibilities combined cannot explain away the ineptitude. We need brains in our architectural schools! We need men of large hearts, luminous minds, rich sympathies; men who can grasp the significance of youth, the social value of democracy and of creative art.

Yet there is a larger test by which these schools may be tested: It is a broad fact, as broad and plain as the land, that, in many other departments of education, teachers have made positive strides in advance. They have been animated in their work by enthusiasm, by devotion, by love; and their noble and earnest effort is bearing daily fruit. These teachers look upon teaching as an art to which they willingly devote their lives. The study of the child, the study of the young has been pursued by them with intelligence and devotion; and the *kindergarten* has brought bloom to the mind of many a child: and all this is the result of a growing philosophy of education. But there is, alas! no *architectural kindergarten* — a garden of the heart wherein the simple, obvious truths, the truths that any child might consent to, are brought fresh to the faculties and are held to be good because they are true and real.

Not only have the architectural schools failed to keep pace with the general progress of educational philosophy and the teaching art, they have, as it were, flouted such progress. Unfamiliar with the immense educational value of metaphysics and psychology as the groundwork of the teaching art, they lack the ground-plan of a naturalistic philosophy of architecture in its historical and creative aspects; hence they fail utterly to illuminate the architectural art past, present, and prospective.

Are you not expecting too much of a four-years' course?

Not a bit. The time is now wasted. It should be utilized. Efficiency is lacking; the impulse is not there; the know-how is not there.

What should be done about it?

What I am doing to you.

XXXI. Man's Powers

If Feudalism be defined as selfish activity of the Ego and Democracy as altruistic activity of the Ego, and if the word, ego, now stand as the determining power of *all* man's powers — let us briefly examine these powers in order to clarify our shaping conception of Democracy, of democratic art and of democratic education.

Let us assume that elementary educational methods have developed much that is praiseworthy.

Let us also assume that the higher education is still tainted with feudal ideas and academic abstractions.

Let us assume that there coexist two conceptions of the function of education — the one utilitarian and opportunist, the other liberal and essentially philosophic.

Let us assume that man is both flesh and spirit.

Let us assume that man is a moral being.

Let us assume that man is not alone.

Finally, let us assume that all the above assumptions are self-evident and valid.

Now we will posit that all man's powers are subjective in the sense that they derive from the ego, and are aspects of the ego quiescent or in action.

Let us group these activities, in order that we may begin to form an idea of the nature of man.

Man's powers mean simply, what man can do.

Therefore let us now see what man can do — what are his powers:

As to his physical nature, man has the power of locomotion, of muscular control; the power to select and manipulate other things, other objects; to surmount obstacles. Therefore is he by nature a wanderer, a toiler, a worker, an artisan, an artist: for these things mean the power to do — to create.

As to his mental nature, man has the urging power of curiosity. Hence he is again a wanderer, an explorer, a seeker, an inquirer, a scientist. He wishes to know the *How.* Hence is his power to do increased by his knowledge *how to do.* His art is strengthened and amplified in its power by his science. Further, man's curiosity wishes to discern the WHY. Still a wanderer, a seeker, a worker, a thinker, he pushes his power of inquiry into new paths; he becomes philosopher. His thus acquired knowledge of the *why* increases his power over the *how,* and hence his power to do: which means a progressive cumulating growth in solidarity: his philosophy, his science, his art mutually strengthening each other. Thus man the worker, the inquirer, the thinker, becomes ever more unitary in the exercise of his powers: he becomes the *greater worker.* But his results thus far may be purely material, strictly utilitarian, altogether objective in the ordinary sense. The exhibit of his powers thus far in action may be purely intellectual and physical: surely a one-sided aspect.

But man has the power of feeling, of emotion: great powers of his inner life: hence man is The Poet.

And man has the power to vision forth: hence is he dreamer of dreams, spectator of visions: *The Prophet!* His emotions and his dreams, his visions and his forecasts, vitalize his thinking, his speculations and his work. They charge his creations with the current of life: and so man rises in accomplished power. He ever pushes back the frontiers. He ever intensifies the near and the far.

And man is a spirit: hence his emotion, his intellectual, his physical need to find union with Spirit. Thus grows he ever in concentrating and diffusing power. (Thus is he metaphysician.)

And man is a moral being: a power of enormous momentum: It is THE POWER TO CHOOSE! (The central power of the Ego.)

And thus is his growth, his unfolding, his self-centralization, MAN THE WORKER becomes MAN THE CREATOR.

We might go on indefinitely enumerating man's minor powers by a continuous process of subdivision of his major powers, and exhibit man for what he is: a fecund marvel of power: and all would seem to be well. But all is not well. There is a fly in the ointment. For the inquiry immediately emerges: *What does man do with these powers?*

Here lies the heart of our inquiry into Democracy. Here arrives the most urgent of all present human inquiries. Its processes and results we call Sociology; which, truly, is the art, the science of gregarious man, the dream of the solitary dreamer, the visionary, the prophet; the world-old inarticulate dream of the ever dreaming multitudes. Thus is the unitary science, poem and drama of Sociology, the precursor of Democracy — its explorer, its evangel.

For, reverting to our definition of Feudalism as the selfish activity of the Ego, is it not instantly visible that all these wondrous powers of man may, for selfish ends, be used individually and collectively for harm? That such use may be directly *unsocial* as we are coming to understand the term? Hence looms the power of choice before us as man's mightiest power for good or for ill — that, in fact, man's moral power is his supreme constructive power.

The inverse of Feudalism — that it to say, Democracy — defined as the altruistic activity of the Ego, definitely posits the moral power as its foundation, and the nature of choice as basic to its welfare. It simplifies and clarifies the concept of moral power and declares that the power of choice shall be exercised for the good of all. It purposes, in short, a NEW CIVILIZATION founded on CHARACTER.

Indeed, it is the business of democratic sociology to simplify and clarify all things, to exhibit and elucidate these powers of man which energize his power of choice and the dramatic consequences of such choice — their high visibility through successive civilizations and in our own. The main and the immediate business of democratic philosophy is to simplify, to clarify and to know itself. Then will aspiring democracy discern its power to create — and to define its goal.

It would avail but little to discuss the matter further here; for the postulates of our theorem should be evident.

What we need in our progress is a further unfolding of our widening view of man's nature and activities; his actions and reactions as exhibited in what he does — the record he himself makes of himself.

But it should be clear at this point that a system of education, to be democratic, must be based on the unfolding of these natural powers in the young, and the power of choice clearly impressed and defined. So doing, the remote things we call art, science, philosophy, poetry and ethics will come near by the very force of attraction, as they are now away from us through mutual repulsion. Then will the science of sociology become the gravitational center of all sciences; and a philosophy or gospel of democracy, the motive power of the world. Then will our art cease to be a wanderer — and come into its own.

Where did you get these ideas?

Where anyone with two eyes might have found them.

Why did not the "anyone" find them?

Because he did not know or use his powers. He was too intelligent to discover them — too busy. He probably believed man's powers to be gifts.

Well, aren't they gifts?

Gifts from whom?

Well, then, say endowments.

Endowments by whom or what?

Then faculties?

Faculties are powers; let us get along about business: for if man has the power to do well, he has also the power to do badly. It rests with his choice. Let us further see how he exhibits choice: what he accepts, what he rejects. Let us test him, anew, by the acid test we now have. Or, if you wish to change the figure: we have surrounded him — let us find him.

NOTE: This chapter (formerly "Education 2") and the next were entirely rewritten in 1918. The word "Ego" was introduced into this chapter in revision; to forestall assumptions concerning Sullivan's reading, it should be pointed out that Freud's *Das Ich und das Es* did not appear in book form until 1923; however, Sullivan's library contained many books on psychology.

XXXII. Eminence

And now in our continuing discussion of social values, let us draw nearer to the Architects: not necessarily the little fellow; not the man who has taken up "architecture" with all its ins and outs as a trade, a convenient-as-any means of turning a dollar; not to the manifestly ignorant and sordid; but, specifically, to the *leaders,* the men in the forefront, whom fortune has favored, whom circumstance has fostered.

These are the men we are now to examine as a class, in the growing light of man's powers. The power-values of these men we will subject to the scrutiny of revaluation. We wish to know if their total value is social in the current feudal sense, or social in the awakening democratic sense.

What can be the social value of eminence if it means not moral altitude: a summit from which rich, far-spreading areas are seen in all their plenitude of diversification — vast vistas whose depths are viewed: an abode in the heights of the spirit, in serenity, power and poise of the Ego: in a *locale* wherein the soul abides far removed above the currents and counter-currents of our daily life, yet conscious of them all?

What can eminence signify without vision, without prophecy, without manifest fulfillment — without convincing works?

Is eminence, as we daily view it, more than a counterfeit? Is it above subterfuge, above intrigue, above the low, mean tricks of the high and the clever cogent tricks of the low? Is it far above the cynicisms, pleasant generalizations and practical satisfactions of those who look on their art as on baled merchandise? By and large we have seen, and shall see.

I have been at some pains to tell you of thought; I have said something of imagination, of function and form, of objective and subjective; I have spoken of value; of growth and decay; I have partly lifted the veil which hitherto has hidden the countenance of democracy from man; and I have taken you into the out-of-doors of a summer's day that you might there live with one of nature's miracles — and interpret as best you might.

I have told of realities. I have told of illusions; and I have spoken of many other things and thoughts and hopes and aspirations. Finally, I have hinted of man's powers.

And of what avail shall be all these sayings if we have not now arrived where we may safely reweigh and revalue the eminent everywhere, in every walk of life, but specifically in our own art — and closely note the response of scales.

Democracy, as you may now infer, is an IDEA. It is a function of such infinite spiritual fertility, it is so unitary, so concentrate, so diffusive, it is so charged with power, that it may well seem the latest and most potent of nature's spiritual forces to arise within the domain of MAN'S DESIRE — even though in truth it be of the primordial and the eternal.

Declaring, as it does, the mission and the joy of the Infinite to the finite; bringing as it does the boon to man of the emancipation of his powers, whereby the spirit shall become free: is it not indeed *that truth* which shall make us free!

Why then does it supervene that our eminent are slaves, not free men? Why do they tell us, in their bondage, of the illusions of bondage? Why do they smile at our quest for freedom? Why are they unaware of fine values and inexpert at weighing aught but heavy current values? Why are they unimaginative, unreflective? Why are they unaware of the all-embracing, all-diffusing law of function and form? Why unaware of the subjective phases of objective things — of the objective possibilities of subjective impulses? Why do they deny or ignore that which is wholly natural, wholesome, self-evident to innocent eyes, and aver that which is limited, bald, desultory, poor? In short, why are they vacant?

To be sure, if you ask them, our specifically eminent will say NO, it is not so! But, look at the buildings! The buildings say *yes,* it is so.

Why argue when the buildings are here? If the buildings were not here, we might argue; but the buildings *are here,* and they are the court of first inquiry. It is to them we go — it is not to the architect. For a building records with naked candor what the architect has done to it. It does not equivocate, apologize, explain, circumlocute, hedge, dicker, divert, or conceal. It simply *tells,* and it tells with awful honesty. We quiver with amazement and are at once aghast at the folly. The man may be a liar, but the building is not; it tells the truth about the liar. For buildings are our familiars, they are indeed loquacious — perhaps too talkative. By the testimony of the buildings our eminent are light-weight. By our measure of height they are Lilliputian in stature.

What other testimony have we? Assuming a man to be equipped with the most complete education it has been possible for him to acquire in the schools (what is called a liberal, a cultural and technical education), assuming that he has added to such education the usual worldly knowledge, insight and experience: where is the *weak spot?* Judged by the feudal estimate there would seem to be no weak spot.

He can talk quickly, learnedly, even eloquently. He is most convincing. We are sure he is right: he *must* be right. He gives us all the facts. He is charming, is perhaps impressively business-like. He may even be sonorous, or very modest. But to us he is *sterile.* We know it because the buildings tell us so. We have the inconvenient habit of listening to what a building says: of scanning the screen of its features: of looking into its soul. The eminent one says YES! The building says NAY!

To our eyes the eminent one is unproductive in the democratic sense. More than that: because of hybridity in the democratic sense, and productivity in the feudal sense, he is reactionary. The output of the mental power he exercises constitutes in each instance a barricade, a deterrent, to free-flowing thought, a menace to advance, a drag upon the evolution of the free man. His efforts tend to render our thought static and his Brahminical. For the effect of such utterances (and a building is an utterance, is it not? All activities are utterances; all visible things are utterances, are they not?) is to place before the mind of the casual and even the cultured observer a *simulacrum* of what *we* mean by power — a false apparition which the man on the street is unable to dispel, if he would, because he lacks sufficient knowledge of man's powers — of their use, of their abuse, of their neglect. His vision of democracy is so obscure that he talks of good and evil in a semi-sentimental way, unaware that they reside, both, in man's power of choice.

Now, *we* say these eminent men are blameworthy — and we are amply and literally justified in so saying, because they have allowed their liberal and technical education to petrify them with culture instead of stimulating them, through strengthened powers, to sane and wholesome, far-seeing democratic activity and genuine utterance.

Buildings such as I have shown you tend to immobilize minds that regard them superficially, and drive them into the land of acquiescence. They tend actively, through their mere presence, to disperse and dissipate the finer ideals of power and accomplishment.

We see these buildings as they are and for what they are, for truth is indeed naked. It is the veils, the trappings, the vestments, that so often conceal the forms and features from the confiding, the unwary. It is our definite business to remove these decoys of vesture, these cultural lures and blandishments, from the eminent, in order, when so shorn, to show the startling resemblance to the man on the street.

You deem this procedure destructive in its insidiousness, iconoclastic in purport and effect? You ask, who are to replace our eminent?

No, it is not destructive except in the prefatory sense of construction. As to iconoclasm — I have no use for idols with clay feet. Your inquiry as to those who are destined to replace our eminent is strictly to the point — it touches upon the quick of our thesis. It is the sole reason why I have spent so much time with you — and intend to spend much more. For not only must we see, hear and interpret things and thoughts as they are: we must outline that which is courageous, creative and beneficent.

If we find the body social filled with weaknesses and strength seemingly commingled and inextricable; if we find it a confused composite of evil and good — we must so expose the nature of man's powers, of his manner of using them, of abusing them, of failing to recognize their integral nature, that the IDEA of personal responsibility and accountability will stand forth, clear and fresh to our vision, as both a revelation and an inspiration.

Indeed, it is the business of the democratic philosopher to widen the scope of an inquiry such as ours until all eminence, all activities, shall be included in its purview. In his application of the universal law of function and form to all social manifestations, he is to discern the forms of social activities and trace such forms to their sure origin in men's thoughts. Men cannot conceal their inmost thoughts from such as I, for thoughts are written in deeds. He must also search out the thoughts, the dreams of the lowly, and note how institutions, how civilizations, rest upon them as a foundation — however impressive the superstructure. In short, he must search for MAN. He must find man in the innermost sanctuary of his secret thought, his elemental powers, and reveal man to himself and to his kind. It has never been done. It is the great, immediate task. Current ideas concerning democracy are so vague, and current notions concerning man's powers so shapeless, that the man who shall clarify and define, who shall interpret, create and proclaim in the image of Democracy's fair self, will be the destined man of the hour: the man of all time. The world is yearning for such man as for a Messiah — the huge world of men, women, offspring: unstable, drifting, dreaming, dumb; a purblind world, an uneasy, aching world, suffering in torment of soul for lack of the one, single, shining IDEA toward which they might look as toward a new, a glorious star rising serenely above the horizon of their long, feudal night, and toward which their hearts might turn.

Such man must have both vision and sympathy; within his spirit must reside the powers of worker, inquirer, thinker, dreamer, prophet; of artist, philosopher, metaphysician — which, all, in condensation, shall organize and propel the utterance of the world's great POET — yet to come.

Of such is true eminence.

Of such is the colossal power of passion!

Here are we now, arrived at a parting of the ways. For we now know and see our way. But we must hold to that road which has been our thesis and is still our choice: that road which leads to an intermediary goal; even though the spectacle of Democracy open as an infatuation so marvelously near us.

Our road will still be rough, the terrain forbidding. But we shall push on to the end.

XXXIII. Our City

Don't you think, my prophet and philosopher, that, in this city of the conspicu-
ously eminent, in this swarm of houses, obliterating from view what once was Man-
hattan Island for the Dutch, we have an epitome of the architecture of the country?

We have nothing of the sort; we have an epitome of New York; New York is
not the country. It is in this land physically to be sure, but spiritually it is on the
outskirts. It is *sui generis* a border town.

How curious are the currents that make up what we call the ocean of life. They
are strange enough elsewhere, but here the name is maelstrom: a whirl that wrecks
and submerges; that draws in and puts not forth; a current, narrowing, ever more
and more madly, toward that vortex which swallows up body and soul — the vortex
of golden vanity. Here money is God, and God is money; a god of gold, of standard
fineness; a god circular in shape, diminutive in size; a disk, that any may wear as
a talisman if he but purge his heart of all else — and cleave unto this.

In days of old, there came now and then an epoch which we call Golden. But
here is a modern instance, not to be outdone — an Age of Gold! An age of ferocious concentration, which cries, once more: After us the deluge! An age, a place,
which cries again: I am the State! Small wonder its buildings echo the tumid boast.

This indeed is an architecture well worth the studying; for its like does not exist
elsewhere upon earth. It is a product of the time, of the place and of the men; and
time, place, men and architecture are all alike. At one end of the island, or at the
other, or in between, it is the same thing. "The more it changes, the more it remains
the same." The barbaric variety, the unrest, the ignorance, the vulgarity, the scholarship, the culture, the yard-stick architecture, the blind-man's architecture, the
deaf-man's architecture, the lame-man's architecture, each gives out its raucous
individual note, and all together swell and sway and swirl into a huge monotone
of desolation, of heartlessness, and of an incredibly arid banality that roars above
a muffled murmur of incompetence and strangulation. For, here, Art is tortured,
twisted, choked, mangled, beaten, bruised, torn: poor Art! For Art is here swiftly
starved, is dying of thirst. For Art is not a god here. For Art is not in the hearts
of men here. Gold is in the hearts of men here and fills arteries, capillaries, veins,
with its maddening stream.

Here indeed is an architecture to be studied! For the roar of the streets is not
louder than the roar of what lines the streets — a quarreling herd, ranged mile after
mile, pressing hard, shoulder to shoulder, tied hands, tied feet, leering and howling
at the passer, or smirking and winking and giggling — an uncanny lot, the most
extraordinary aggregation in the world's vast menagerie. Oh, this hocus-pocus, does
it not sicken one in his heart! Does one not blush to the roots that he, too, must
go by the name. Oh, the sadness of it! The wearisome pessimism!

Think of the generations to come, when once they shall realize to the full the
nature of the blight that has thus been laid upon them by a generation which says:
After us the deluge! It will surely be a deluge of tears and bitterness, and a contempt toward this generation of Manhattanites. They will curse the eminent and
the shyster alike, for they will find no rational pretext to discriminate between their

works. Oh, the pity of it! the pity of it! the pity of it! When a noble art is so near to the hand! Oh, the pity of it; the pity of it all! The boundless pity of it all! The awful desolation of it all!

But you do not specify, dear Master!

Why should I specify? Are your eyes veiled? Are your ears sealed? Have you forgotten your lovely week in the country, companioning among real things, living things? Have you lost to mind the bounty, fertility, chastity, strength; the beauty, the mobility, the serenity of nature? Have you forgotten the storm? Have you parted with the calm? Have you forsaken the yearnings of your heart? Have my outpourings fallen upon vacancy? Have I in vain led you through a wilderness? Have I all for naught given you a glimpse of a promised land: of a land I faithfully promised? And you would have me specify! Have my words been as a puddle of rain-water rather than the river I thought them; or have you been as gravel, not the fertile garden I thought! Where is your imagination, my laddie, where are your eyes, where are your thoughts!

Must I then specify? Must I show you this French château, this Château de Blois on this street corner, here, in New York, and still you do not laugh! Must you wait until you see a modern man come out of its door, before you laugh? Have you no sense of humor, no sense of pathos? Must I then explain to you that while the man may live in the house physically, he cannot live in it morally, mentally or spiritually, that he and his house are a paradox? That he himself is an illusion when he believes his château to be real. Must we go again to our ABC? Is it not self-evident to all but the man and his kind that the "château" is a *humoresque* — and he another? That château and *their* kind were in place and time only in France?

Must I show you other and similar curios of this period and that period, and that period, and this and that "style"! Faugh! The word makes me sick! Will not the *one* suffice? Are you not a bright youngster? Can you not translate? Can you not generalize? To satisfy you must I take you to see another maudlin riot, called office-building, with one barbarism heaped upon another until the incongruous mass reaches the limit of its idiocy in height, and culminates, perchance, in a Greek temple? — a solecism more extravagant, if possible, than the château?

Must I show you another library, or it may be a court-house, or a bank: with its piddling classic, its awful niceties, its refinements, its everlasting misconceptions, its kickshaws of culture, its jejune wool-gathering?

Must we really begin our ABC? Must I speak of the power of rational thought — do you find such thought here? Must I tell, once more, of imagination, the wonder-worker — do you find imagination present here? Have I failed to impress you with a sense of realities: in this city of illusion can you find reality except it be pathological? Have I not told you of values — do you find value here, or poverty, in all this wealth? Have I not dealt with growth and decay — in the physical growth here can you not discern spiritual emaciation? Have I not impressed upon you that a building is a screen and that behind the screen is a man, and behind that man, other men, and behind them, others?

Have I not let you see for yourself something of the organic processes of nature? And what do we find here, the eloquence of organization or the brawl of disorganization? Have I not talked of ferments and of leavens — is there leaven or ferment here?

So is this populous island, with its huge, ostentatious spread of material wealth, a thing of poverty and rags to him who can weigh values in the balance of sanity. It stands for the stertorous negation of democracy; the cancellation of that which is best, noblest and enduring in the heart, in the mind, in the spirit; and for the asseveration of that which is paltry and transitory in life's values. So stands this island. Let not its contagion spread!

Well anyway, the blooming town is quite satisfied with itself; quite complacent: it isn't moulting — that's sure.

Indeed it is not! Its feathers are all there; and they are bright, and clean, and gaudy. But the voice is the voice of Macaw!

Tell me: Why did you bring me here? I have heard this before.

To show you, in a larger way, what I mean by the perversion of power. To show you, as a spectacle, a drama, the cumulating power of choice: gigantic energy gone wrong. To show you how the people of a city portray themselves in mass.

Note: Fig. 8 has been chosen as an appropriate, rather than specific, illustration.

XXXIV.   Another City

And what, doctor mine, shall we say of this flat smear, this endless drawl of streets and shanties, large and small, this ocean of smoke? It is a thousand miles away from New York. Is *it* then an epitome of American civilization, an index of our art? Is *this* a true exponent of democracy? You have told me of thought — is thought here? You have talked to me of imagination — is imagination here? Are filth in the air, and slime under foot, or dust in the nostrils, indices of enlightenment; or is Chicago a *sui generis* in turn? New York may be revolting to you, but this Chicago thing is infinitely repulsive to me. *There* at least was a physical if not a moral cleanliness, an outward if not an inward cheerfulness. But this foul spot on the smiling prairie, this blotch on the fair face of Nature! Why have you brought me here again? What have I done to deserve this? I thought it well understood that no one stays here who can get away; that it is no place for a civilized human being to live. What are we here for?

We are here because I wish to show you the pole-opposite of New York; because I wish to show you extremes, in order that, as such, you may fix them in your mind indelibly. Because a study of these extremes will fix for us certain definite psychological boundaries.

Chicago is indeed a *sui generis*. Seventy years ago it was a mudhole — today it is a human swamp.

It is the *City of Indifference*. Nobody cares. Its nominal shibboleth, "I will" —

its actuality, "I won't"; with the subscription: "Not how good but how cheap"! Impoverishment of heart and mind are here conjoined. They seem to glory in conjunction.

It is the *City of Contrasts*. Cast your eye over the sumptuous beauty, the color, the spread, the open-far horizon of Lake Michigan, and then turn to this ugliness and horror on its shore. On a Sunday, if the wind be from the Lake, there comes into view as a revelation the pellucid, the delicately beautiful atmosphere with which Nature canopies man here. On a Monday morning, behold, how he pollutes it with his mental outpourings, his moral murk!

I have taken you here to show you once more, and in a way just as characteristic, just as convincing, that a city is but the material reflection of the character of its inhabitants. That a city, in turn, is but a screen; and behind that screen are the men, women and children who will it, who suffer it to be, whose thought it is. It is their image, their materialization. It is an impressive enlargement in bulk of the notion that behind the screen of each building is a man. The type is subjectively and objectively fundamental — and remains ever true.

If this city is sunk in solitary gloom, it is so for reasons; and these reasons are clearly and logically related to our central concept of democracy, which, as I have most insistently cautioned you, implies the immediate responsibility of the individual; not response to coercion, but response to that inner prompting, that rectitude and pride, which make for self-respect and self-control.

If, as you wander dejected but inquiring over this immensity of pollution, you find civic cleanliness, pride and self-respect, and capacity for creative self-government woefully absent, you will find it is specifically because cleanliness, self-respect, and pride and desire for creative self-government are thus absent in the mind of the individual — the so-called man on the street. If everywhere substantially you find a physical display of apathy, it indicates a common spiritual apathy. I have warned you over and over that for every physical effect there is a psychic cause. You see the effect — the cause is just as visible. Can you imagine that Man is here made in the image of his Almighty, when he pollutes that which the Almighty, as it is said, has given to him — when he pollutes even himself? This is not democracy, my lad, it is modern American inhumanity. This is not civilization, it is CALIBAN!

There are libraries and universities, and schools and art galleries here, to be sure; but what are books but folly, and what is an education but an arrant hypocrisy, and what is art but a curse — when they touch not the heart and impel it [not] to action.

What are the leaders doing here? What are the eminent doing, what are the cultured and the scholarly doing? What are they thinking? What are their standards — if they have any? They are doing just what the mob are doing, just what your "herd" are doing — that is to say, in vital substance, nothing: there is no tangible, forceful great ideal, physically, broadly, to be seen. And yet the Great Lake and the Prairie, emblems of pride, fertility and power and graciousness, encircle and enfold the city as a wistful mother holds a subnormal child. This City of vacant, sullen materialism, brooding and morose within the splendor, presents a spectacle unparalleled in history: the spectacle of Man's abject spiritual beggary. The Big City dreams.

There is a leaven here, I WILL! (there are ferments here), but it is, ah, such a little leaven now — still, it may leaven the mass — who knows, who knows? There is a little thought, a very little; a little imagination, a very little — a little unselfishness, just a little. These seeds may germinate: who knows? The materialistic humus may have already made a fertile soil: who knows? The rose springs from decayed things, and betimes it blooms in a passionate outburst of beauty. But you will say the rose blooms only in a pure air, and in the sunshine — and that is so; that the soot and murk may suffocate these seedlings, or they may be trampled under foot heedlessly — and that is so too; that is all true! The voice of I WILL is faint.

But the case "Chicago" is not any more hopeless, seemingly, to him who can weigh values, than is that of the architectural art at large; it is not a whit more impoverished, spiritually, nor inept physically; not at all more apathetic, more dismal, more pitiful; and if we may hope for the latter as we do, why not for the former as we may? For Chicago at least has youth, and where youth is, there is always hope — and where there is hope let us cling to it. Its sins and sicknesses of youth have been fierce and debilitating, and almost fatal; but there are a few sparks remaining in the ashes of its short life. Fate may perchance fan them once more into a flame of democratic fire. It is a chance — a chance only — but youth is here; a tremendous under-strength is here. The critical turn is at hand — we shall see what we shall see — and we shall see it soon.

The case "Chicago" is not the case "New York" and is not to be judged by it; there is no common standard of comparison — New York is old — its sins are fixed, the damage is done. Chicago is young, clumsy, foolish, its architectural sins are unstable, captious and fleeting; it can pull itself down and rebuild itself in a generation, if it will: it has done and can do great things when the mood is on. There can be no new New York, but there may be a new Chicago. As you look out on the dreary murk, this may seem a fantastical dream; perhaps it is — who knows? If there are to be dreams, there must be dreamers to dream them — and there can be no greatness unless dreamers dream of it! Still, it may be a foolish dream; a dream born of the incomparable Lake and the strong, silent, lovely prairies — who knows? One must indeed be incurably optimistic even momentarily to dream such a dream. Yet the Lake is there, awaiting, in all its glory; and the Sky is there above, awaiting, in its eternal beauty; and the Prairie, the ever-fertile prairie is awaiting. And they, all three, as a trinity in one, are dreaming — some prophetic dream: I am aware: even as the Big City dreams its sordid introspective dream. And he who looks upon them, all in one, in pulchritude of his heart, in rejuvenescence of his spirit, may perchance in turn dream something of their dream — who knows? There may be unknown dreamers here!

Thus we are rounding out our absorbing study of Democracy. Thus, turning slowly upon the momentous axis of our theme, are we coming more and more fully into the light of our sun: the refulgent and resplendent and life-giving sun of our art — an art of aspirant democracy! Let us then be on our way; for our sun is climbing ever higher. Let us be adoing; lest it set before we know the glory and the import of its light, and we sink again into the twilight and the gloom from which we have come. So much for New York. So much for Chicago.

III. *Another City*

XXXV. A Survey

And yet, my boy, even if Chicago and New York stand in a certain polaric opposition in our civilization — or, if strictly speaking they are not poles, but perhaps
nodes, or at the least nodosities — the contemplation neither of one nor of both of
them will give us that just notion we are seeking of what America is in reality, or
whither the true drift of its civilization. We can do little more, in studying them,
than arrive at a certain understanding of boundaries, at the furthest limits of the
eccentricities of our civilization. If we wish to locate the true center of gravity we
must seek elsewhere. For while the great cities are great battle-grounds, they are
not great breeding-grounds. The great minds may go to the great cities but they are
not (generally speaking) born and bred in the great cities. In the formation of a
great mind, a simple mind, a master mind, solitude is prerequisite; for such a mind
is nurtured in contemplation, and strengthened in it. In the quiet, in the silence,
alone with itself and Nature, and alone with the subtly interchanging influences and
aspirations of Nature and of Self, it grows: and it grows because it is undisturbed
— just as the wheat grain in the soil grows because it is undisturbed. There is no
deeper psychic law than this: that the thoughts which mold and make a civilization
come into being in solitude, and are there nurtured and gestated. All great thought,
all great ideas, all great impulses, are born in the open air, close to Nature, and
are nursed, all unknown, all unsuspected, upon Nature's bosom. The great are the
unknown, the unsuspected, perhaps the despised, during all that formative period
wherein the destinies of the world are taking shape in them. Then in time they
emerge, and come into the battle of life; and by instinct they seek its fiercest battle-
grounds. So are the great cities merely great battle-grounds whereon strong minds
gather together, and clash in the fierce rut of ambition. Or the master mind may
remain, of choice, in the solitudes, and breed there storms of momentous power
which in time overspread us: or, as a sequestered mountain lake, it may reflect the
infinite in a deep calm of the spirit, that another, passing by, may behold how serene
in power is a soul at peace — and bear that message to his people.

The big cities are breeders of distraction, of noise, of racket, hurly-burly, turmoil
and worry, jostle, wear and tear, by-products of a most intense pitch of mental and
material activity.

The vast open country, the great out-of-doors, breeds its minds, its hearts, as it brings
forth its wheat, its trees, its rains, its rivers and its lakes, its mountains and plains
and forests, its glories of the seasons, its poems of the night and the day, its expanse
of the heavens, and its repose of the earth.

So must we know our values; for a great impending civilization, a great impending art hangs upon the justice and the even balance of our view. Our synthesis is
now under way; we begin to build. And, to build well, we must know our foundations, our boundaries and our limitations; we must know what lies without those
boundaries as we must know what is and is to be contained within them. Our foundation must be so deep and so securely laid that those who come after us may build
thereon without fear, and above all, without reproach, as they rear the superstructure of our dream-edifice into the clear heights of beauty, within the broad light of
day.

Do you mean to say, then, that a very great mind cannot originate in a city?

I do not say so dogmatically, for that would be to deny my own thesis: and, moreover, to become dogmatic is to become foolish and top-heavy; but I say that the chances are enormously against such a happening. Still, a great mind will find its solitudes anywhere, city or country, just as it will find its multitudes anywhere, even in the desert. Yet I bear in mind the parable of the camel and the needle's eye.

But then why do you lay such an especial stress upon the open country? I like the country, I might go farther and say I love it — but I don't know it very well, in fact, I scarcely know it at all, except as I have told you in my feeble way. I have seen it, of course, but I haven't seen it with eyes like yours. And yet I feel, HERE!, vaguely, and wistfully, what you mean! You mean that the city is a small matter in comparison with the country. That the city is indoors, so to speak, and the country is the mighty out-of-doors. That we go to the city for activity and strife, and to the country — by which I assume you to mean Nature — for strength and re-animation. That the country, the out-of-doors, is the prime source of power; and the city, the arena in which that power is dissipated for good or ill; or, to broaden the view, that Nature is the true source of all power of the heart and the spirit, and likewise the source of the power of the great cities.

You have said that pretty well.

And I have noticed, too, that our people, rather generally, have something of that feeling for out-of-doors; else why this love of golf and country clubs, this annual flowing of people to the parks, to the lakes and woods, to the seashore and the mountains?

That is instinctive and shows that we are not indefinitely to remain a nation of city-dyspeptics and weary melancholics. It is a part of our semi-conscious need of racial self-preservation; a slight disturbance of that nightmare wherein we dream of devouring the unwary and the unfortunate. It might seem that we need a convulsion of Nature to awaken us to a recognition of her solvent, recreating power; but it is not so: the very quietude, the placidity, the restful, expansive beauty of this continental spread is a token, an augur, of a power within the race of men who abide and shall abide with it, such as the world has not known. It may be a premature prediction, but I will say this to you now: that here, on the soil where we are, will arise the greatest race of creative artists in history; creative minds in every walk of life; and I predicate it on the soil, the waters, and the air, and on the spirit of Democracy which has mated and shall fully mate with them. Democracy, and the open air of a serene continent, shall bring forth this superb race; and the eminent, the thinkers, poets, artists of that race, in turn shall bring forth in their works that which the urge of Democracy and a luxuriantly vital continent have imparted to them and to their people. But I anticipate, so eager am I to build.

He who in studying American aspects and tendencies confines the range of his vision to the narrow field of the few cities, is in danger of arriving at conclusions deepening into a hopeless pessimism. And he who would found an art philosophy on American latent capacities, instincts, tendencies, and aspirations, must therefore make doubly sure that partial and local truths do not sway him, but that his view shall be broad and comprehensive as the land — and deeper than the mere superficial aspects of his people. If our view could reach no deeper and no higher than present aspects, or if such aspects were to be taken as final and conclusive, the study would not be worth the while, for it would end in a negation or a nullity. But such is not my view and never has been my view. I have in my heart a profound reverence for the great self-centered body of the American people, for the inexhaustible activity and imaginative flexibility of the American mind, for the wealth of sentiment resident in the American heart, and for the inexhaustible energy of the American continent, which, after the subtle manner of Nature's processes, is slowly infiltrating the American heart, mind and spirit. To take a less broad, less vital view of our land and people, would mean inevitably that the art philosophy which I am expounding to you would rest on a basis less broad and less vital than the land and the people. I am unfolding to you a philosophy of art simpler and deeper than the world has hitherto known, because, through my love of my land, of my people, of Democracy, and of the Infinite Creator, has come the insight and the power so to do. My conclusions have been reached not in the racket of cities, nor in the study of garrulous philosophies, nor in libraries, nor in schools, but in the bounteous open air, within the infinite peace of Nature, alone in the solitudes, where the soul in contemplation became peaceful as the dawn, and mirrored the infinite in its own calm. I have communed more with trees than with books, and have exchanged greetings with the broad sky and the broad sea, with snow-capped mountains and the far-flung plain and prairie, with river and lake and tiny pool, with the sun in his rising, his high course and his majestic setting, with the moon in all her infinitely sweet, sad moods, and I have as a devoted lover followed the seasons through their beauteous rhythm, and have known the modulated solitudes of the starry night, and the brilliant ever-varying glories of the day. And I have been with that hitherto enigmatic creature we call man, in all his complex attitudes of heart, of mind, of soul. And from the contemplation of these has slowly emerged into the light of our day and our land, the conception of a creative art of, for and by the people, which I am now engaged in imparting to you. Its basis is too simple, too natural, too unaffected and too straightforward for a schoolman or a man of "culture" to understand, to grasp, or to sympathize with. For its dissemination I need minds and natures like your own, that have not as yet become wholly sophisticated, artificial and inert.

Such minds exist in abundance among the American people; particularly in the rising generation. And just so soon as the immense feudal scare-crow of scholarship and culture and eminence is destroyed for them, the ground cleared, and the ideal of a personal spiritual freedom conjoined with a personal responsibility and accountability is reared for them, they will grow, expand, and bring forth happiness, as the Great Creator intended, and their land and their people will be the better and the happier, for it will be in poise and at peace.

So let the orbit of our philosophy shape itself according to the deeply attractive, the profound, the abiding forces of our land and our people — heedless of the petty aberrations. For destiny is shaping here vast potencies, the which it is the part of wisdom to note and to heed.

In Nature's infinite simplicity, in her chastely fecund variety, in her silent inexhaustible power, in her exquisite adjustments, in the depths of her placidity, in her inscrutable divinity, in her master-work, Man, whom she has brought forth out of her silent depths that he may utter the yearnings of the abysmal solitudes — solitudes teeming with speechless life — in these has a little seed of regenerative sentiment slowly germinated and pushed itself upward into that atmosphere we call the mind. So has my philosophy germinated, pushed and grown from regions of the wordless, into formal speech — and so would I have it grow through the expanding seasons of your mind into a graceful, rugged tree of thought, spreading forth its leaves toward the midday sun, and abiding placidly through the winters and the nights of your span of life, and thereafter to remain with men generation after generation.

And thus in our thematic elaboration, Chicago and New York cease for us, as we progress in our synthesis, to be material cities as such, and become in our view psychic discords whose disturbing influences we must resolve, through an organic modulation, into the basic harmony of a gospel broad and inclusive as the people and the land. For our key-note is that deep, universal aspiration which animates the land, the people, and the world-force — Democracy.

To do this and to expand our thesis in such wise that we are never to be out of touch with the simple, the natural, the human; ever near on the one hand to man, and ever as near to the Great Spirit; paralleling that out-of-doors which I so love, with an out-of-doors of the spirit which I love still better; and keeping ever in mind the dignity of man, a dignity which can comport with nothing short of self-respon- sibility, and that self-government which are the seal of complete manhood: Such is our task. And to fulfill it we have to go no further for documents than to the commonest weed by the wayside, or to the smile of the nearest child, or to the stars shining forever and forever through the silent depths of the night.

Accepting, therefore, New York and Chicago as representing certain miscarriages of democracy, each group so distinctive in its way, that I have called them the oppo- site poles or nodes, expressible of certain phases of degeneracy afflicting our land and people, we have but to turn, to regain our balance of view, to the country at large and the people at large. In passing, let me say that I am not disposed to ignore or minimize the sane moral and mental and emotional forces, within those cities, which make for righteousness. Far from it, I gladly recognize them and hope that some day they may prevail. But I do say that they are not characteristic of those cities, and the balance of forces at present is heavily against them.

Such regenerative forces as do exist in these cities, I will class therefore with the upbuilding forces in the land and the people at large, to which they bear a much closer relationship.

Nor will it assist us materially to study the other cities large and small — for, strangely enough, they lack definition of character to that degree which makes them typical from our point of view, and therefore useful to us. The originally vigorous Puritanism of Boston, the Catholicism of Baltimore, the Quakerism of Philadelphia, the slave-holding oligarchism of New Orleans and other southern cities, the "river" epoch of Cincinnati, and other "river" towns, the mining craze of San Francisco — were forces now long ago on the wane, and no definite rehabilitation of aspiring energies has led, in any of these instances, to a new and marked definition of char- acter. The transition stage has been singularly protracted. Therefore in view of our fixed purpose to study contemporaneous, not historical, American architecture and civilization, they can offer us but little of suggestion, except in a negative or neutral sense.

The two cities of aggressively modern individuality, however harsh and discordant, are unquestionably Chicago and New York. The other cities resemble one or the other of these two more or less closely or remotely, but in no wise do they differ actively enough to offer us a third node. The country and the people at large are to stand, in our view, for the characteristic force against which these two cities must be balanced — and that force is so vastly more powerful than they, although much less noisy, that our reckoning with it must of necessity take time and care — and will be interwoven with many allied themes, and by renewed unfolding of themes which we have already partly deployed. But I may say to you now, that such synthetic progress, as it rises through the various stages of its elaboration, will be based, ever, on my profound, my abiding faith in the American people.

And so, my young friend, if I am spared for a few more suns, we shall leave these crowded tenements of the mind, musty and too long inhabited by squalor, to go abroad again into the open air, into the out-of-doors of the spirit, under the bright blue sky.

XXXVI. Autumn Glory

Arise, *Fidus Achates!*
Unglue slumber!
The sun has bloomed like a great red rose in the garden of albescent morn!
Awake! I say! For I am Chanticleer, crowing the peak of a new day!
Like Faust, I cry: "Another day — and yet another day!" But mine is in a major key — my song.
Awake! Awake the somatic splendor of this wonderous day! For morning is singing a crisp, cool, cheery song, so full, so full of sweet Autumn's beauty and delight! Oh, hear its song; and hear my song, dull sleeper!
Have done with slumber's dreams and come along and dream and dream with me the waking dream of a golden autumn morn!
Arouse, I say! Arouse!! Make answer to my canticle, my cheery little matin roundelay! Come on, come on; put your head forth at the window and take a good, awakening look at lusty youth and on the crispy day!
What obsolete and unoiled wheel without — that creaks so dismally?
It is my song, dear pater. Do I not sing like a robust bird?
You sing like a capon, if such, indeed, be a bird.
Oh, fie upon you! Such a snarling mood for such a gracious morn! Unsour yourself, kind friend, and open wide, and open very wide your eyes, and try, and try as hard as ever you can to smile on me, your boy, and on this bracing and vivacious day.
Come, hurry down! Let us break our fast. Let us "dash it in pieces like a potter's vessel"! The forest is awake; the hills are awake; would you still wallow in the trough

of sleep? What are vain and fitful dreams in the balance with the lightness and the brightness and the sweetness of this autumn's glory — of my heart, ensconced within this autumn morn! Come! Come!!

You are making a most terrible racket.

Of course! I'm noisiest when I'm hungriest! If you keep me waiting but a little longer, I shall climb to the top of yon tall beech-tree, stand on my head, and let myself fall into the sky — and then you'll be sorry — oh, but you'll be sorry when I'm gone.

You are an *enfant terrible!*

Papa, you said that out-of-doors was good; and it is good. I cannot tell you how my heart expands and exultates within the opening glory of this autumn day. To walk into the ample air, to open wide the portals of the soul, ah, that is something like! When first you told me that the true architectural art was to be sought and found not in books, but in the out-of-doors, I honestly thought you crazy. It seemed the most absurd statement I ever had heard; but out of respect for you — that is to say, out of a prudent regard for your sharp-pointed tongue — I said nothing: It seemed to me I could afford to wait. But now, now it's all different. How truly you said that the power of understanding lies in the imagination and the heart; that without imagination, without heart, we cannot grasp, we cannot understand; that to receive is a greater gift, a greater function, than is to give. When I heard you say that the heart is greater than the head, I again thought you a little foolish, a little unbalanced, a little too much of a dreamer; and again I said nothing, preferring to wait: But now this autumn day comes as a revelation of your meaning, and I find your doctrine sound to the very core of my own heart. How serene in her loveliness is Nature here today, in her opulence of gold and red and brown and yellow, with infinitely varying shades and changes, and the quiet note of evergreen. Last summer, Nature frightened me with the intensity and depth of her life; the marvel of it all upset me: for I was alone; but here, in the quiet abatement of her rhythm, in the solemnly joyous preparations for her long winter-sleep, it all seems easier for me to understand, or I, perhaps, am more easily reached by her sweet, sane influences, and more placidly impressed by them. For out of the long, elaborate, and for me vastly too-rich discourse that you have thus far unfolded to me, certain great and beauti-fully-connected truths are becoming now apparent to me, and tangible. Slowly they have arisen within me — as it were that I might have moved into a landscape in the night, without knowing much of it; but now comes the touch of Nature, and Sympathy begins to illumine these shadowy forms, as the great sun, rising this morn-ing, has brought light and definition of form and color, to the spacious landscape about us. So does the heart, I believe it, throw warmth and light upon truths hitherto obscure and sombre to the mind. How marvelous is the rhythm of Summer's close: for Autumn, I take it, is but the ending of Summer, as Spring was its beginning: and Winter is her sleep. And how truly, for me as you said they would, is the sub-jective becoming the objective, and the objective making itself known to me as the subjective. For they are twin brother and sister, a beautiful pair, each as real and as beautiful as the other, each as necessary to an understanding of created things. It is all so clear, so transparent in the mind here, as we stroll in the nipping, bracing air, just tinged with the last warmth of Summer's winsomely departing smile, with the brown and the pied leaves just beginning to gather a little under foot, as we walk through this stately grove, the rugged trunks, and the branches far uplifted, seeming so stern yet kindly, and wondering, one might almost say, why we have come here among them. And over all, through the openings, the brilliant, blue and cloudless sky, and the view now and then of the valley and the river below, and the gorgeously crowned opposing range of hills, brilliant here, but moving and undulating away, until, far off, they pass into a thin delicate haze, which little by little deepens into purple. And all so still, so silent, under the softening sun, so wonderfully calm, so majestic, so content. The spread of it exalts and overpowers me. And when I think that this is but a little part of it all, takes a new hold upon me, and the splendor, the beauty, the serenity of Nature's moods and rhythms come to me more and more, and my thoughts go out as upon wings, far and far and far over the land. For is this not the gorgeous heralding of winter? Is not this his breath from the far North, is not this the vast subsidence of Summer's wave of power, its ineffable declension, its exquisitely balanced modulation from moving into quiescent life? Is this not Nature's very utterance of logic: then what can logic possibly mean? If these are not thrilling illustrations of cause and effect, then cause and effect are two empty words. If this is not rhythm, why use the word at all? If this be not harmony, what is harmony? If this be not proportion, why babble idly about proportion? If this be not a process utterly organic, what does the word organic mean — what can it mean? If this superb spectacle, this third act in Nature's great drama-of-the-seasons, does not stimulate thought, does not awaken imagination, does not soften and reanimate the heart, what then can work these wonders — books? Can books go so deep as this? Can that which I get at second hand go so deep as that which I receive at first hand — that which I receive copiously, in far-flung abundance, in abundance under foot, over head, round and about, and near at hand? It is all coming near and clear to me — what you mean by the out-of-doors of the spirit. Hereafter great Nature's out-of-doors shall be my temple, far, far more beautiful, more holy, than the temple of the Roman or the Greek; and now and hereafter will I worship therein; and in the great out-of-doors of the oceans and lands of the world, of my own land and my own people, shall my spirit freely move, as a breeze through the forests and through the sky, by the light of the sun and the light of the stars, over land and sea, over river and plain. Why did not the fools in my school tell me something like this and work away at me until I understood its significance, instead of cramming me with pedantic stupidities, for four, long, weary years! I begin to have a rage against them, myself, the asses! What I knew at the end of my four years you saw only too well — nothing but presumptuous dudishness, and a veneer of artificiality which concealed a little of the weak ignorance underlying it all. Well, it's of no use crying over spilt milk; the mischief is done; we must rectify it, if it be not too late. They made me weary enough, at the time, with their finical, farcical notions of architectural grammar, which consisted chiefly in an attempt to bring unrelated things together and force them or cozen them into not quarreling too roughly; but one good, loving look at a big tree here knocks all that nonsense out of me — there is grammar *there*, and syntax too, a-plenty, and logic, and function and form, and organization, and rhythm, and proportion, and above all *vitality!* LIFE! The harmonious expressions of a Divine Creative Energy! No quarrel there! You can bet your bottom Dollar this giant oak-tree, here, never has stopped to inquire, in its oakley soul, how a pine-tree grew, or beech, or hickory. No sir! It has been true to its acorn from the time that acorn sprouted among the leaves it fell in; nor is it now fretting and whining because the leaves of the pine remain green — believing therefore the pine to be a superior tree — as some people I know would do under like circumstances. If I am wrong, correct me, master. Tell me your view.

No, go on. I prefer to listen!

Then, if I grasp the essence of your thesis, it signifies that we, in our art, are to follow Nature's processes, Nature's rhythms, because those processes, those rhythms, are vital, organic, coherent, logical above all book-logic, and flow uninterruptedly from cause to effect. And that we, being greater than trees — at least we think we are — and possessed of heart, imagination, mind, and the sympathy of mind, and above all, gifted with spiritual insight, should use those faculties to give to our art a power, a vital, a creative beauty, that shall make with Nature a harmony and not a discord.

Well said.

And that if a man, by accident of birth, or some concurrence of latent forces, be gifted, in imagination, mind and skill above his fellows, he should use those gifts, in his peculiar province, for the good, and not for the ill of his people.

They won't offer you a professorship either in a university or in an architectural school if you talk heresy such as that.

Oh, they be hanged —

What, your Alma Mater too?

Y-e-e-s-s — See there! a little breeze is blowing! Oh, the music of the forest! And how gently the big trees sway and turn their boughs, and the golden leaves let go, two, three, a dozen at a time, and flutter and float downward, and more follow, and more and more — the air is alive with them! What a marvelous shower! Like a myriad-flock of gaily-colored birds, they wing away on the stiffening breeze, and nestle in the grass and weeds. And now they come fewer; the wind is slackening; now they come in tens, sixes and twos again, and now in ones, and the music dies away, and the fluttering ceases, and all is calm and serene and content once more.

I think we had better turn about; we are quite a few miles from the inn. Ah, that puff of wind was the first blow to Autumn! See how much thinner the leaves are, on the trees, how much thicker under foot; how they rustle as we plow Nature to provide such a carpet for us two! Just think of Nature's lavishness — of her patience. I wonder that she tolerates man — they so blaspheme and flout her. But that is another evidence of her bounty — that she tolerates men.

That was quite a climb over the hill! How rich the fragrance of the woods and the earth; how spice-like but cool; everything cool and growing cooler; a sharp frost, tonight, I should say; and the sun is bending low; and the air is taking on a deeper chill; let us walk faster!

See yon orchard of apple-trees; how their boughs, heavy-laden, sweep to the ground; and the heavy layer of windfalls underneath. How faithful is the apple-tree under its load of fruit; how patiently it has borne them, through the long summer while they slowly grew and ripened day after day, week after week, month after month. Why may not man emulate such infinite patience and content, and let his thoughts ripen, with time, as they hang from the boughs of his mind; and so come to a full fruitage in their due season! See! 'Tis only a few, short months since the tree was leafless amid winter's snows! But the power to bear apples was there. And when the springtime came it burst most joyously into bloom — and now we see the ripening fruit!

Ah, here we are again at the inn! What a gladsome day this has been for me! In the cool and calm of its glory many a thought has clarified for me. How glad I am that we came here; for there has come to my understanding, never to depart from it, a clean and a wholesome sense of what you mean by the out-of-doors of the spirit — a thought, crystalline, beautiful and serene as has been this autumn day.

XXXVII. The Elements of Architecture: Objective and Subjective (1) *Pier and Lintel*

You may recall that in the course of my talk on values, and of the objective and subjective aspects of values, I stated in effect that the great painter transferred to canvas and paints something of the world and something of himself; that he caused to become subjective that which was before objective; that he thus sublimated material things and gave to them a new value — the value of personality and being; and that this power to inspire material element we call genius, talent, skill, etc., according to the relative values of these powers. I said moreover that it would become a vital part of our undertaking to revalue the accepted values in our contemporary so-called art. This latter we have done in a measure, and on the surface of things. We must now go deeper, we must search the past to lay bare the elements, the basic origins of our art — elements and origins independent of time, of period, epoch, styles, or style. For, what canvas, paints and brushes manifestly are to the painter, the objective elements of our art must manifestly appear to us: the rest, as I will show to you, is an added or infused subjectivity, a personality, or a racial propensity, made up of sensibility, of thought, of imagination and of the power of expression — the objective aspect of which latter is evidenced by technical skill.

To understand ourselves well, we must arrive first at a simple basis: then build up from it.

That we have seen things badly done, or done in a vacant, helpless spirit of imitation or reminiscence, has a broad value for us now. It has enabled us to see through the uninspired. On the other hand, we have been out of doors, and you have seen how inspired, how eloquent is Nature. You have felt the glow of her presence, and have found in your heart a response thereto. These two aspects, one of man's errancy, the other of the eternal urge and freshness of nature's creative power, have been placed, for the moment, in a sufficiently marked contrast.

Therefore let us begin to seek out those manifestations in our art, which, because instinctive and impulsive, may well be called *natural:* and little by little to discern — to discover, as it were — why they are natural. To begin a constructive study of the art of expression, or even an analytical study of historical monuments, without a prior investigation, summary and understanding of underlying elements, would be illogical, would lead us astray. To begin the serious study of architecture by a scholarly examination and analysis of its finished forms, as exhibited in certain periods of the past, or its artificial academic forms, the present-day echoes thereof, is a method I leave to the schools, their professors, and their joint folly: for it is evident they arrive nowhere.

Now let me impress upon you again, let me inspire you with the idea, that everything you see around and about you, however near, however remote, however minute, however vast, however complex, apparently bewildering, confusing or awe-inspiring, has a simple basis. That all you feel within you has a simple basis. The greatest utterances or works of the greatest men past and present have this same simple basis: whether they know it or not. And while at the end of the subtlest and furthest-pushed analysis we shall surely find this basis to be not material but spiritual, we are not to go that far now. We have not as yet arrived at the time for a logical elaboration of this theme, although its form is already apparent by inference.

Sufficient for the moment will be for us an examination of the simplest physical beginnings, the rudiments, the naked elements as yet without definite organization — as nearly formless as possible. Of these, as we casually know, the simplest is the vertical element, the PIER — regardless of its fortuitous shape or material. It rests upon the ground, it thus has support; but it already aspires, for it rises vertically from its ground-support into the air. It is stable, for it has both weight and strength. It is serene because within itself are balanced the two great forces, the simplest, elemental rhythms of Nature, to wit, the rhythm of growth, of aspiration, of that which would rise into the air: which impulse we shall call the Rhythm of Life: and the counter-rhythm of decadence, of destruction, of that which would crush to the earth, of that which makes for a return to the elements of earth, the Rhythm of Death.

This pier-form or entity is, for this reason, the simplest of architectural elements. It is in equilibrium — at seeming rest. While it seems aspiring, it seems also solidly founded: it impresses us as immovable, as static: as timeless. Simple as it seems and is to our sense of sight, it is nevertheless compound; for it is the field of operation of the two synchronous forces — downward and upward; yet it is as near to the utterly simple in physical practice as we are likely to arrive: the absolute-simple, as the absolute-anything is an image in metaphysical thought. We might, for pictorial purposes, have presupposed our pier as a tree trunk or a long stone, or a number of stones lying on the ground; but that view applies perhaps more significantly to the second element, namely the LINTEL. Our pier may stand alone as a monument, a memorial, a boundary, a guide; even as a boulder; yet with it the architectural art literally begins. But with the lintel comes into view a radically new element, a most subtle, strange and abstruse element. Alone, lying flat on the ground it is functionless, useless: (it may become a pier). That it shall definitely assert a function there must pre-exist two piers. But the moment this lintel (this latent thing), is laid upon the two piers and connects their activities — presto! by the subtlest of conceivable magic, instantly the Science of Architecture comes into being, as surely, as inevitably as, when two chemical elements unite, a new force or product at once appears. This phenomenon is, in Nature, the exact opposite of catastrophe or sudden death — it is sudden, instant, BIRTH! We have no true name for it in the language. But if you fix the phenomenon well in your thought, the absence of an exact word for it need not matter much. And be sure that you do, for later on I shall have much to say to you in further subjective elaboration of the two great rhythms of growth and decay, or of life and death — as you may choose to call them — and concerning the innumerable rhythms born of them, exterior to man and within him.

So, when the lintel is placed upon the two piers, architecture springs into being not only as a science, and a useful art, but also as an art of expression; and the Architect comes into primitive being with this primitive beginning of his great creative work, with this simple, ingenious union of two elementals. You see it is all plain and natural; there is no immediate physical mystery in it — however inexhaustibly deep it may be as a spiritual manifestation. You see how spontaneoussly architecture is born of Nature and man, how it emerges from his need and his power: how it fulfills his desires. That the lintel is essentially unstable in fact and in time, however placid in appearance, you well know; and how complex are the forces at work within it, modern science teaches us. In simplest terms, reposing, both, flat on the earth, pier and lintel cannot be distinguished one from the other: their potentiality is the same. (It is only when by man's touch they are slightly differentiated, that they are separable, in evident function.) Yet when erected into place by the power of man's mind and body, in response to his need, his desire, supported all by the kindly earth — a new, a primitive FORM appears without and within man. [Fig. 9]

To recapitulate: The pier and the lintel, elemental in nature, form, in combination, the simple visible origin of our art. To be sure, you may think the wall more primitive than the pier, but that is of no real consequence; you may look on the wall as a lengthened pier or on the pier as a shortened wall; it does not signify. The essence of each is that it is a vertical mass resting on the ground, and capable of support.

What is essential is to note the entry of the personal or human element at the earliest primitive beginnings of the art; and to note, with high concentration, how, by virtue of the inexhaustible powers of the expressive mind, have sprung, from the simple elements — pier and lintel — architectures of great beauty, yet differing emphatically from each other in rich and vivid display of poetic expression, fertile fancy, and dramatic power: witness the Assyrian, the Egyptian and the Greek architectures. How eloquent, how characteristic, is each, of its race; and yet each and all of them arose from the same simple elements. It shows what man can do. It exhibits, as in a moving panorama, the splendor of his powers: the vast scope of his needs; the powers that reside within his structures reside within himself.

It is related in Genesis that the Lord God formed man of the dust of the ground, and breathed into his nostrils the breath of life; and man became a living soul. So did these peoples — the Assyrians, the Egyptians and the Greeks — and in the same allegorical sense — make their varied architecture of the dust of the earth, and breathe into the simple elements, lintel and pier, the breath of life, and they became living art, filled with the soul of the race, with the soul, the identity of those who made great architecture out of the dust, as the author of Genesis made man out of the dust.

These simple elements, lintel and pier, are yours. Extrinsically and intrinsically they belong to no time, no people, no race. Go, breathe into them the breath of your life, that, formed of the dust, under the urge of your need and your will, they become inspired of a living soul! You were born with spiritual power; for the Lord God, now as ever, breathes it into the dust from which man is continually making. You were at birth a living soul! See to it that that soul does not die within you. But more of all this later. At our next talk we will carry further the study of our elements.

XXXVIII. The Elements of Architecture: Objective and Subjective (2) *The Arch*

Picking up again the thread of our theme: It appears that three great civilizations of the past evolved their diversified, and highly characteristic, architecture from pier and lintel; that they amplified the expression of these two primitive forms, and their combined form, with the expansiveness of their life-experiences, and that thus they builded wisely, graciously, even fatefully.

Yet, how it happened I know not — whether the caving in of a troglodyte's home, the stones over the roof becoming wedged into a certain roughly-spanning shape, or what not — certain it seems that at some time in the purple dim of the past a primitive imagination wondered if stones might not be braced against each other to span over something or other — a cave or what not. Doubtless the beginning was as rude as man himself. But, however it happened —and that matters not especially — some man at some time, or successive men in successive times, by a series of rough approximations conceived and carried out the idea of wilfully placing stones, the one against the other, to span over something or other, and gradually through the course of time the process was elaborated, and defined. [Fig. 10]

So came into being the ARCH. It is difficult to conceive the arch as a creation of a single mind; I do not recall an instance of creative power approaching this in sublimity. To the reflective mind the arch is a wonder, a marvel, a miracle. But, come it did; and it is with us; and has been with our predecessors for thousands of years. It is the third and last of our elements — or elementals.

We need not stop to discuss inconsequential imaginary or romantic origins of a form so primal, so masterful and yet so winsome as the arch; but I feel pretty sure of this, in my mind: that it came in its primitive form about the time pier and lintel came. How many thousands or tens of thousands of years ago the three appeared, I am not inclined to hazard a thought. But when they came into being, as such, in man's experience, there came also into being the three physical facts, the three symbols, I might say the three letters, which constitute the alphabet of our art — the briefest of them all. I wish deeply to impress upon you this simple fact; for it is of the utmost importance that you carry its significance ever in mind. It is a triune fact, the simple germinal phenomenon from which has arisen the vast, splendid, sumptuous Art of Architecture.

More subtle, more intricate, more subjective than either pier or lintel, the arch has just so much more of man in it. We may therefore view it both as a triumph over an abyss and as the very crystallization of that abyss itself. It is a form so much against Fate, that Fate, as we say, ever most relentlessly seeks its destruction. Yet does it rise in power so graciously, floating through the air from abutment to abutment, that it seems ever, to me, a symbol and epitome of our own ephemeral span.

The Arch is, of all constructive forms, the most emotional. It is susceptible in possibility and promise to the uttermost degree of fulfillment that the creative imagination can forecast. Its plasticity is limitless, as that of man himself: he may turn to it the most hard, the most delicate, the most imaginative use. It responds to every need. Under man's hand it becomes what he will. In all its power it is a form so frail in essence, so gracious, so ethereal, that it must need ever touch the heart attuned to Nature's mysteries.

The Romans held it in bondage, as a useful thing. The Chinese used it more graciously as a useful thing. The Saracens, the Hindus, the Persians, said lovely words with it and about it. Its soul was partly known to them. In Byzantine, Romanesque, medieval times you see it again as it was needed and understood. All such uses, however, were local, limited and typical. Nowhere do we see a full grasp and intensive comprehension of the arch as such. That is why I am endeavoring, ever more fervently, to impress upon you the simple truth — immeasurable in power of expansion — of the subjective possibilities of objective things. In short, to clarify for you the origin and power of BEAUTY: to let you see that it is resident in function and form.

So is ugliness, isn't it?

To be sure.

Is there anything that does not reside in function and form?

Not that I have been able to discover.

Why have you said nothing concerning the cantilever?

Because it is not primary. It belongs among those secondary structural forms which may be classed as expedients. It is neither one thing nor the other; neither pier, lintel nor arch, though it seems curiously to partake of their functions in a reverse or imitative way. It may assist pier, lintel and arch. Its essence is overhang. The pier, lintel and arch are in their simplest forms primary propositions. The cantilever belongs in the province of morphology.

What would the modern bridge engineer do without the cantilever?

That is his business. What he does with it does not change its nature, however wonderful the performance. The same may be said of his impressive development of lintel and arch. Because of his needs, and in response to his needs, he has raised the primitive cantilever to a position of high importance, but its nature remains unaltered. But I am not following the development of the science of engineering, however fascinating the topic may be. It is our immediate business to deal with the art of architecture. So let us return to the road.

Then perhaps I may put in a word: If I get the drift, the abutments of the arch are esssentialy piers; and the two abutments, with the arch rising between them, form a triune-simple which does not differ in essence from the triune-simple you have visualized as a resultant type-form of the two piers and a lintel.

Very good; but what do you infer?

I infer this: that you, in your philosophical, psychological, metaphysical and somewhat poetical way, wish me to conclude that these two triune-simples are so similar in their nature that they evidently derive from the single function SPAN.

Very good. You have saved me time.

Shall we go further?

Not now. Time's up! You may dream about it.

I fear I shall: and of the variants.

XXXIX. Illumination

I have dreamed and dreamed. Dreamed of the pier, the lintel and the arch as you have set them forth; and I have mused upon their implications, so subtle, so manifold. I have evaporated in speculations, and condensed and descended again upon the humanities. How great is man, how manifold his power! How he recreates himself in what he does! I am beginning to see and to feel. It is all wonderful—too wonderful: you are setting forth man in a new light — a light at once tender and clear — a light suffused by his own grandeur, his instability, his folly. I have been as it were in a trance, filled with thoughts that come from where — I know not. Thoughts that seemed to arise from the depths and suffuse my vision. Gradually this state has passed away, leaving, however, its immemorial impression. I have come at least to know what the word subjective contains, implies: that it is a word immeasurable as man, immeasurable as the universe. I have come to understand, what I could not possibly have understood hitherto; I have arrived at last where I may understand the plastic nature of the objective. It has taken you all of these talks to get into my head the meaning of two words which, at first, I regarded as pedantic and technical. Now I see that they are human — immensely human. That to grasp these two words means to grasp two great powers. And so it has been with the word function and the word form, and the word power. You have uncorked the flagons that held three words in bondage, and now they fill the earth and the sky: and now they fill the soul. I begin to understand what you have said about words. How they come to us with their contained power: how they may be surcharged by us with new powers, new meanings, how they may be recreated. I have come to learn with startled consciousness how terrible a thing is a word. How immense, how world-wide may be the power of a single word, for good or for ill. In such sense I am coming to understand the word Feudalism and the word Democracy. The world is beginning to live for me. The world of the present, the world of the past: the great world of man flowing through space and time: the world of his dreams and his deeds. It has become all so human — so passionately human. It elevates, it depresses: I could almost faint, as in the solitude of my soul I view this far-flung panorama of man and the earth his home. It is all so human, so utterly human, so stupendous in grandeur and folly — as man alone can be. So man begins to live for me. Within my dream he is coming into his own. He is coming true.

That's pretty fine for a youngster.

Thank you for waking me. I came here to ask a few questions and immediately I began to rave, to speak in a strange tongue. Is that what it means when it is said that sometime in his life a man may have an illumination?

That's exactly what it means. I have been looking for it in your case.

Well, if that is so, then I can come down to earth and not lose my dream — my vision?

It will remain with you forever. You are born again. For illumination is but that cataclysm of birth of which you have heard me speak.

Then you think I can safely ask a few questions and make a few suggestions — I am very nervous.

Why certainly. Quiet down and go ahead.

Then I will begin: Let me start with the pier; taking as a basis the pier in its rudest form, its most primitive significance, any ensuing change in form or significance is due to man's touch or manipulation, to his plastic power as a worker. That as the pier gradually takes on definition, or perhaps I had better say CHARACTER, it does so because of its *own* plastic nature, for all materials, however refractory, yield to the will of the craftsman man. Now why does the objective material, once it has yielded to the subjective will, at once assume human characteristics? Would it not show finer feeling, deeper insight, if instead of saying the material yields, [we were] to say that it consents; that it has awaited the will of man? Is this metaphysical moonshine or is it an immediate vital proposition in our art and in our regard of the art of the past? Is it not more fruitful of result to aver this unison of craftsman and material than to posit them as separate and isolated: has not the time come to discriminate between force and power? For have you not been exhibiting man as power, not as force? Am I spinning too fine a thread: if so, it is my own, and I believe it to be strong as a cable in its every-day application and use. I see you are not disagreeing, so I will go on: What made man *wish* to make changes in the simplest form of the pier? Was it not in response to some need — physical, intellectual, emotional? And was not and is not the need at bottom of all needs the need, the desire to procreate his own personality, temperament: the need, the desire that the creations of his hands, of his brain should *fit* him — that he might feel at home with himself? That when he looked upon his creations they *satisfied* him: else why that singular allegory that the Lord God looked upon his works and declared them good? Are not all works to be judged by this basic standard, independent of what the word good really means: taking it only as implying satisfaction of a need, of a desire of the exercise of a power! Now, assuming this much, were not all changes in the pier, subsequent to its primitive shape, essentially morphological in their nature: following man's temperament in its manifold metamorphoses? And are we not to read in all the changes in structural form the artistic treatment of the pier, in all those manifold subtleties of changing shape, in involved and evolving character, are we not to read in them a record of man's changing moods, of his ever shifting attitude of mind and heart, of his response to the world of nature, to the world of men and to his own inner world? If this is so, does not the historic spread of our art through the centuries resolve itself into an unceasing flow exhibiting the flow of man himself! From the character of a pier may we not discern the character of a race: and from the slowly changing character of a developed pier may we not discern the temperamental changes taking place in a race: its growth, its fulfillment, its decay! Has man at any time, can man at any time, can he now lay his hand upon anything, can he focus his mind upon anything, without leaving upon that thing the impress of his character? Is it not evident that under modern social conditions a man may impress upon materials the character of his mind without even touching the materials with his own hands? Is it not evident that though he may lose actual physical contact with materials, he need not, he must not, he shall not lose actual, emotional, intellectual, spiritual contact with them any more than though seemingly isolated he shall lose contact with his people, times — contact of heart and spirit?

Better than I could have said it! You have ardor; the ardor of youth. The world is new to you, but you are beginning to see it.

Passing that sweet saying by — is not what I have said and implied concerning the pier and its morphology applicable in full measure not only to lintel and arch but likewise and in even fuller measure to the triune-simple based upon pier, lintel and arch, and the structural and expressional morphology of these triune-simples?

It is certainly the case.

Then if such is certainly so, we may view and interpret all manifestations of the architecture of the past and present in the light of man's temperamental changes; they become for us demonstrations of character, episodes in manner, indexes of civilization and the changes of mood within civilization; and by this light those architectural manifestations we moderns rather foolishly, rather emptily, call the Historic Styles, appear to us as luminous symbols of the past; and the past thus lives for us again — even while we know it to be past. Now I come to the crux of my proposition: How is it, why is it, that we of the present, in contrast to those of the past, seem to have no present of our own except in a materialistic sense? In any other sense we seem empty and amorphous — without form and void, as the scripture has it. To me this is the great modern enigma. Does it signify decay, moral stasis, spiritual degeneration, or does this marvelous materialism really signify a new epoch, a gestation period of spirituality within the huge body of materialism; is that body really pregnant, does this vast materialism signify and prophesy a terrific cataclysm of birth? Can it mean, in its immensity, the coming release of the heart from its bondage to the intellect? Can it mean this or am I hoping against hope? It is all like a huge high wall to me. I cannot see through it or over it or around it. It seems as though I were living in a cocoon, a cocoon spun by the thought of the ages. I can dream of the past, I can, as it were, see the past and live in the past, but I cannot see the world about me. I feel as though I were at the edge of an abyss — I totter.

You are not at the edge of an abyss; you are climbing a summit. You are high enough now to see something of the past. Climb higher and you will see the present.

Is that really so? Then I feel better.

NOTE: This chapter, rewritten completely, was in the earlier version entitled "On the Historic Styles."

XL. On Scholarship

If then, the historic modes of building, those attitudes, emotional and mental, expressed in materials, we call the historic styles, were and are what we deem them, that is, records of an eloquent past, a memorandum of states of feeling, active and purposeful in their day, having definite direction in their day, but not possessed of these specialized qualities for us today — what shall we say of those in our day who try — and they try very hard, it must be confessed — to duplicate, imitate or plagiarize these historic monuments expressive of moods gone by, and in the doing, believe, or affect to believe, such impertinence of forgery to be the chief end and aim of modern architectural endeavor?

An architect is, literally, according to the dictionaries, a chief worker, or something of that sort; at least, I take it, a person who directs the making of something germane, of something useful, of something timely; an individual who has the brains to imitate, to propel, to lead in a work, in a constructive plan of operations, deriving from actual needs, and resulting in a building definitely organized in every sense for a predetermined specific use; and standing as the full attainment of an end.

Now to simple unadulterated minds it would seem that the chief usefulness of an architect, that which should justify his name, must lie in the initiation of a building; in fostering its growth from germinal conditions; in securing its maturity. That is to say, the architect must be, first of all a clear, comprehensive thinker; he must have that mental grasp of things material and spiritual, which shall provide him the power to initiate, to supply that emotional impulse and that creative energy which shall result in a building coming naturally, logically and graciously out of its conditions physical and social. That to be a thinker in this sense, such a man must be possessor of a bold, well-controlled, fertile and accurate imagination, sympathetic understanding, and an intelligence calm, well-trained, accurate, alert and cognizant, and a high social aim in a complete accomplishment: no cultural factor overlooked.

But this, while a simple enough conception for us, at this stage of our progress, is not the current view; particularly is it not the view obtaining among people of refinement, cultivation and good manners — setting aside for the moment the newly rich, the vulgar rich, and the hard-headed, practical business man — he who is never mistaken.

Their cultivated view, indeed, is quite the opposite of that which I have set forth briefly as ours. They hold — perhaps without consciously voicing it — that there is something vulgar, or at the least unrefined, in the actual conditions of the life and civilization of our day: in its unshapen elements, in its very quality of transition or sturdy growth, in its eddying currents of thought and feeling, in its unrest, its fierce urge, its ceaseless ferment and ebullition. To them all this clamor and disturbance is chaos — forgetting that the world was ever thus — and they turn, with a genuine desire, to find something manageable, something culturally domesticated, something that will stand still, something in repose and stationary: with wistful gaze toward those periods of the past, the ebullition and roar of whose life has settled into the calm and the silence of permanent rest. Such minds, to be sure, are not masterful, they are timorous; they ache to be correct. They seek a sleek peace, not achievement; tranquillity, not strife; problems that have been solved, not disturbing problems that must be solved. Therefore do they turn to the tranquil records of the past; forgetting or ignoring that these very achievements, so serene as it would seem, were, in their own day, the output of strife, or tumult, of ebullition, of uncertainties: that the timorous and finical were there also.

Hence, comes also from this neurasthenic, fastidious, precious feeling, or inclination, or revulsion as it may be, a desire to find strength in the past; and, while thus delving for countenance and support, to exalt the values of all the findings, even to the extent of appraising unearthed commonplace as treasure-trove. Depreciating the immense powers of our day, they belong to the class that may be called ashamed.

Far be it from me to underrate the studious habit of a serious mind in whatever channel it may choose to run. When sincerity and simplicity of heart are handmaidens of such a mind, and a positive, definite purpose really useful to us is its goal,. I am the last to say nay.

But that is not the point; and we must carefully discriminate between semi-honesty and semi-dishonesty; between seriousness and frivolity, between strength and weakness, between boldness, cowardice or evasion of purpose.

Every and any field of inquiry is a legitimate province of activity for a certain mind of a certain cast, provided the results of such inquiry are couched in terms distinctly germane, and reached with entire mental candor. But when such inquiry is made under dubious pretenses, and its results couched in terms that are irrelevant or misleading, such procedure can be classed only as egoistic and reactionary: in short, as mental dishonesty.

The desire to take refuge in the past has both its honest and its dishonest aspects; and, generally speaking, the desire to live in the past and to taste its fruits in solitude is called scholarship; but little discriminaton has thus far been made, by cultivated people, between candid and uncandid scholarship: between the scholarship of stealth and the scholarship of courage. Particularly has this held true of architectural scholarship. Once it was innocent; now, with us, it is vicious.

Therefore must we be resolute to separate true scholarship from pseudo-scholarship in our art.

In the Roman-Temple-Bank, the Doric Column, and the College-Library-Building we have seen the astonishing insincerity of commercial scholarship. In these structures, as I sought to show you, irrelevance is carried to the limit of credibility.

Of the drift of true scholarship I have sought to give you a hint in my talks on the Elements of Architecture and as well, inferentially, in other talks. Briefly, it is evident that results of scholarship, to be true, must bear a relation of unmistakable value to the day and generation of the scholar — otherwise he has no function, no excuse for being — he becomes a parasite. Nor does this view ignore on the one hand the exceeding complexity of our modern civilization and on the other the recondite nature of a true scholar's labor.

Aside, therefore, from the great touchstone, Democracy, we have this broad test of the value of modern scholarship, namely, that to be true it must bear a genuine relation to the vital, aspiring thought of our day and generation. And thus, specifically, the highest, the truest, the most useful, the most sane scholarship for us Americans of today is that which tests the past; which draws from the recorded life of the past such inspiration as will stimulate us and animate us; strengthen our own hearts and quicken our own minds to solve, and wisely solve in our own temperamental way, the pressing problems of democracy which confront us, and which daily seek so urgently for a salutary solution. If this be true in a broad way, it is acutely true in an architectural way. In a nutshell; we learn that, in the eminent periods of the past, which we so sincerely admire, people did things in their own way. By this test, when we ask an architect to make for us a bank building and he gives us a weird imitation-Roman-temple, he is not a scholar, he is a plain fraud!

So, when we ask an architect to build a memorial to the Great Lakes, the primeval forests and the hardy *voyageurs* — and he gives us a Doric Column, he is not a scholar, he is a faker!

So, when we ask an architect to build a twenty-odd-story office-building, and he throws up a swaggering mass of Roman remnants, he is not a scholar but a brute.

And so, when we ask an architect to make a library building for a modern American university, and he gives us fragments of what the Greeks did, and guesses at what the Greeks might have done, he is not a scholar, he is an aimless pedant: selling his modern birthright for a pseudo-scholarly mess of classic pottage.

In short, when we ask a modern American architect to solve with candor any one of a hundred directly and distinctly modern American problems hitherto unsolved, and further ask him, in the doing, to bring to bear upon his solution the highest qualities and powers of a trained and active sympathy, (true fruits of scholarship), and thereupon, he, shrinking, shirking the vital issue, builds for us ineffectually, after the manner of civilizations long since gone, though not forgotten, which had little or nothing in common with our own specialized needs, and soulfully dubs his work as of such and such a "style": such man is not a scholar, he is a plain public nuisance, obstructive alike of our growth in democracy and in spiritual welfare. And yet I have known such an architect, yea, an eminent one, to smile and shudder at the mere thought of liberating the creative impulse.[1] If his conception of the creative impulse is on a par with his conception of scholarship, I smile and "shudder" with him.

1. Details of this incident are given in Appendix C, because it is probably characteristic of an artist's relations with exponents of the status quo and it explains the sense of premonition and the recurrent tone of urgency in *Kindergarten Chats*.

My boy, if this is what current scholarship results in, in our specialty, you were better off without it, and to go it alone. But that sort of hybridism is far away from what democratic scholarship means.

Think of it my lad! — and take it to your heart: an architect, a gentleman and a scholar who can find nothing great, nothing inspiring in his own land — his own times, his own people! Think of it: a scholar who has seen the creative impulse spontaneously liberate itself amongst us in so many fields of activity and bring forth results under his very eyes that have made his country great among the intellectual and moral and material forces of the world — and yet this "scholar" dreads and "shudders" lest this same vital, energetic, creative American mind seek and find liberty for the exercise of its power in the field of a genuinely productive, temperamental architectural art! So much for the education you and your predecessors have received.

True scholarship, my son, is a sane and beautiful thing. It is born of reverence and of love, and fills the mind with wisdom, the heart with tenderness. No true man can look into the mysterious depths of by-gone days, as they pass in solemn procession through ever deepening twilights into the impenetrable abyss of oblivion, without being overcome by a profound feeling of awe and tenderness and wonder and inspiration at the power and the glory of that Infinite Creative Impulse, which has evolved from itself these countless generations of men upheaving and subsiding in waves of civilization. And to him surely will come the companion reflection that we, in our turn, are a new wave of civilization, huge and portentous, rising and slowly swelling toward its crest; and that the impulse of that wave is not militarism, not feudalism, but Democracy!

You and I are but the minutest of passing wavelets in that uprising sea. We come and go — none knows whence or whither — out of the sea and into the sea! Little wavelets we — a breath — and we are gone! But souls have we which blow from the same Infinite Breath that upheaves the sea; and to those souls we will be true while the swell of the wavelet lasts.

So, my lad, do not falter though others fall. Of true scholarship you can never have too much. It never burdens and wearies, nor does it dull the mind and dry the heart; rather does it give wings to the spirit, serenity to the mind, and to the heart eternal youth!

So opens to us something of the richness of the human mind: the ego: that marvelous agency of power under the arching sky! It is Nature's most glorious achievement in simplicity: the power of powers: the marvel of marvels! So should you hold Nature in ever growing reverence and love; for she is the eternally fruitful mother of the great race of Man.

So move we a little further forward in our theme. Its ever broadening harmonies appall me as they come, like springtime, surging into view. And I am dismayed. For how little of their indwelling life have I the power of speech or e'en the power of love to unfold. Alas, how weak is utterance!

XLI. On Culture

What strange and wonderful things words are. I have been thinking of the word, culture. What a puzzling word it is. What is its real meaning at the core?

It often happens that a certain word, through oft-recurring unimaginative use, becomes so glib that its significance blurs and dissipates and we dull to its active meaning. It loses tang. How surely, for instance, the word, war, loses its terrible meaning during a protracted time of peace. How soon does the word, poetry, part company with its loftiness among a prosaic people: You can readily see how, little by little, it falls from its high estate, degenerating into a mere synonym of rhyme, or, at the highest, versification — falling, ever lower, until at last, among a dull people, it becomes little else than a covert term of reproach. Through what extraordinary vicissitudes has the word, God, passed! To what depths of banality and common-place utility has it descended; through what Saharas of materialism has it wandered, forlorn and forgotten, when a spiritual night has fallen. Into what quagmires has the word, art, floundered — yet from them it has often struggled forth.

So, know that words hold only that which is continually imparted to them. They are vital when those who use them vitalize them. They expand with the expansion of a thought; they decline when that virtue or power they stand for declines in a people. Bear this in mind: words are unreal, the most illusory of symbols; yet have they an objective life and story of their own, both as a race of words and as single words; wherefore is it that each and every word in our language, or in any language, is, at any given time, in its own special condition of health or decline. Yet in each case, the condition of the word is an index of the subjective status of the people who use it, collectively and individually. So when you listen to talk, or read in a book, listen with the inner ear, and see with the inner eye; thus will you sometimes be amazed, sometimes disheartened; sometimes you may be inspired thereby.

So too when you, in turn, use words, make sure that you possess the wherewithal to charge them — lest you be a bow without an arrow — a seedless husk from which no living thing can sprout. See to it above all that when you use the term, creative art, your mind, your whole being shall be charged to saturation; and when you speak of the liberation of the creative impulse, be doubly, trebly sure that you are not an empty husk! Of arrowless bows and seedless husks Lord knows the world is full. But of all the words that are just now ill unto death, fallen into decrepitude of neglect, of emaciation, the word, culture, seems to me the most pitiful.

Stop to recall, my son! — Did I not promise I would be your gardener, and that you should be for me as a fair garden under the glad sun that shines for all? Did I not say that, after plowing and harrowing the fallow field, I would plant, in the soil of youth, seeds of many thoughts; and, further, when they had germinated in the darkness, and sprouted forth in tender eagerness, I would water the tiny shoots with the water of life?

I have not, to be sure, said much to you directly or indirectly of culture as such; but I have said much to you of manliness of head and heart, of clarity of vision, of indomitable courage. I have sought with all due insistence to impress upon you, as a maxim, the simple truth that the heart is greater, worthier, nobler, finer than the head: that the heart is the sanctuary of the Temple of Man, the head its portal. That from the heart comes forth Sympathy into the open: the subtlest, the tenderest, the most human of emotions; and that of Sympathy is born that child of delight which illumines our pathway, and which we call Imagination. Yet withal, have I said little to you of culture: for you could not then grasp what true culture means; you would be last in the crowd of masqueraders, nonplussed by the varied camouflage.

Openly though wearily have I shown you disease, that you may the better know what health means. I have shown to you the aspects of decay solely that you might the better grasp the wholesome meaning of growth. I have given you a glimpse of cynicism and pessimism that I may the more surely lead you on the path to stable optimism. I have shown to you the damnable folly of greed and selfishness, and how it kills the soul, that you may eventually and surely grasp the wisdom of altruism, that your soul may live its life — yet have I said to you little of culture.

I have spoken, at some length, of Democracy, because I know and deeply feel how greatly the meaning of the word needs expansion, in every heart and mind.

I have striven, in a measure, as far as you were ripe to understand, to make the sense of reality known to you — the flowing reality of past and present: the reality of man. The reality of his powers. I have been helping you to form an idea of man, and to feel for yourself how greatly that word, also, needs expansion, until it shall meet our pressing need.

I have taught you something of the nature, the use and the value of thought; yet have I ever prudently outbalanced human logic with the exquisite logic of Nature's powers and deeds. I have shown to you the difference between things unorganized, miscellaneous, complicated, involved, and things organic, single, simple, complex: and again have I taken you to Nature for her proofs.

I have warned you of the pitfalls of words and phrases, and have impressed upon you, directly and indirectly, that the highest thought is not only wordless, but of necessity must remain so. Yet has language its wondrous uses.

I have talked to you of the training of the senses; and have assured you that the physical senses are the only avenues whereby the outer world can reach your inner world; that the senses have a higher and a lower range, the one called physical, the other spiritual — or objective and subjective, as you prefer; or outer and inner, as you prefer.

I have talked of values; and have urged you ever to discriminate between those values which are enlightened and those which are unenlightened. I have intimated to you that all values are weighable strictly and surely on the amount and force of their contained subjectivity or spirit; which explains to you why a building is merely a screen behind which resides its *real* value, great or small — a personality — and that such weighing in the balance will reveal the spiritual poverty or wealth, the humanity or the inhumanity, the democracy or the undemocracy of that personality. And yet I have said to you little of Culture! And why not? BECAUSE THESE THINGS ARE OF THE SPIRIT AND SUBSTANCE OF CULTURE!

Would you plow and harrow, and plant no seed? Is that culture?

Is it culture to let the fallow field revert to weeds and brambles, when plowing and harrowing are done?

Would you put a young man's nose in a book, say to him: this is finality? Would you show him without rational explanation, completed, complex documents he cannot in his immaturity understand, because they do not, unaided, find their way directly to the intelligence and the heart? Is that culture? Is it culture to conceal from him his native powers, if not indeed to belittle them — because you fondly believe genius to be exceptional? Would you show him great works and refrain from telling him these works are man — and that he too is man? Would you dare tell him these great works are unapproachable by us? Would you so belittle us all? Would you so belittle universal human powers you fail to understand for lack of heart and brain?

Would you narrow his mind, or would you seek in every way to broaden it? Would you enlarge his sympathy, or would you constrict it? Would you intimate to him that his own times, his own land, his own people are valueless, hopelessly vulgar and negligible, or would you tell him that they are what, during all his life, should and shall be nearest and dearest to him — that they are his home? Which view stands for culture?

Would you in utter rashness, seek to make of him in your various image a pedant, a fashion-monger, a phrase-maker, an attitudinizer, an opportunist, or would you awaken in him the creative thinker that surely is within him — the truly productive worker — the real man? Which result would stand for culture?

Would you tell a young architect that democracy has nothing to do with his art, and his art still less to do with democracy: that no one ever heard of so strange, so preposterous a notion; or would you tell him that in that very democracy lies an inexhaustible wealth of inspiration needing only the open eye, the open mind to receive it, to interpret it, and to convey it? Which course would stand for culture?

Would you tell a young architect that the enormously varied problems large and small of building, under modern American conditions, material and social, are to be met and solved, not by personal, individual force of sympathy, intellect and will, but by the application of an artificial memory of things past and gone; unsympathetic now, and inapplicable! Would that be culture? Or would you say to him, as I now say to you: My son, the world is seeking now, more than ever, men of force of intellect and strength of character: MEN OF CULTURE. It needs them; for it has much for them to do. Supremely does your own country need such men in all walks of life; it sadly needs them, it as sadly needs confidence in them, to make for it its buildings. Such men it needs in every walk, in every function, in every activity, in order conclusively to express the realities of its destiny, the realities of its racial wisdom and character, the realities of the land and the time — the genius of the people: once it believes in them it will welcome them. You are in truth not asked by them to tarry with superficialities, to be their flunky; you are expected to go intimately deep; to come intimately near; you are expected to be wholly, not partly, efficient; you are expected to sympathize, to understand: you are expected to be obviously human and true.

Now just so long as our educational institutions above the grade of the kindergarten and kindred aspects persist in foisting a feudal and hence now artificial system of thinking and feeling upon an active-minded people, just so long shall we continue to be characterized by spiritual poverty instead of spiritual wealth in our civilization and in our art. For our art cannot differ materially from our civilization, and our civilization cannot essentially differ from our thought, our education. Hence, we may seek and find the existing center of gravity of our art within the nature and tendencies of our educational methods. I am gratefully aware of important movements for educational betterment, even though they be sporadic. I know the brilliant minds impelling these movements — striving against the inertia of academic convention and the languor of habit. The leaven is working, and some day will surely work largely.

Thus, my son, do we obtain a general view of the orderly form and content of true culture, in contrast to the relative shapelessness and emptiness of what, amongst us, passes for culture. Culture to be real, to ring true, in this day and land and for our people, must become democratic: as they must become. It must justify itself as the most simple, impressively obvious output of the spirit of democracy in its subjective aim and social form. Otherwise, culture for us is an illusion, a delusion, not a power. When two such words as Democracy and Culture are conjoined, there arises from the conjunction a new idea, a new sense and vision of power — a new world wherein Democratic-Culture shall signify man's highest estate.

True Culture means the full opening of the heart: its veritable blooming. Without this — all else is vanity and vexation of spirit.

Now we are beginning!

He that endureth to the end shall be saved!

XLII.   What is an Architect?

What's on your mind this time?

Pater, this is, for sure, a weary world! I cannot reach the heights of it: I am hung up by the middle. Suspended in the center of a minute vacuum of my own, by a string invisible, the end of which reaches up beyond my ken. Yet do I gravitate by my own weight, feathery tho' that be; and if the string were cut, I flutter, like an autumn leaf, and settle upon the solid earth of another vacuum unreal and intangible as this Infinite of which you speak, illusory and elusive as the democracy of which you speak, unreal and intangible and yet just as commonplace as the land and the people of which you speak — fugitive and furtive and evanescent as the realities of which you speak.

Ah, that which is near at hand is farther off than mountains! Why did you tell me that the near-at-hand might be grasped? The nearer at hand the farther away! It is only illusions that can be grasped and held! Realities escape our every touch; they recede as we advance.

We are creatures of illusion and must remain ever such — for realities, as you have said, are divine; they are of and for the Infinite; they are not for us.

Yet am I not sad, nor cast down, but resolute — I am merely out of focus; for no man can look forward and backward, up and down, right and left, near and far at the same time.

Go on, pater; I have girded up my heart! I am your hardy mariner O.K., but it is a heavy, foggy calm, and dead-reckoning is no joke! No; I will not be a porcelain ship upon a porcelain sea! Let the waves break and roar! Better to drown in turbulent waters than collapse in a tenuous air!

I am a seed deep in the dark ground! Would that I might sprout, and my spear shoot into the lambent light and air, and delicately pierce the melody of spring!

Realities, realities! What are realities to the living-dead! What are sights to the eyeless! What are sounds to the earless! What are joys and sorrows to the heartless! What is the Infinite to the mindless! What is man — to man the beast?

Ah, it's all very fine, very fine indeed to be out of focus; especially when you know it. What does it comfort me that most men are out of focus! — for they know naught of the open air, while I — I have had glimpses — I! — only to lose them — except in memory's hold! Verily life has every weather, every water's depth!

Why is it farther to the nearest dewdrop than to the moon? Why is the nearest man you know unreachable as the pole? And yet, and yet, we press a button and a current flows that did not flow before, and there is light — an artificial light to be sure. But what are all our lights but artificial lights?

While you have been talking, I have been thinking, pater. Perhaps my thoughts were tinkling bells — who can say! Time alone can tell, and Time is rudely silent thereupon. Will she consecrate or will she blast — I do not care! For I am stubborn, now, with Fate, and must push on!

To what depths must we dig to find a solid soil! What a ridiculously elaborate scaffolding must we erect! And when our little structure's done and the scaffold down and the tools and the rubbish removed and our darling left to the world, the Stupid says: "Oh, how stupid: I could do that." I do not care; even though to move a people is harder than to move a rock! I suppose when Moses struck the rock and the waters flowed forth, that was another oriental allegory. I don't care whether it was or not, if it has to be explained. Why must we be eternally explaining things! Why don't things explain themselves! Why don't we understand without these everlasting explanations which explain nothing! We either see or don't see, don't we? And that's about the beginning and the end of it, isn't it? We are a dull crew all of us, and I am superlatively dull! When will the scales stay fallen from my eyes! When shall I be born again in strength! What avails it that I think, if my thought is sterile and brings forth not something fruitful into the light! Yet what do I care! Why should I care?

What is an architect, anyway, pater? I mean a real architect? I know what the common breed is. What sort of unusual hocus-pocus is he? From what particular heavenly menagerie is he supposed to have escaped, that he is to roam thus, as you intimate, through the wilderness of our land and day? You implied that he comes as a storm; and I think your whole storm-business was merely an occidental allegory. Allegories are all right if you are talking to an imaginative people; but — stop to think!

That a poet should arise as an exhalation from the spiritual agony and drought of his people, to condense, and return the waters, and after that that there should be rainbows and other beautiful things is fine, but it's too metaphysical. It's taken me three months to get it through my head. I thought, at the time, that you were talking and rhapsodizing about the actual physical storm we saw and felt. How could I know for a certainty that you were at the same time talking about a storm that I did not see and could not feel? But let that go, I want to think about it some more.

The main question in my mind is, what is an architect? Just as another question is: What is American; or, for that matter, what is an apple, a horse, a pine-tree — and, of course, ultimately, what is a building? And, again, more ultimately, what is architecture, what is a man, what are you, what am I, what is God, what is anything, and so on and on, around and around the circle, only to go around and around again, like a moth fluttering around the reality of a candle flame, which after all is only an illusion for the moth — the reality comes when the moth is burned.

Pater, learning this metaphysical business is a good deal like learning to control an aeroplane: the main thing is to keep your balance, not lose confidence, and go ahead. I shall learn the vertiginous game after a little, because I've made up my mind to it, and because I'm beginning to see that there is a deal in it that is useful in the way of aerial observation.

But for the moment let's bar it. Tell me what an architect is in fact, in reality, so to speak. I'm getting my own mind pretty well made up, after what you said on Culture, but I want to hear your view first — just to see if it's right, so to speak — you know. I want to get down to the practicalities.

Now don't look wistful, and tell me that if I want to see what an unreal architect is like to go look long and steadily in a mirror and learn by contrast. I don't like these sarcasms. They hurt now, for I have growing-pains; I am beginning to take myself very seriously, and flippancy scratches. From the duplicity of your heights, where contraries unite, you may treat serious matters with a certain irony and disdain — or am I entirely mistaken! In any event, kindly bear in mind that I am the shorn lamb and that you have shorn me; so temper the wind while I gather new wool — for what is art but wool-gathering after all?

But I digress. What I want to know is, what is an architect? Let's get down to business — or perhaps I might ask: What is an architect *not*? Shall we proceed by elimination or by cumulation, by frontal or by flank attack? And please bear in mind, pater, that I am an architect. Pardon me — don't look at me like that — I hasten to amend — I *think* I am an architect and—

Oh, let up, boy; you tire me to death. Bottle up that effervescence and save it for your next fit of blues.

That's right, daddy. I kiss the hand that chastens. I don't believe that an architect is a plumber, or a bricklayer or a mortar-mixer, or a teamster or a quarry-man, or a woodchopper, or a saw-mill, or a railroad, do you?

Of course not?

Nor is he a tinsmith, a glazier, a drain-layer, a roofer, a stone-cutter, a marble worker, a tile-layer, a jack-carpenter, a cabinet-maker, a wood-finisher, a painter, a derrick hand, a wire cable, or coal, or water, or the earth on which the building rests, or the air in which it grows — is he?

No.

I intend no allegory.

Go on, go on!

I am speaking objectively.

Will you go on!

Nor is he a moulder, a blacksmith, a forge, an anvil, a miner digging in the mines, a blast furnace, a rolling-mill.

Well, what of it?

Why, this: All these men and all these things enter as a genesis into the creation of a building, do they not? And yet they are not architects.

First rate. Go on.

Neither is he a surveyor, a mechanical engineer, an electrical engineer, a civil engineer, is he? Otherwise why are these men so called? Why are they not called architects?

That is well put.

Nor yet is he a builder, else why the name builder?

Very good.

And yet as regards a building the builder has his function, the engineer has his, the blacksmith his, the stone-cutter his, the man with a shovel his, the railroad trainman his, the railroad president his, the steel mill superintendent his, the banker his, the merchant his, the policeman his, and so on and on and on in an ever including and widening *cyclus* which extends ever outward and inward from the center to the borders of our civilization, and from its borders to the center. And why? Because Man has a desire to shelter himself and his products from the elements. Yet, so far, we have no architect. And why? Because none of these people and none of these things is called architect. Yet there is a name architect, therefore there must be a function architect — a real function — a real architect — an architect *solus*.

I have been thinking this out all by myself. You see, I want to isolate the architect and study him, just as biologists isolate a bacillus and study *him*. The bacillus is not the fever, the bacillus is the bacillus. So the architect is not the building, the architect is the architect. The bacillus *causes* the fever by acting on the body corporeal; so the architect *causes the building* by acting on the body social. The simile is not a nice one; in fact it's rather crude; but it gives you an idea of what I'm thinking.

But, on the other hand, the architect is a *product* of the body social, a product of our civilization. This you have shown me clearly. My simile breaks down here in a measure, but let it go — I'm through with it. So we approach him from two sides — as a product and as an agency; so of course I come at once to his true function, namely the double one: TO INTERPRET AND TO INITIATE!

That's very well done. You are beginning to show that you possess a logical and a perspicacious mind, and that you know how to use it.

Thank you. That's the first sincere compliment you've paid me.

It's the first you have earned.

Well, now, if our architect is at once a product and an agency, and if his function is at once to interpret and to initiate, *what is he to interpret and what is he to initiate?* What is it that justifies the name architect, what is his special, exclusive function? What is he expected to do, and what is he, alone, assumed to have the capacity to do, under our scheme and arrangement of civilization?

I hereby wave aside from the inquiry the hybrid-architect: the architect who believes himself an engineer, a carpenter, a merchant, a broker, a manufacturer, a business man or what not — and never stops to inquire if he is or is not an architect. If the merchant, broker, etc., were architects they would be called architects. They are not architects and that is why they are not called architects. Conversely, the architect who deems himself merchant, broker, etc., ceases to be architect and becomes hybrid, just to the extent that he believes it.

Of course, I assume that other men than architects may be and are products and agencies, and interpret and initiate. The dramatist may be such, the merchant such and many others: in fact, in the broadest sense, all are such, in larger or lesser degree, under the terms and conditions of modern civilization. But not one of these is expected to interpret the wants of the people with a view to initiate buildings. *Hence the true function of the architect is to initiate such buildings as shall correspond to the real needs of the people.*

Very good. Have you finished? If —

No, no! Let me talk. I have thought about this a great deal, in my own way. I am coming to the crux of the discussion; it is this: if it be true, as I have declared, that the true function of the architect is to initiate such buildings as shall correspond to the real needs of the people, how shall I infuse such unmistakable integrity of meaning and purpose into the word, *initiate,* the word *correspond,* and the phrase, *real needs of the people,* that mutton-heads and knaves can't use them for their own shameful purposes, by effecting a change of significance in the formula?

My boy, formulas are dangerous things. They are apt to prove the undoing of a genuine art, however helpful they may be, in the beginning, to the individual. The formula of an art remains and becomes more and more dry, rigid and shriveled with time, while the spirit of that art escapes, and vanishes forever. The bright spirit of art must be free. It will not live in a cage of words. Its willing home is in boundless nature, in the heart of the people, in the heart of the poet and in the work of the poet. It cannot live in text-books, in formulas, or in definitions. It must be free, else it departs as the light departs with the setting sun, and the darkness of folly is upon us.

Yes, I feel that, and I am beginning to feel in a very practical way the truth of what you said concerning the trickiness of words. Yet what am I to do — I must make others understand what I mean.

You can never make others understand what you mean. It's sheer folly to think of it. That, my boy, is an illusion — a fetish of the learned.

You understand what you understand, and another understands what he understands. You can't understand him and he can't understand you — and that's a beginning and an end of it. There exists between you and every one of your fellow beings a chasm infinitesimally narrow, yet absolutely uncrossable. The heart cannot cross it, the soul cannot cross it: much less can words cross it. Thus do you, thus does every human being live in the solitude of isolation — whence comes the word *identity.* This isolation is unreachable and unescapable. It is for each one of us a dungeon, or a boundless universe according to the largeness or the littleness of his soul; and around every living thing is there such an infinitesimal yet impassible gulf: around every tree, around every animal, every insect, every bird, every plant. Yet, within the confines of that circling chasm, lies an identity, a soul — unreachable, inscrutable; the ultimate reality; the very presence of the Eternal Spirit — a spirit of such infinite marvel that it brings forth an infinitude of infinitudes of identities — wonderful! wonderful! Spirit of the Universe! The Eternal Sun!

So, my boy, do not trouble yourself as to whether or not others understand your words as you do. Seek rather to understand yourself — regardless of words; and in due time, if so it be written in the great book of destiny, others will perceive in your works more or less of what you, more or less adequately, have thought, felt, lived, loved and understood.

Yes, that's doubtless all true, although I had never thought of it in just that way. Moreover, it's a rather creepy and scary thought — this notion of an invisible, impassible gulf which separates you from everything and everybody, so that you even cannot understand a friend. But still that shouldn't prevent me from attempting to define myself with a reasonable degree of clearness. So again, let me try to be explicit concerning the words *interpret,* and *initiate,* and the phrase, *real needs of the people,* as I understand them. To my own statement that the true function of the architect is to initiate such buildings as shall correspond to the real needs of the people, I now add your statement, that he must cause a building to grow naturally, logically and poetically out of its conditions. Now all of this means, and practically all that you have said to me means, I take it, in a few words, that the real architect is first, last and all the time, not a merchant, broker, manufacturer, business man, or anything of that sort, but *a poet who uses not words but building materials as a medium of expression:* Just in the same sense that a great painter uses pigments as *his* medium of expression; a musician, *tones;* a sculptor, *the marble block;* a literatus, *the written word;* and an orator, *the spoken word* — and, like them, to be truly great, really useful, he must impart to the passive materials a subjective or spiritual human quality which shall make them live for other humans — otherwise he fails utterly and is, in a high sense, a public nuisance instead of a public benefactor. Isn't that so?

It is indeed so.

Well, then, if it is so, and if it is true that this is the core of the matter, what's the use of talking about the so-called practicabilities. It can go without the saying, can't it, that a knowledge of administration, construction, equipment, materials, methods, processes and workmanship are part of his technical equipment whereby he has the efficiency and power to express the poetic thought — just as language and a knowledge of words are the technical equipment of the literatus. It is not, I take it, the words that make the poem, it is the manner in which the words are marshaled, organized and vitalized, that makes a poem a poem. And just so with building materials; they must be organized and vitalized in order that a real building may exist. Therefore to vitalize building materials, to animate them collectively with a thought, a state of feeling, to charge them with a subjective significance and value, to make them a visible part of the genuine social fabric, to infuse into them the true life of the people, to impart to them the best that is in the people, as the eye of the poet, looking below the surface of life, sees the best that is in the people — such is the real function of the architect; for, understood in these terms, the architect is one kind of poet, and his work one form of poetry — using the word in its broad, inclusive, actual sense. And if this view of the function of the architect be the true one, the real one, I can now understand what I did not fully grasp at the time, namely, your views concerning the methods of our architectural schools, your exasperation at the professor, and your contempt for what is currently called scholarship and culture. Truly it is inspiring, when one begins to acquire the faculty of looking at things with the inner or spiritual eye! Truly such an eye illuminates that which it sees, and opens to the inner view, and to the grasp of understanding, the great world of realities. This is, substantially, about as far as I can carry my thesis, with my present incomplete understanding of it. I suppose I have dropped a few stitches in knitting my argument.

No matter about the dropped stitches, for the present. You have done very well. Keep on observing, thinking — in the back of your head, in your spinal marrow, in your blood corpuscles, in your heart, liver, stomach, little finger, or wheresoever or by whatsoever real thinking is done — I don't know — and, slowly, but surely, you will find your thought grow, develop, personify itself and take on the inscrutable quality of identity: just as a plant grows by nutrition, assimilation and organization: and, when your flowering time comes — ah, my lad, when your flowering time comes! — your thought will flower and exhale the perfume I call architecture. You will be a real architect; sound of spirit, head, and clean of heart.

That is very kind. You fill me with hope. But don't you wish to take up my thesis where I left it and carry it on to a full and fine conclusion?

No, that isn't necessary. As I told you, long ago, you must do your own thinking. My task is simply to coach you a little, in calling your attention to certain things, certain conditions, certain powers, that exist in nature, in the world of men, in your land, in your people and in yourself, and to point out to you certain things or essences that are eternal. My chiefest joy, and my greatest care, has been and is to protect you, until you are really strong, against illusions, delusions, and that self-secreted poison we call self-deception; and to inspire you with courage, manliness and an abiding sense of personal accountability. In such regard my work has been, is and shall continue to the end a work of love, born of reverence for youth and of fidelity to country and mankind. But I repeat, and should repeat over and over again: all the rest you must do. I cannot do your thinking, your living or your growing for you. I cannot define your personality: I will not delimit it. The true work of the architect is to organize, integrate and glorify UTILITY. Then and then only is he truly MASTER-WORKER.

Moreover, we still have far to go, through shadowy valleys, over chilling heights, through flowering meadows, before you shall be prepared to reach, by yourself, the threshold of the hidden temple of our art. Indeed, I fear lest as we come in sight of it that temple will recede, like a fearful rainbow: for of all things elusive, the fair spirit of art, whose abode is that temple, is the most unreal in the evanescence of its reality. If it come at all, it comes to us; we cannot go to it. And that it may come to us, that it may desire to come to us, we must ever truly seek it within the boundless power, beauty, and the sumptuous, fertile chastity of Nature. We must seek with fervent minds, with open hearts — in the *plein air* of the spirit.

Amen! I see I have some *job* before me. The architect is now hovering in my maturing imagination, not as a super-man, but as a real man — a philosophic man of the world: as the creating, guiding, sustaining SPIRIT: to the end that the finished building may and shall be an ethical TOTALITY — however large, however small.

XLIII. On Criticism

It was said, of old: For what shall it profit a man if he shall gain the whole world and lose his own soul: An inquiry — doubtless as old as inquiring Man — which arises ever again when the Questioner speaks within the heart. Asked, of one's self, it is the perennial query addressed to one's self by one's self concerning poise, balance, symmetry in life: concerning one's life value considered as a totality. It may be transposed into many forms; but its essence always is: If I gain this and lose that? It is a question ever intensifying as the years go by and the reckoning-day approaches. It is a progressive or retrospective weighing of values, material, moral, spiritual. It is the question of maturity, of advancing age — it is the question born of experience, retrospection and introspection; it is seldom asked by the young. It is the ultimate question of proportion, of an attempted adjudication and adjustment of values in life's long account — an account scrutinized all too often in the nearing end, with the calm eye of sorrow and infinite regret — and the yearning to begin anew: or the yearning to die speedily and to close the false account forever — to blot it out.

Man is unbalanced through the extravagant force of his mental perversity and by pressure of education and circumstance. He is a sorry victim of varied impulse, of callousness, of short and dim sight; and irrational to an incredible degree, if not always consciously brutal. Youth is his period of diffused illusion, hyperbole and romance; middle age his period of concentrated illusion, of specialized insight, judgment and narrowed sense of reality; and old age the period of statical illusion, of infinitely useless regret, of a sorrow more or less delicate, more or less roseate, more or less sombre, more or less terrible as his sun sinks nearer its horizon, and the coming twilight brings the refrain more or less unvoiced: What profiteth it a man if he gain the world and in so doing lose his soul? Self-criticism in old age may be mellow or futile; in middle age vigorous or futile; in youth it is doomed to futility as a flower is doomed to fade: unless — yes, unless! This *unless* is the motive power, the interpretation of all I have said and shall say: the germ of my constant purpose to unify for you the outer and the inner life: to define the power of choice. For Man's great historic search has been for poise, for balance, for anchorage in his universe, for a stable foundation on which to base his hopes. From lack of such balance and [of] a knowledge how to adjust the lack comes to us by far the greater part of the ennui, the disenchantment, the cynicism, the pessimism, and the disgust and hollowness of our lives: the weariness, fever and pallor.

If the fullness of life be an ideal, so shall the fullness of work be an ideal; and the work is to be judged by us solely as it may approach in its flow of expression that fullness of life which is assumed by us to be the ideal of all arts of expression, and the implications of which ideal we have been extending to all social activities, considered, in their turn, as democratic arts of expression, or expressions of a democratic art. And consequently, civilization itself looms before us as an expression and an art of expression; and, finally, Democratic Civilization as the complete art of expression by, of and for a people.

By way of illustration, note the flower of the field! How resonant of life! How eloquently complete in expression! How rational and exquisite in structure, function and form! With what consummate organization and unfolding has it arisen with its purpose from the seed and the soil; expanding in sunshine, watered by rain and dew. Can you not vision forth its extended counterpart in a civilization?

By way of counter-illustration, turn now to the nearest every-day building — large or small. How melancholy the contrast! And yet we speak of the wayside flower as a weed — unaware that in sanity of procedure we have not succeeded in rivaling the weed, much less in surpassing it. We allude to the weed as common, as wild. It may be "common" as we say, it may be "wild" as we say, but it is a miracle nevertheless. It is a most impressive symbol.

Now why does the work of a given man, why does the work of society as a whole, compare thus with the work of a given weed? Is it not a genuine function of modern criticism to make this inquiry?

One answer is obvious: It is this: The weed is of the work of Nature, remains with Nature and is, therefore, "natural" as we say. The man, strangely enough it might seem, has departed from Nature whence he came. Strangely he has, in pride of intellect, denied INSTINCT: called it a weed, and wild, as it were. He has become "educated," sophisticated, perverse, inverted; and, in a span, he has come to despise the Mother Nature that bore him, and has become an Ishmael. Is it not a function of criticism to inquire into this? — to note wherein lies this abnormality of intellect?

Now and then, a man-child remains with Nature, and *thence* puts forth, as she does, the utterance of his heart in one or another form: music, words, sculpture, philosophy, ethics — or other voice of that fathomless subconscious world which is Nature's own.

Now why does it almost invariably happen that at first he is ridiculed as a human weed and wild? Why was Nature's greatest man-child crucified? Is it because he is as it were the Ugly Duckling, because he seems not like his kind — for men know not the child of Nature? But Eternal Nature knows her man-children and will not be gainsaid! When she speaks through one of her chosen she will not be denied! Only through the voices of her true ones can her message to her recalcitrant brood be conveyed.

So, in time, after hardships and sufferings and despair (because he is not like his kind, and can be none other than himself), the Ugly Duckling is seen — *by Swans* — to be a SWAN! And thus the Child of Nature, the master-worker, the wonder-worker, at last is glorified, or his memory is glorified, by the sons of men, who hail him — when they may no longer deny him — a visionary genius: a benefactor of his race. Why is he a genius? Is it not of the high power of criticism to inquire into such phenomena and to widen the inquiry to the limits of knowledge and understanding. Must not criticism itself partake of Nature's quality?

If under present conditions one man in a million may keep in touch with Nature and be inspired by the influence of her subtle power, may not two in a million, three in a million, ten, one hundred, five hundred thousand, or *all* — under SANE conditions?

If sophistication, waywardness, perversity and inversion mark the half-man, if naturalness, simplicity and truth mark the whole-man, why are there not more whole-men? Is it not a function of criticism to inquire deeply into this?

If tradition, education, are, in any measure, responsible for half-men, and I believe them largely responsible, is it not a high function of criticism to inquire closely into the basis, the spirit of our traditions, of our educational methods — and to inquire why such tradition, such methods, make or tend to make half-men?

Now does current criticism generally and seriously busy itself with such investigations, or with cognate subjects? In so far as I am aware, scarcely at all. Architectural criticism surely does not: It busies itself almost solely with externals, with superficialities, with literal, verbose, petty things, with refinements which refine nothing widely valuable, with analyses which analyze nothing to the core, with discussions which disclose nothing essential to our need. It busies itself with empty shells of human life. It deals with the littleness of "styles," not the largeness of humanity — the urgency of propositions! It seeks and finds small truths among the mutabilities of things done. It does not search the heart of man for the native why and wherefore of these things done. If criticism in other departments of activity excels, I leave it to you to discover, by experiment and comparison.

Truly, my lad, we need the whole-man critic as urgently as we need architects gifted with whole-power to create. For the high function of the critic is to reinterpret to the people the works of such as truly interpret the people: to make plain to them who have not the leisure, or the special training, themselves to undertake the work of sifting wheat from chaff, the real nature and the true drift of the architectural art, the real nature, the true drift of democratic civilization: to show to them clearly, concisely, what elementary education may become when based upon a knowledge and understanding of man's power to absorb and to create. Then the art of architecture will cease to be a sealed book, and the greater book — the art of civilization — will open to our gaze.

XLIV.   On Knowledge and Understanding

In your talk on Criticism, you so interested me that in my absorption I forgot to ask questions. And, for that matter, it has happened before. But this time I have been reflecting, rather than dreaming; or perhaps dreaming with open eyes, seeing, as it were, a dream coming true, and at the same time seeing other dreams fading away as in a grand transformation scene. What impresses me particularly at this moment is the fact — very considerably disturbing and yet expectantly inspiring — that, when it would appear in my judgment that you have brought your general thesis substantially to a close, you begin anew, and a new flower of thought blooms forth in my consciousness as an instinctive response. You have, for instance, added a new work to my vocabulary — the word Criticism. You have charged it for me with a richness of meaning I had not supposed it contained, that I had no idea it could contain. As a result, I am led to climb higher up that summit of which you spoke and which, when reached, you said would reveal to view our modern world. You have set more thoughts agoing in me than I can ever work out in a lifetime.

The landscape is clarifying in the light of the modern sun. But is there to be no end to these beginnings, these unfoldings of one truth from a preceding truth; these ever greater, ever expanding rebeginnings: new births from a parent idea, I might call them? Is it really true, as my instinct tells me you imply, that our very world of men is now actually at the beginning of a new beginning, that civilization is about to emerge from its past and begin a new advance, with a new, inspiring, luminous thought, a thought born not of the deep valley, but of the summit of altruism? Is there no end to the new beginnings, the new unfoldings of man's powers? For truly I am beginning a new beginning. I am beginning to see Man in the light of his powers. To see what he may accomplish if he but choose aright. Tell me some more. I am hungry and athirst for knowledge, for understanding.

Then let me tell you, now, to choose your words with greater care as you advance. The phenomenon you mention is not a beginning but a becoming.

Isn't that a rather fine metaphysical distinction?

No. It is a metaphysical clarity. That is what metaphysics is for — to be put to human use. There is all the difference in the world between beginning and becoming: one is almost mechanical in import, the other deeply spiritual. A similar difference exists between two other big words you used, namely Knowledge and Understanding. My ostensible thesis has been Architecture as a social function, as an art of expression. My real thesis underlying that one and all others of all other men is that within man, a spiritual being, resides a spiritual power capable of infinite unfolding, unnumbered beginnings and expanding rebeginnings — truth out of luminous truth. That power in its becoming I call Democracy, and hail as man's becoming.

I think I see fairly well what you mean, and accept it as true because you say it is true.

You will accept nothing as true because I say it is true. Why fall again into the pit out of which I have dragged you — the worship of authority of dogma? If you say you accept provisionally as true what I say is true, well and good. If you *see* it is true, so much the better. The proof of all the statements I have made lies not in me

145.   *On Knowledge and Understanding*

but in the broad populous world about you, present and past. With open eyes you will see; with veiled eyes you will not see. But bear in mind this: It is not sufficient to have Knowledge alone; one must have also UNDERSTANDING.

Is this to be a logic-chopping expedition? Let us return to the poetic side. I understand it better. Close thinking tires me. I prefer to dream.

I wish to broaden your dream: to expose something of the drama of the ages — the drama of man. Let us climb the summit somewhat higher.

Yes, let us climb together. What will you talk about on the way? I can't yet grasp the idea of becoming.

I shall preach a sermon on the text you yourself have selected: Knowledge and Understanding. For of what avail is Knowledge without Understanding? And yet Understanding is begotten of Knowledge — but not by it. The world is filled with Knowledge; it is almost empty of Understanding. For, let me tell you, Knowledge is of the head, Understanding is of the heart. Knowledge is of the intellect, Understanding is of instinct. To a person older than yourself this might seem a wild and weedlike statement, in view of world accomplishments. To you, for the moment, it may mean nothing. But be patient. I do not question that fullness of Understanding may and should follow upon fullness of Knowledge; increase in Understanding upon increase in Knowledge. But has it in the past? Does it today? I do not question that in their native qualities they should mutually react to the increase of joint power. But have they? Do they? Or has Knowledge far outstripped Understanding, or has Understanding lagged? It seems strange that Knowledge and Understanding should not have gone forward together hand in hand. It seems a far and tragic separation, or has Knowledge overestimated itself, or Understanding failed to assert itself, or has Knowledge, so to speak, bullied Understanding? Or, has the intellect domineered over instinct and suppressed it? It is a strange, strange drama, a drama beginning with the dawn of civilization and extending even to this day, this hour. It is true there has arisen a power called Reason, but reason has failed thus far to effect a reconciliation, assuming that it has ever made the attempt or even recognized the disparity. For reason prides itself upon its coldness, its pulchritude, it calls itself pure. And intellect aspires to this selfsame purity; it tends even toward abstraction. It is strange, a strange role in the strange drama, that intellect, proclaimed by man his highest power, tends ever to forsake man; and man, following this motile star, falls in the ditch; climbs out, falls in again; and again climbs out and again pursues. For Knowledge, man says, is power. He also says — after a fall — that a little Knowledge is a dangerous thing. Now is it to be supposed that if man were to extend his Knowledge he might arrive at a knowledge of Understanding? I do not mean to say or infer or imply that man has not arrived at a fair understanding of some things; that he has not made some use of the vassal. His knowledge certainly is phenomenal in so far as it represents immense and patient labor, and the stored-up results. It would seem almost as though man's knowledge were sufficient unto the day. With indefatigable energy, patience and perseverance he has extended his perpetual curiosity far into the limitless vast and far into the limitless minute. He has drawn up Leviathan with a hook; he has loosed the bands of Orion; but he has not bound the sweet influence of Pleiades, nor has he sought to guide Arcturus with his sons. He has tested, analyzed, classified. He has enumerated and computed; he has weighed and measured and recorded. As man the inquirer, he has stood back of man the worker. With admirable ingenuity he has extended his powers of observation, of analysis, of synthesis. With unceasing industry he has formulated. He has given his findings with generous, overflowing hands to the world of active work. With equal abandon he has given over his findings to those who create from them systems of thought, systems of procedure, systems of explanation — theories and hypotheses and speculations — whereby it is purposed to elucidate man and his universe. Man's intellect has examined all things piecemeal, it has examined man minutely in his body and his mind. It has erected extraordinary systems in explanation of man's soul. It has produced vastly erudite accounts of man's career, historic and prehistoric, biological, sociological, emotional and intellectual. It has erected its own conception of man in its own intellectual image: THEREFORE, it has utterly failed to understand man. It neither sought nor found him. What it sought and found was an abstract intellectual concept — a complete inversion of the reality.

And yet man has been face-to-face with man for untold ages. True, here and there through the past came men who caught glimpses of man. But they were neither scientists nor logicians, nor philosophers, nor theologians; they were compassionate dreamers overflowing with love. The wise could not understand them. Only the common people could glimpse an understanding; for the multitude also are compassionate — they are near to the earth. If ever there has been an example of that pride which goeth before destruction, and that haughty spirit which goeth before a fall, it is this unique colossal failure of the intellect to discern and welcome man; to reveal him to his own perturbed and anxious self. And yet it could be confidently stated a *priori,* without this preamble, that intellect could not but fail in such search; for such search, such recognition, such acclaim, lies in the specific province of INSTINCT. It is through the primordial power of instinct alone that we may seek and find man. Intellect, having forsaken instinct, is at present unfitted for such fine work. That work must be done through the HEART: for it is the heart alone that understands; it is the hand-maiden of Instinct — pulchritudinous and pure. When we, perchance, momentarily cease our labors with the electron, and the double-stars, we may perhaps predicate the appearance of a new double-star within the human firmament, the star of intellect and the star of instinct each in its orbit, and each and both responsive to their common center of gravity. When such star shall shine within man's soul, his becoming will increase and glow in splendor. He will be prepared to know and welcome Man.

Hence it is today that every vicious attitude of man's intellect, every cowardly brutality, every cold-blooded cruelty, every stupidity it perpetrates is attributed to his instinct. Hence it is that ignominy upon ignominy has been cast by man himself upon the better part of himself, in his intellectual fear, in his fatuity of misunderstanding. The unique characteristic of intellect is that, alone uncontrolled and unsupported, it is peculiarly unstable; it tends ever toward insanity, toward self-destruction. It leads man to cataclysms of downfall. Those diseases, selfishness, greed, domination, suppression, usually attributed to the heart, are distinctly attitudes (not attributes) of the intellect in its unbalance. To speak of a man as hard of heart is foolish: to speak of him as hard in intellect is the truth. For ages man has been the victim of his intellect, and such victim he is today. In his folly he has denied to the heart equal partnership. In his utter folly of intellectual self-hypnosis, he has become socially mad. No wonder modern man does not know man when he sees him. No wonder he is this very day in the tragic throes of intellectual agony, that this is his cataclysmic hour of bloody sweat.

Long, long ago in the dawn of proto-man, when the function, man, was seeking form and power within a hostile world, it sent forth out of the abysm of instinct a sub-function which we now call intellect. This new-appearing power sought form and activity that it might watch, ward and direct; that it might assist in the self-preservation and self-assertion of the ego — that primordial power seeking form and assertion in the beginnings of man's becoming. As proto-man, in evolving, approached the form and contour of primitive man, intellect became more and more active, more and more dominant, while instinct as steadily declined in outward manifestation of power. Ego chose intellect for its counsellor and guide, through fear. And here began selfishness, here Feudalism began its long career. Here began man's downfall, so vividly portrayed in Genesis in the impressive spiritual allegory of the garden. Here man parted with his innocence. Here began sin: the sin of intellect. Verily he tasted of the fruit of the tree of Knowledge. What a price he since has paid! For when man parted with Instinct the conserver, the preserver, the sure sustainer, he parted company with himself, he lost himself, and became a wanderer and then a seeker, as one going with outstretching arms and half-closed eyes, seeking to recall an all but forgotten dream — seeking himself — seeking man. Instinct was not dead within him. It slumbered. Hence man in his hunger sought with his intellect to create a companion, he became dual. He put forth an image of his loneliness which took shape in dual philosophies, dual religions, dual civilizations, by way of compensation and balance. Thus man in becoming dual lost his integrity. But unitary ego was not dead, rather was it in a trance. It slumbered and put forth intellectual wonders and aberrations: now and then dreaming gently of its own integrity as a holy dream within an all-enfolding illusion. Meanwhile the heart yearned, it knew not for what. It yearned for surcease, it yearned for peace, for happiness — it yearned in silence for an understanding: while the intellect strutted, raved on in an ecstasy of ambition, and civilizations rose and civilizations fell. The intellect, with all its power, could find no stabilizing thought; Knowledge and Understanding were far apart. The heart from time to time burst forth in storms of emotional protest. And ever and again the intellect laid flat its chilling hand and gloried in itself. Meanwhile man worked wonders. Self was his guiding star. He emitted glories, he exalted himself astoundingly. He drew Leviathan with a hook. He loosed the bands of Orion. Meanwhile the multitudes dreamed that this was their dream come true. From time to time they awoke in horror — to slumber again and dream anew. For man had not found man: had not found his forgotten self.

Such was the past; such is our own day, merely with new names, new agencies and change in local color. The essence is the same, for man has not yet found man: though the multitudes of earth, suffering in sleep, are now dreaming a new dream: heavily dreaming of a brotherhood of man; fitfully dreaming of the man that was lost and must be found; dreaming vaguely of man's integrity; dreaming deeply and more deeply of man's becoming: dreaming the long-, long-coming dream of Democracy. Dreaming, perhaps, that some day man shall understand. For it is out of the dreams of the multitudes that civilizations arise and institutions unfold. It is thus that the mighty arose and held sway; they were true to the dream of the multitude.

Tell me, tell me quick! How shall Knowledge and Understanding be reconciled?

There is but one agency, SYMPATHY.

What? So weak a thing as sympathy!

You mean *so great a power* as Sympathy.

Sympathy is that power, long dormant in man, which may harmonize all his thoughts, all his outward activities; which may integrate them, which may establish for them a valid center of gravity, an arbital self-impulse as our world moves through the infinite depths of space, carrying its precious human freightage. For Sympathy is of Spirit. It is at once the Searcher, the Visionary, the INTERPRETER. Its ethereal power underlies and enfolds both knowledge and understanding — were we but aware of it. It is man's greatest unused power. You may call it intuition, you may call it inner-sight, you may call it vision, you may call it the sixth sense, if you will. You may even call it Love, if you but sufficiently expand and charge that word. What you call it matters not: for it contains, encloses and sets in motion and guides to a definite goal, all that is of human value — all of man's powers and the output of those powers. Sympathy is the long-awaited modern Messiah. It is the essence and vital form of compassion. It tempers all things, it inspires all things when it comes forth as a suspiration from newfound man. Viewed from the summit of Sympathy the world to the clear eye of the prophet, the poet, the world of today changes its dull, forbidding aspect and becomes a revelation.

I was in despair. It all seemed hopeless. It seemed like a huge incubus of pessimism, like a vampire, a ghost from man's own graveyard of the past seeking the blood of the man of today, sapping his life at his heart.

And so it is, in the uninterpreted surface facts of the world's feudal life, present and past. But it has been our business to peer beneath the surface. In our progressing function as constructive critics, it is precisely Sympathy that has so clarified our vision that we might see man behind the screen of his acts, his institutions, his edifices, material and immaterial. That we might, as we have done, see through the screen of a building to the man behind. That we might discern ever multiplying, ever enlarging screens, and behind them the realities. To see, is worthless, unless we interpret; it is in this sense that sympathy is interpreter. To possess knowledge without understanding is not only a misfortune, it is socially dangerous: and here again Sympathy interprets Man. Once inaugurate, the power of sympathy in its solvent action ever increasingly interprets, explains, stabilizes and guides, world without end. Its gentle, clarifying, mellowing, illuminating power is man's most precious possession. May he henceforth and forever hold it such. It will mean for him his emergence from his age-old cocoon, self-spun of his sophistries, and the coming forth of his spirit, on radiant wings, into the open air of the humanities.

It seems to me, (or is it a hope?) the chrysalis is stirring, even now.

Then shall its age-long imprisonment be our inspiration, now and forever.

NOTE: This chapter was completely rewritten, 1918.

149. *On Knowledge and Understanding*

XLV. On Citizenship

It were idle, in these times, to discuss architecture as an art did not such discussion lead with certainty to the architect as a man. And it is idle to consider the architect as man in name only. We must follow him to his function and place as citizen. His citizenship must be outlined and defined as a function of democracy: for democracy is our universal, constant medium.

Conversely, if a full-grown sense of personal responsibility and of personal accountability be of the essence of sound democracy, if sound individual choice and self-poise be its key, so must these be of the essence of sound democratic citizenship; and if the architect is to be in truth a citizen, such powers must in turn abide in him and be outpoured in his works. He must show by his works that he is doing his share in the upbuilding into visible fact of the great World-Dream, Democracy.

If knowledge without understanding makes, as I aver, for mischief — tending ever away from democracy and toward anarchy — the burden is upon him to prove, by his works, that he is not a mischief-maker.

If knowledge *with* understanding makes for highest usefulness, his works must bear witness that he is sincerely striving.

If imagination and reflection are powers or aspects of human power, his works must show by a radiation of these living qualities that he is a well-wisher to humanity at large, not a stranger to it, and heedless of it.

If thought is a power, his works must reveal him man of thought. Lacking this, he lacks usefulness in the actual upbuilding of democracy.

If sympathy be the beneficent and fruitful quality of spirit I hold it, his work must show that sympathy has illumined his path in illumining his heart, and hence his understanding, and that he has desired the good of all in seeking and finding an expression of aspiring democratic life. By this test his citizenship may be tested.

If, as I hold, democratic scholarship is of high usefulness in that it implies wealth of vision, knowledge, imagination and sympathy—hence understanding—his works must so reflect such scholarship as to prove his fealty to understanding, to make evident and incontestable that his scholarship is used as a means toward attaining wholesome ends: that his scholarship has been applied for the good and the enlightenment of all the people, not for the pampering of a class, the misleading of that class and all others. His works must prove, in short (and the burden of proof is on him), that he is a democratic citizen, not a lackey, a true exponent of democracy, not a tool of the most insidious form of anarchy.

If democratic culture be, as I hold it to be, the very flowering of heart and mind, the fine expression of personal and collective poise of heart and mind, of completed power of graceful, natural self-government, the fullest index of the spiritual democratic type because of the boldness, the breadth and the warmth of its understanding, its nearness to all and its power to comprehend and unify the aspirations of all — his works must show beyond cavil that his culture is true. By this test shall his citizenship be tested.

The highest scholarship, the most enlightened culture manifestly may not be, in their completeness of finished expression, within the reach of attainment of all the people; but the simple, noble principles animating such scholarship and culture are not only within the reach of all the people, but most certainly they live as ideals within the hearts and minds of the people. The universal desire for education shows this. The aspiration for democracy is eloquent of it.

Per contra, there can be no surer test of the spuriousness, the falsity, the narrowness, the venom of an alleged scholarship or an alleged culture than this: that it holds itself aloof from the people, above them, exclusive, aristocratic, assuming that it is unintelligible by the people, and meant only for a self-sufficient, withdrawn and supercilious class. Such scholarship, such culture, is barren, because self-centered. It brings forth no fruit other than the shriveled fruit of popular ridicule, contempt and distrust.

If it happens that a given man be gifted, as is said, with stronger brain, more resolute will, a more fluid imagination, and greater natural powers of concentration, of comprehending, prophetic vision, of organization and of expression than his fellows, let him pause to reflect that these powers are not truly speaking his alone, that he did not make these original powers, but that they make him, by inspiring him to consciousness of them, and that they came to him out of the long birth-and-death struggles of the people of all times, were born, through the race, in him, and that he is answerable to all people — to the world — for their prolific democratic use. It is precisely here that there must enter into the drama of democratic life the dominant roles of personal responsibility, personal accountability and self-government, if the powerful equipped man is to be a blessing to his time and not a curse. Turn loose upon a people such a man lacking in such self-imposed restraint — and therefore feudal — and you are turning loose upon them a beast of prey: for he will use these powers for their exploitation, their suppression and his dominating aggrandizement. This is not, politely, called anarchy; but it is in fact, to the reflective mind, a form of anarchy so insidious, so powerful, so undermining of the social fabric and so destructive of democratic principles, that the ranting of a few professional anarchists is as the sweet singing of birds in comparison.

Hence in a democracy there can be but one test of citizenship, namely: Are you using such gifts, such powers as you possess, for or against the march of spiritual freedom, the emancipation of man, and his powers, the unfolding of his knowledge and his understanding? Are you for or against the people? For or against Democracy?

To be sure, this view can be quibbled with, juggled with, sophisticated and generally obscured and turned to contrary designs. But to the mind seeing squarely and steadfastly with clear eye, to the seeing eye which discerns totalities, the question cannot be begged and can be answered in but one way and that the RIGHT WAY.

In a healthy democracy the individual may not, cannot, have TWO systems of ethics: one for his private use, and one for business, professional or political uses.

Yet the active existence of this DOUBLE SYSTEM OF ETHICS is the direct cause of most of the diseases from which our body-democratic long has suffered and now suffers; it is specifically visible to us in the greater part of our architectural output. It is equally visible in other activities.

The remedy I have already indicated to you. It lies in that SINGLE STANDARD OF ETHICS implied in the idea of direct personal accountability — here and now.

It is for you to accept or reject that SINGLE STANDARD!

It is useless to quibble and to say: If one man denatures the food he makes, why may not another man denature the architecture he makes? It is fatuous to say the eminent denature thought and adulterate ideals. That we are a nation of adulterators. That we believe in makeshifts. That we temporize.

The question is: WHAT ARE YOU GOING TO DO?

WHAT ARE YOU GOING TO DO?

And just so, it is useless to multiply instances. The principle is as clear with two as with two hundred.

No democracy can long survive that does not rest upon a sound moral principle endorsed by its people — and the people means you!

If our civilization is showing signs of internal disintegration, the corrective can be found only in the counter-power of change of vision, change of choice, and of the establishment of sound popular education: an education which shall inculcate, as its basic element, that simple, wholesome moral sense that makes for true citizenship and a resultant sound, noble fabric of individual, communal and national democracy.

This, my son, is the essence of all my preachments to you on the ethical aspects of a truly democratic architecture.

We are at the grand climacteric of our national growth, of our continued existence as a democratic people.

If you have the soundness of this growth, the continuance of our ideals at heart, do what is RIGHT and you will have done your share. That is all that can be asked of you!

You may have thought that I have dealt roughly with our aimless architecture and specifically with some of its structures. And so I have; but I have endeavored to deal with knowledge, with understanding, and justly.

You may have thought that I have dealt savagely with our architectural schools. And so I have. Who would not, that had the intelligence and the sympathy to perceive the damage they, in their stiff-necked or feeble imbecility, are doing to this land and people! You may have thought me unkind toward the public. Quite the contrary. My heart goes out to them. They are suffering from an imposed and artificial culture, from an utterly inadequate system of education: from a pest of eminent demagogues and cultured weaklings. The people wish to be expressed. They wish for national self-expression. In the finer sense this has been denied them by all those who have proved disloyal to Democracy and its aims.

In a democratic land, architecture can have no value, no significance as a plastic art unless it reflects, with high sense and fine quality, the true life of all the people and their institutions: unless its deep life is their deep life. To this end, architects in a democratic land must be not only competent artists, as the word is currently used, but such superb artists as fine citizenship and its accompanying sense of high artistic responsibility and accountability to the people implies and demands.

I trust that it is rather superfluous at this late day for me again to remind you that those architects who have been and who are now applying to our democratic life and institutions the unfit, the unbecoming garments of other days are not of this class. They are masqueraders in a graveyard. They fear the truth as though it were an upstart ghost.

But go your way: and, at times, when your path seems too rough, and too desolate, and insurmountable, think — not only of your architecture as your chosen art, but as the chosen expression of your citizenship!

XLVI. Pessimism

The mind has its day and its night.

When Sympathy illumines, there is the light.

When Sympathy departs, comes on the twilight, the deepening darkness; and therewith the obscuration of those things which in the light are real.

Then sees the mind darkly, for all is in shadow.

A long, long night comes to some minds.

Then, to them, the dark things become real, and the darkened mind wanders and prowls with a certain cunning among sombre shades and phantoms.

A certain night-sight comes to these minds; and in time they declare darkness the one normal and permanent fact of being.

For them, the soul of man is black; the heart is black; the mind is black; all lightness, unfathomable, perverse, and doomed to despair and dissolution.

For them, Humanity, with all its hopes, is but a Niagara of the night, endlessly pouring its vast, ceaseless volume of wretchedness over the gigantic precipice of Fate, descending, as a huge cataract of folly and sin, into the abyss of eternal night.

For them, all tenderness is folly; love is a delusion; and honor a gloomy jest.

For them, Man is born in sin: thrust by a mighty, but malicious hand into a world of hopeless illusion and corruption, and there to be propelled by an irresistible, an unseen, power, through that long, dreary agony he calls life.

For them, Man may not prevail with Destiny more than a rain-drop may prevail with the hurricane in night's engulfing folds.

For them, Man is a futile thing; corrupt in his body; corrupt in his mind; corrupt in his heart; and worthless as to his soul.

For them, Man is the incarnation of evil.

For them, the springtime is Nature's time of pessimism: the folly of procreation. The mania of survival. The grandiose delusion of love. Over its tender, joyous efflorescing they spread the shroud of denial.

For them, winter is Nature's single moment of sanity: the resolve to die — amid the chill of ice and snow, and sullen frozen skies. A wise resolve, endlessly renewed; but which the folly of Spring again and again dissolves in carnal orgies.

For them, all life is cruel; and Death, Man's only friend.

For them, all men are cruel; and no man has a friend.

For them, the best in the heart is the worst, because it is a deception.

For them, the best in the mind is worthless, because powerless.

For them, the soul is a sorrow which intensifies our sorrow.

For them, God is Evil: and this God they dread and revile.

For them, whatever is, is wrong, and but food for discontent.

For them, Man, created in the image of his God, is therefore evil; and will corrupt and betray his neighbor until the crack of doom.

For them, honor, loyalty, fidelity, love, are words invented by Man, in his evilness, that he may the more surely betray his neighbor.

For them, personal responsibility and personal accountability are jocose phrases — evolved from the folly of the heart, the tempter — phrases, like poison-flowers, attractive in form, alluring in color; but, inhale their odor, and you sicken and die. Phrases meant to catch the unwary, that the wary may gain.

For them, all virtue is folly and weakness; for evil reigns: evil is normal.

For them, hope is the idle dream of folly: sorrow is our lot, and despair our birthright.

For them, the end of all thought lies in nihilism and disgust, in bitterness and negation.

For them, two and two do not make four — two and two make nothing whatsoever.

For them, Knowledge is a chimera; and Understanding, a mirage.

For them, Man is the supreme traitor.

For them, all human thoughts and acts are born of selfishness, nurtured in cynicism, and mature in perfidy.

For them, failure is normal; success, a caprice of Fate.

For them, it is normal that Man should war upon man; for folly and evil are our common curse.

And so has the mind its seasons; as it wings its flight about mysterious, attracting life — the dark sun of existence for some, its radiant orb for others.

But winter comes also, when that sun retires; and the heart shudders, the dread chill falls upon it; ice locks up the laughing waters; snow floats down from lowering skies. Summer has long since departed; leaves are fallen and forgot. All is rigid, lifeless and forlorn.

Pessimism is that winter which falls upon the mind when sympathy has flown.

Pessimism is that winter which congeals all affluence of thought, which freezes all unselfishness of feeling, which nullifies understanding, which locks up the waters of life's well-springs, and many a cadenced rivulet, and broad, sweeping stream.

For pessimism is the winter of the mind, the winter of the heart, the winter of the World.

And yet pessimism may become a passionate protest.[1]

We have not yet reached that pitch of agony where we must moan with Job: Let the day perish wherein I was born, and the night in which it was said, There is a man child conceived.

For indeed it must be an unfathomable pessimism which holds within the solitudes of its darkness no regenerative seed.

1. This sentence, added by Sullivan in revision, stands in place of many further paragraphs inveighing against pessimism.

Why do you drive this murky cloud across my vision? Why do you put my great hope in eclipse? Why do you affright me when I was beginning to feel sure?

Because my soul is sick: I must have air: I must seek the open.

But it is winter.

Nevertheless — I go.

Then I go also.

XLVII. Winter

O, pater, what a gloomy day is this!

How sad and saddening is winter, here, in the open country!

This leaden sky of late afternoon. This vast coverlet of dull white. The tops of the fences, only, visible here and there in their long, disconsolate lines. The trees, standing, bare and dusky, on the low hills here and there; standing, melancholy and still, against a still and melancholy day.

What ineffable, what unspeakable sadness here!

And the dreadful silence of it all!

What miserere is Nature chanting, here, with numberless voices unbearable to our ears?

Oh, this vast, universal sleep; this torpor; this profound subsidence of life!

Why are we here!

Is it not depressing; is it not sorrowful!

It is not more depressing, not more sorrowful than is the present state of our art throughout the land.

The thought of THAT brings winter to *my* mind — winter indeed!

And I must have sorrow, would that I had not *this* sorrow!

For in *that* seems to lie no hope.

In Nature's winter there lies ever a hope.

No spectacle is more depressing than the torpor, the silent wintry sleep of the human mind.

No spectacle, more sorrowful, than a leafless art in which the sap has ceased to flow.

No spectacle, quite so pessimistic, as an art in the winter of its decline.

I have lived to see this!

Shall I live to see aught else?

Winter! Winter! Winter of the heart has fallen, like the pallid pall of winter here!

Winter has fallen upon our art!

Winter now falls upon my soul!

Leave me; I would commune, here, with that Infinite which dwells within the winter, here, in the broad expanse.

155. *Winter*

I will not leave you.

I would be alone, here; alone with that Mighty Spirit which fathers all the seasons, and whose breath is the breath of life and likewise the breath of death.

I would fain talk with the God of this leaden sky, of the leaden snow, of the sombre, silent trees, of this freezing air.

I would fain immerse my spirit in his spirit.

I would fain question God, here, in this wilderness; for my soul is become such a wilderness — a solemn, wintry wilderness in which no voice is heard:

Lord of this vast o'erhanging sky, Lord of the wintry heart, Lord of every sombre tree and pallid snowflake! Why hast thou let a winter fall upon my soul? Why are the seeds of my spirit dormant? Why are the fair flowers of my fancy moribund? Why are the well-springs of my heart congealed? Why do they no longer ripple and murmur in sunshine and gladness?

Spirit Sublime! Why hast thou let a winter fall upon the hearts of my country-men?

Have I not lived for my art? — an art grown up in praise of thee.

Must I then die for it?

And, dying, leave nought behind else a few precarious, scattered seeds, overlaid with the snow — when my heart was so filled with fertility, in thine honor, and in response to thine everlasting glory and power.

Must I repeat the ancient cry: Oh, for a daysman between thee and me!

Mysterious Power, why dost thou bring agony to them that bring forth in they name?

Why art thou silent as birth, silent as the tomb, when the heart cries out to thee in its extremity of sorrow?

Inscrutable Presence! Why hast thou caused me to know sorrow, 'less it be that my soul shall be pregnant of Sorrow — and give birth from Sorrow?

All-bearing Spirit! Why dost thou suppress my spirit? Why is it locked up and sealed, in winter's ice; as thou dost lock up the violet and the wind-flower in winter's tomb; as the lily and the gentian are rigid and still, under the snow; as all life, here, is so silent under the silent snow?

Do they dream of thee, as my soul dreams of thee in this silence of winter? Or are they, thy children of the woods and fields, soulless, and dreamless under the pallid coverlet of white petals fallen from the sombre garden of the clouds?

The strength of thy spirit is the strength of thy winter which, as a white breath, breathes over the broad earth; for it, also, is the breath of thy spirit. But in my winter is no strength; no spirit; no breath.

For thou art Lord of Death. For Death, also, is the breath of thy spirit. For thou art all in all.

But what is Man! What shall he know of Death, other than to see his shadow, to see his smile!

So little is man, in his understanding, that he knows not whether Death be the child of Life, or Life the child of death.

But thou, Inscrutable Spirit — in thy unfathomable purpose, why leavest thou man to his sorrow as thou leavest him in his joys? Thou disturbest him not in his living death!

Man may see thee, thou seekest not man — but leavest man helpless before the inscrutable mystery of his own soul.

Why dost thou not seek man?

Why dost thou not cross the chasm of his isolation?

Canst thou not cross?

Why dost thou leave man a riddle to himself?

Why dost thou leave man helpless and perplexed before the mysteries of thy works:

Helpless and torpid in the winter of his soul — the emptiness of his mind?

Why hast thou made the soul of man an endless marvel to himself, yet but a speck among the myriad works of thy hand?

Why hast thou sent a night to darken the mind of man, that he has set up gold for god in thy stead?

Why hast thou filled man's eyes with ugliness, that he ignores the endless, radiant beauty of thy works?

Why hast thou estopped man's ears, that he hears not, day by day, the beauty of thy voice, the ceaseless melodies thereof?

Why hast thou let man so go astray that he praises thee with lip-praise, not with heart-praise, and the pæans of his spirit, the adoration of his mind, the works of his hand; meanwhile praises he himself with overpraise.

Why abidest thou, in the winter, here, silent and grim, imperturbable, passionless, voiceless?

Dost thou speak, and I hear not?

Dost thou call me, and I am unaware?

Unspeakable mystery! Where art thou? What art thou, that thou dost affright and fascinate me here? That I cry out, and the wintry silence alone answers me — that the chill and the torpor alone answer me — that no man, no thing answers me; that mine own soul answers me not! That thou dost answer me not!

Alas! there is no answer; save the merciless and sombre gloom — the falling snow!

So, must I go my way.

So, must I seek my way alone — if way there be.

So, must my soul abide its wintertime.

So, must the tiny, hidden seed of hope await its day.

For man is unto man alone!

God hears him not, God sees him not in his winter — in the fatal winter of his soul — nor does God see him in his springtime — in the springtime of his soul — nor in the summer thereof, nor in the autumn — God sees not man.

Man surely is alone — and so must he be his own and only god — his only god; aside from Thee!

Oh, master, do not speak in this way!

It appalls me!

See how the snow is gently falling, with wet, heavy flakes, as if in rebuke to you.

And the twilight is falling upon us, and upon all nature, as in explanation and re-buke.

Darker and darker it grows!

I see you now but dimly!

While more steadily and heavily the snow falls in infinite gentleness.

A sleigh passes in the dusk. A tinkle and it is gone; muffled up and quieted in the growing night.

So is Man's little life, but a tinkle that is muffled quickly in eternal night.

Oh, say not so!

How dark it grows! And the snow falls and falls upon us. Why do you not stir? Why do you not speak? Answer me! I no longer see you — I can but feel you with my hand. Answer me! !

So would I speak with God, and feel him with my hand, but God will not answer me!

He sends me for answer the silent darkness and the snow: so touches he me with his hand.

But 'tis enough! It is enough!

It is enough for darkling Nature here. Why not enough for me?

For the snow falls likewise within my spirit, and darkness quiets it to rest.

And my spirit is stilled within me, and sinks into its winter-night.

It is enough, it is enough!

Enough for me, is winter and the winter's God.

For I am as but a flake of snow within this winter's night; slowly settling to my rest, among the myriad of flakes; asking no more; seeking no more; questioning no more — accepting all.

You appall me, master!

Why should I appall?

I should think you would despair!

Why despair?

Oh, in this mournful winter night, and all that it implies!

And so I might, were not, likewise, implanted in my heart THE BELIEF IN SPRING!

XLVIII. On Poetry

Why, master, did you lead me with you into the winter night?

To refresh my spirit, and to reveal to you something of the limitations and the boundaries of the mind: to bring you face to face with the wall against which men have broken their hearts.

And why did you appeal so despairingly to the Infinite?

To show you the unhappy limitations and the far-off boundaries of the soul. To show you at once man's solitude and his power. To try your soul. To test your strength, to fortify your courage.

And why did you all of this?

To help you make of yourself an interpreter, a poet.

And why should I be a poet?

In order that you may evince power of interpretation, and extol poetry in your useful art.

And how can I express poetry in my art?

As one expresses poetry in anything — by first living it. For poetry is life. To express life we must know life, and understand it in its bearings. To know the simplicity of all life we must grasp its complexity; we must view it from many angles, envisage its many moods and seeming contrarieties; and to know its complexity we must grasp, with all the power of understanding, its deep-down simplicity. To know the soul we must arouse the soul. To know the spirit we must liberate the spirit and let it face the open and move in the open until it knows not fear.

So have I striven to round your view of life; and will still strive to expand and to round it, to the end that, as your knowledge increases, your power of interpreting, understanding and expressing may keep pace.

So have I taken you to Nature, and shall again take you to Nature, to show you how our moods parallel her moods; how her problems parallel our problems; and to bring you directly to the one unfailing source, the visible effect of creative energy, that you may find there, now and evermore, the key to solutions; to make plain to you what man may read in Nature's book, to the end that her processes may be our processes: that we may absorb somewhat of her fertility of recourse, her admirable logic, her progression from function into form — her poetic finalities.

For Nature is ever the background across which man moves as in a drama: that dream within which man, the dreamer, moves in his dream; that reality which is man's reality.

For all life, collectively is but one vast drama, one vast dream, and the soul of man its chief spectator.

For I would also give you some knowledge, some understanding of rhythm. I would cause you to feel, in your inmost conviction, that man cannot stand alone: that man must seek and find within his own spirit a sure anchorage within the visible and invisible universe, upon the earth, his home, and in the world and the hearts of his fellow men.

For in man's rhythmical adjustment with Nature and his kind lies his happiness; in discord, lies his misery.

I would give you of your art some persuasively adequate notion of its latent, unused beauty, its inexhaustible capacity for utility in expression, its fluency, its lyric quality, its fervent interpretative dramatic power — when once it but come, within your spirit, into kinship with Nature's rhythms: when once you have aroused to the sense of uniting her power with your own. And how can you know this to be true unless you have felt its approach? How can you understand it in its workings if you have not sought to know it? How can you hope to express it unless you have LIVED it and understood it?

159. *On Poetry*

Here is shaping perpetually before man the spectacle of Nature's affluent, changing moods; of those gloriously varied rhythms, those equilibriums born of the union of Sun and Earth: a myriad progeny taking visible organic form. Should man do less in satisfying his utilitarian needs! It is the function of the poet, in whatever walk of life, to regard these things; to make them his own; to express them in his works: whatever those works, whatever his special activities may be. Thus do we enlarge our working conception of the nature and utility of the poet. On the other hand, you cannot express, whatever your walk in life, unless you have a system of expression; and you cannot have a system of expression unless you have a prior system of cognate thinking and feeling; and you cannot have a system of thinking and feeling unless you have had a basic system of living.

When all is said and done, the great masterpiece, or the little masterpiece, whatever its kind, is but the condensed expression of such philosophy as is held by the worker who creates it. It stands for his views, his more or less ripened, organized and rounded views of Nature, of Man as an entity in nature, of his fellow men, of an infinite pervading and guiding Spirit; of his views and convictions concerning the human mind, the human heart and soul, and the progress and destiny of the race: in short, his philosophy of life.

These views, such philosophy, may not be expressed categorically as in a catechism, but they are of the initial determining impulse of such works; and indeed a great work — whatever its kind — is scarcely conceivable which is not the expression of the philosophy of life held by its creator.

To assume that a man may at his pleasure create a great work, without in his own way having held communion with the flow of life, as he may have vision to see it, without having in his own way contemplated humanity as he may have vision to see it: its trials, its entanglements; the fleeting frailty of individual life and the profound duration and import of the great life — would be but to express crudely what is crudely thought.

To fancy, languorously, that a man may create a great work by reproducing a Greek temple, or any past vital work, is an example in such crude vacuity of thinking: indeed, the misapplication of the very notion of thinking. It is simply minus-thinking.

For a great work, for us, must be an organism — that is, possessed of a life of its own; an individual life that functionates in all its parts; and which finds its variations in expression in the variations of its main function, and in the consequent, continuous, systematic variations in form, as the organic complexity of expression unfolds: all proceeding from one single impulse of desire to express our day and our needs: to seek earnestly and faithfully to satisfy those needs. To make our world a pleasant place.

Now the popular method, the mere setting together of ready-made fragments, parts, or features, the setting together of ready-made ideas, of conventional assumptions, is a mechanical, not an organic, process; it is, indeed, the very antithesis of an organic process. It may tax the mind; for it is, essentially, a species of unwholesome compromise; but it finds no place for the exercise of the higher faculties of thought and feeling, which lie at the base of an organic or creative work, an enterprise, an adventure of any kind.

Hence, if the aggregative or miscellaneous process be called scholarly, as it is so called, by many, such a term but brightens our image of a creative or poetic art: utilitarian in foundation, harmonious in superstructure.

To be sure there will ever be temperamental variation, in time and place, amongst those who produce great works. This must be so, for such variation lies within the nature of individual identity — and a great work is, always, a great individual expression; the expression of a single thought or a single mood born of a contemplative, active, clear-sighted creative mind.

Hence, how impotent does the imitative method become to a normal view. It needs as foundation no philosophy of life, no serious resolve, no sense of adventure: it needs only a myopic view of the past, a blurred, an unseeing view of our day.

Nor does it avail to say that such imitation professes the reproduction, in our day, of forms, of procedures of ancient origin, which the world has long held in high esteem. That is a mere begging the question. For, in the first place, you can reanimate nothing that is passed: the men who created these works in their image have gone to their fathers. Those men alone could have made other works in the same SPIRIT. In the second place, if your mind is lofty enough, sympathetic and honorable enough, to come into a genuine companionship and communion with theirs, you will wish, through such communion, to emulate them, not to imitate them, to do what they did, namely, to reproduce: to interpret the life of your own people, the spirit of your times, in terms of knowledge and understanding.

Hence, to a serious mind, to a mind honestly intent, the entire fabric of imitative art and imitative procedure falls to the ground — and is shown to have been but too manifestly the resort of the weak of will, the unresourceful, the inconsequential.

It does not profit here to talk of "veneration for the past," for such talk will not change the aspect of facts — and we are dealing with the psychic as well as the physical facts of our contemporaneous civilization, and its specific architectural aspect or expression.

Do not mistake my meaning, nor my attitude toward the great works of the men of the past. None can, I believe, venerate them more sincerely than do I, nor more clearly and gratefully discern their beauty, their worth, their inspiring evidence of what man can do when he wills. But such appraisal, such enthusiasm would go for naught were I to stultify both myself and them by denying them their privacy.

> For, my lad, beauty has not really departed from the sons of Earth.
> Nor is high thinking but a memory of days gone.
> Nor is the winsome art of saying done for.
> Nor has the power of man forsaken him.
> If he has lost them, on his way, he has but to call to them:
> They will answer and come gladly.
> His spirit will revive.

XLIX. The Art of Expression

In the springtime, greeting the sun when ice and snow are gone, sap mounts within the trees, seeds awaken, a new utterance of life begins. Out of the darkness, out of the silence of winter, comes a song. The filigree of Nature's resurrection reappears. She chants of her deliverance.

And thus, the dormant soul of man awakening to the sun of sympathy, he puts forth the beginning of his springtime — the utterance of things long forming, long hidden, long obscured, long unfelt, but now stirring toward the light, seeking form, seeking growth, seeking expression.

Thus does Nature, thus does Man burgeon the promise of fertility.

Perhaps, my lad, never with truly open welcoming eyes have you beheld the springtime!

We shall see it, soon, together!

Then will my last word be said.

For, if the moving spectacle of spring shall not invade you to the depths, you may never truly learn how sonorous are the great words in our art; how fluent, how satisfying the lesser ones; how sweet the many minor sayings.

An art of expression must flow from an inner reservoir. It must be the gathered and stored force seeking outlet. It is not as a garment — a something to be worn or not worn — it is inseparable from life, a symbol of life.

Hence, an Art of Expression should be the earliest upbuilding element to enter into the curriculum of a thorough education. It should grow as the body grows and mature as the will evolves. It should evidence human capacity and human possibility. It should open the mind, open the heart, to direct impressions at the very beginning. These are to the human what sunlight, soil and rain are to vegetation. Then, let utterance of these impressions begin so soon as it is evident that they are impressions. After which, new impressions, then new utterance — ever continuous, ever reciprocal, ever broadening, surely organizing, unfolding, ever growing in power more coherent, more plastic, more fluent; ever growing in receptivity, ever growing in aspiration; ever growing in mobility, ever growing in serenity; ever growing more complex — paralleling the complexity of life; ever growing more simple — paralleling the simplicity of life; ever gaining in strength, ever gaining in delicacy; ever in ferment, ever clarifying those elemental powers which are so subtle yet the most potent of all — the power of receiving, the power of uttering!

Then, in clarity, one may see not merely over the surface of things, but into the being of things, and of man.

Then may one express life, because he has lived.

Then will one's work be poems, for they shall spring from life, its needs, and its desires.[1]

Now it has been part of our work to expand and concentrate the meaning of words, of phrases. To extricate them from their provincial confinement and let them go free in the world of men. Such a parlor-phrase is now before us, namely: the art of expression. Its use has been limited almost exclusively to the so-called fine arts and

---

1. From this point, the chapter was completely rewritten in 1918.

perhaps particularly to the art of writing poetry and prose. That is to say, it has retained a strictly feudal meaning, in the sense that it is a direct expression of the ego in a quite limited aristocratic and sub-sufficient sense. I call it provincial, not because it is so in actual fact but because it is so in actual use. Like almost all feudal words and phrases it ignores the needs of humanity, it centers in a narrow egoism. The phrase therefore needs liberation. It must take on a great expansiveness and power of symbolism. It must be exalted into a universal guiding principle and power: else shall it fail to satisfy and inspire the brain, the heart of a democratic work. In short, we must change its significance from feudal to democratic. We must so broaden its scope that it shall include every human activity. For it is the function of Democracy to liberate, broaden, intensify and focus every human faculty; to utilize every human power now unused, abused, or running to waste. This is high democratic efficiency. For Democracy in its heart would abolish all human wastages in their tortuous windings, in impasses, in sorrow, in vicious misdirection, expressed in the phantom word, Prosperity. It would, in its efficiency, its thorough-going knowledge and understanding, establish universal productiveness and racial poise; the first fruits of its vision, of its discovery of man and his powers. Its conception of the art of expression is founded on man's evident spiritual integrity, and his high moral power of choice. It proposes to guide him, to organize him, in the exercise of his various powers of Worker, Inquirer, Thinker and Dreamer. It purposes that man shall sense himself and realize himself. It knows and understands why feudal civilizations have ever ended in downfall and the wreckage of disaster. It knows and understands the soul of feudalism. It knows that the thought, the feeling, of the world of man is slowly, surely passing out of that domain of provincialism of the mind which the word, the thought, the deed Feudalism surely signifies. It knows that man's heart is essentially pure, his mind essentially clean. It knows that man thus far has lived by fear alone. In its own courage, Democracy would abolish fear, would banish it, would dispel it as a fetid ghost. It would blow down, it would dissolve, the wall that Fate has seemed to rear, it would expose the world to man's clearing vision.

Thus is it necessary in a democracy that men in all walks of life (especially those who assume to be leaders in thought) qualify, each in his way, in the all-inclusive art of expression. For Democracy has real things to express, it insists on their expression, it will make sure they are expressed. The steady gaze of Democracy pierces all feudal screens, all veils, all pretense, all subterfuge, all hypocrisies, all cant. It sees through them and beyond them to the feudal realities of our day. But the will of Democracy lies in its wish. With ever cumulating power it is seeking and will surely find expression in social function and form. It is seeking and will find a consistent, highly diversified, highly organized expression springing with superb logic from the contained power of its germinal idea: the sole social idea that stands for complete SANITY, the sole spiritual idea that is worthy of man and his powers. Therefore the art of developing Democracy into a complete, complex yet simple, working civilization is the one great art of expression confronting man today. It is the one art including all arts, all activities, individual and collective. It is in the development of the technique of such art that modern man is to concentrate his thought, bend his faculties, and exercise his superb powers as creator.

163. *The Art of Expression*

It is needless that I should go further into detail. The implications should be obvious. The great world-need is sanity.

In regard to yourself, my object all along has been, first, to isolate the architectural art as a specialized social activity and then to show how inextricably, in its genuine state, it is interwoven with the needs, the thoughts, the aspirations of the people, that it cannot have a real life without them, and then to raise it into the higher realms of interpretation. That, to become a real art of expression for us, it must be inspired by the democratic urge, it must take its vigorous origin in the direct practical, utilitarian needs, must avail itself of all modern resources. It must first fully satisfy the needs, fully utilize the resources. Then and then only is it justified in entering the realms of sentiment and poetic imagination; and then only for the purpose of giving to the utilitarian its needed aspect of beauty, thus contributing its share to the happiness of mankind — to the poem of Democracy. Then and then only may architecture worthily be called an art of expression.

Much less do I need to go with you into the technical details of our art. Nature furnishes the materials and you have but to use them with intelligence, and feeling. All geometric forms are at your disposal, they are universal; it is for you to utilize them, to manipulate them, to transmute them, with feeling and intelligence. Engineering science has substantially solved all problems of construction. The industrial arts, the so-called fine arts, mechanical skill, craftsmanship are at your disposal. The organized building arts, transportation, communication are at your disposal; language is at your disposal. Nature's manifold expressions of function and form are at your disposal. What more do you need as a medium of expression. The rest is "up to you," as it is said.

To make these things, these instrumentalities, plastic to your ends is your business; indeed it is to be your career. I have carefully avoided laying down any rules — they tend merely to circumscribe and repress. What I have attentively laid stress on is underlying principles; I have shown you how simple, how universal they are. I have shown you also something of the complexity of their unfolding.

Inasmuch as these general principles are universal and proceed from Life, they are at your disposal to apply in your own instinctive way with intelligence and feeling.

However, inasmuch as you will have problems to meet and solve, let me give you this pointer: Every problem contains and suggests its own solution. Don't waste time looking anywhere else for it. In this mental attitude, in this mood of understanding, lies the technical beginning of the art of expression.

L. The Creative Impulse

You have a singular habit of assuming, when you suddenly make a compact statement, novel in character, that I am capable of digesting it at once. For instance, I
am still puzzling over your statement that every problem contains and suggests its
own solution; and that to seek the solution elsewhere is a waste of time. Now I can't
see that a problem contains its solution; still less can I see that it suggests it.

I admit the impeachment. It is likely to happen, when one has given years of
thought to a particular subject, that his working idea concerning it is apt to concentrate into a statement so terse that, while axiomatic to himself, it is not self-evident to others.

That is just where I stand: it is not self-evident to me. My training tended the
other way. And yet the suggestion excites my vivid curiosity. It sounds neat if nothing more.

I have come to regard as valuable those truths only which are universal. And it
is a bit surprising to note how many truths are universal or may be expanded into a
universal application. I don't suppose that anyone who succeeds in solving a problem
really goes out of it for the solution; and this assumption doubtless also accounts
for innumerable failures. And the failures certainly are self-evident: the world is
filled with débris of this sort. Particularly is this characteristic of the intellectuals.
The unsophisticated man is often better qualified to go straight to the core of a
matter: by a process of feeling to sense its reality. Now to give a very simple case:
if you are given a peanut-pod and the problem is to find the peanut, you simply open
the pod and there is your peanut. The conditions are extremely simple, but the truth
is there: the germ of a universal truth, which, with sufficiently extended experience
will formulate itself in an axiom, or what scientists call a law: for to scientists, truths
are laws: in which little word you may incidentally note the survival of an autocratic
notion of the universe.

If we gradually enlarge our problem, we find its husk of conditions becoming complicated, and its contained germ of solution less and less obvious. But when we have
solved our problem by confining our attention to it, we find the "law" holds good.
And when we have had further experience, we become aware that the very nature
of the limiting conditions suggests to us what must be the nature and the limitations
of the solution. If you are searching for a peanut you come to know by experience
that you will not find it within the burr of a chestnut. Thus a given problem takes
on the character of individuality, of identity. And you become aware that your
solution must partake of that identity. If you come across a problem which does not
possess an identity, you know by such token that the problem is not a problem but
a figment. As the problem becomes more complex it becomes the more necessary to
know all the conditions, to have all the data, and especially to make sure as to the
limitations. Now suppose we extend the problem to its broad human limit and pose
it as the problem of Democracy. The conditions seem enormously complicated and
complex, and sternly limited by what is called human nature; the solution not only
doubtful but nowhere in sight. Yet, let us but patiently stick to our "law," and we
finally, perhaps after many years, penetrate this vast husk of humanity and fictions,

and find the germ of the solution to be individual man himself, and the fundamental nature of man within him. Having discovered one man, his spirit and his powers, we have discovered all men. Having discovered man, the problem reverses, takes on a new, a constructive aspect; an aspect and purpose born of the desire to create. So I will leave you to make your own specific applications of the "law" as the need arises, and proceed to talk about what is uppermost in my mind, and yet which will grow rather naturally out of your inquiry. And, by the way, what sort of problem do you fancy you presented, in your precious self, when first you came to me?

What I want to talk about concerns this query: What underlies man's desire to create? It surely must have in it much of the nature of his problems.

To begin with, man must originally have had the notion that he could make rather than that he could create. His idea was to do something, to fashion something, for his immediate use; to satisfy his immediate physical wants. And this germinal notion still survives, in its simplicty, through all the complexities of ensuing civilizations, up to the present day of our calendar. Hence we may assume as a basis that the idea of doing something came into being before the idea of creating something. That man the worker, in biological sequence, preceded man the inquirer, the thinker, the poet — the creator. We are probably justified, moreover, in believing that the power to work and the power of emotion, while contemporaneous in man, were not equally satisfied, that in man's emotional nature lay a germ, an unshapen idea, which gradually grew in assertiveness within him and sought outward realization. This germ was the inarticulate beginning of the desire to express himself wholly; the earliest indication of his need of an art of expression; the latent beginning of the CREATIVE IMPULSE.

Now, the particularly delicate point involved is: Why did man wish to create? Was it not that he felt lonely? That he desired emotional, psychic companionship? Was not this subdued and shadowy anxiety, a problem shaping for him, gradually but vaguely pressing for solution? Now, how did early man solve this unique problem which would prostrate a modern mind if it were suddenly new? Still guided emotionally by instinct, he sought the solution by instinct, and found it precisely where it was — within himself. He did not formulate laws on the subject; he simply acted out his instinct — his instinct of reproduction. He infused his bare work with the quality of his emotions and thus found in them the companionship he yearned for — because they were of himself. His growing intellect might have gone on satisfying his physical needs and amplifying their expression. Instinct alone, in inspiring the work of his hand and his intellect, could satisfy the craving of his heart, the hunger of his soul. Thus man unconsciously began to create in his own image. His work slowly grew in power of impulse, in power of expression. As civilizations arose, man's work in those outwardly differing civilizations evinced his temperamental variation. In some, the intellectual force predominates, in others, the emotions. Seldom have they approached a balance. Never did they achieve it. For such achievement was beyond the range of the feudal mind. It lies in the domain of sanity.

In our own day, sadly enough, as I have told you, Instinct has departed, in form if not in substance. To its beautifully varied powers we, unconscious of their origin, give many beautiful names; to the primal impulse which we emptily call instinct we apply terms of obloquy and reproach. And we do this, not because we are over-civilized, but because we are half-civilized. We have given to intellect a loose rein, utterly regardless or ignorant of the fact that in the end it would surely run amuck and attempt to drive us like sheep over the precipice or into the morass of social suicide.

Now, therefore, arises again, this time for us, the selfsame problem that confronted early man. There exists in us the same power to make something, the same vague, instinctive yearning for emotional and psychic companionship, the same inarticulate desire to image ourselves forth. But intellect has long held repressive sway, while Instinct has been biding its time. We have been "practical" so long that what we have imaged forth is relatively monstrous, and by sane standards unreal, untrue to man's oneness: true only to his dualism. Modern man is a traitor to himself in suppressing one-half of himself. In a measure he realizes this, and makes attempts at betterment, as he calls it, feeble, miscellaneous, and misdirected, employing but a minute part of his power in endeavoring to effect that consummation he so devotedly worships and which he calls Compromise. In other words, he is attempting the impossible task of eating his cake and keeping it. It is true that he is constantly putting forth multitudinous intellectual images of himself and the unique character of these works indicates the corresponding status of his intellectual reach. The fact that he is not putting forth equal works based on instinct shows as clearly his intention that the intellect shall continue to dominate the heart: that he is practical. Therefore modern man's attempts at solving the basic problem of life have been unsuccessful, because he has looked everywhere for a solution, or a suggestion of solution, except within the problem itself.

It is always fatal to a solution to approach a problem with a preconception or fixed attitude of mind; with a mind made up as to what the nature of the solution will be, must be, ought to be, shall be. And yet modern man has made this specific, particularly grave blunder. He has begun by surrounding the husk containing the germ of solution — a husk already thick enough — with a fibrous super-husk of intellectual misconceptions concerning man, his powers and his relation to his fellow man. In other words, he has attempted to solve a problem wholly altruistic in nature by the application of methods wholly selfish and therefore external in nature. In fact, we might pause here to say that man, throughout his history, has preponderatingly sought explanations in the external instead of seeking them as he should, in the internal. This mental attitude accounts accurately for the phenomenon that man projected out of himself that vast sombre and inexorable image of himself which he has called Fate.

The man of the past has shown to us his power to create multiform images of himself in his feudal status. These images arose in actuality of physical form, or as marvelous airy fabrics of his emotional dreams, his spiritual hunger for companionship, directly from the need, the impulse, to create. Yet he did not know (though doubtless he may have felt) that these many things he created, these many systems he created, the many gods he created, were but sublime projections of himself into the outer world; which creations, as visioned forth by him, awakened a reaction within his inner world; and that, in his simultaneous outer and inner world he found the companionship he sought; he felt at home among the family of images of himself —

his veritable progeny. And thus his civilizations, with all their contained institutions, were the collective image of the multitudes, the instinctive unconscious output of their powers, the visible glorifying symbol which the voice of nature — Instinct — told them was theirs, but which Intellect assured them in their waking, toiling hours could not possibly be of them but was a gift to them from on high. And as the lowly as well as the highborn were under the sway of intellect, the multitudes believed and consented. Hence there is not and never was such thing (except in passive moments) as a government existing independently of the consent of the governed. The feudal governments, past and present, have rested upon the foundation [of the] feudal thought of the people. Our civilizations have thus been superstructures erected upon such intellectually and emotionally ethereal, yet physical solid, foundation.

However — and let this be particularly noted — when the massive thought of the multitudes changes, the civilizations, the institutions supported and sustained by that thought, correspondingly change with it, for no civilization, no institution, can long exist after the creative impulse, the emotional desire, the intellectual consent of the multitudes, is withdrawn. For such civilization has by such token ceased to be their image. It no longer responds to their dreams. Or, it may be, their dream fades, and the image fades or is destroyed. Usually in past times these changes have progressed slowly. In modern times there is a visible tendency toward acceleration. And, be it further noted that in all the glory of the past, man had not solved the problem of man.

Now comes to us a new yearning, a new sense of loneliness, a new anxiety for companionship. The old images, the old gods, the old procedures no longer satisfy. Slowly there is awakening and stirring in modern man, a new desire, a new, a vaster creative impulse, a new movement of instinct. This is what makes the aspect of our world today so thrilling, so dramatic, so potent in new solutions, in new creations. The thought of modern man is swiftly shaping itself, with self-impelling power, upon the new-appearing center of gravity within himself; about a new conjunction of Intellect and emotion, a new assertion of Instinct, a new and concentrated creative impulse; a new desire to see his new self imaged in new institutions, giving him a new satisfaction, a new sense of fulfilled companionship. Engrossed now in the analytical stage, he soon will enter the constructive stage. For the creative impulse, intimately subjective in origin, fulfills its function in objective realities.

All this may seem a digression from our main theme, but I have made it purposely, that you may locate wide boundaries and concentrate upon simple initiatives. That you may see the day that man will soon, with open eyes, find himself confronted by portentous images of himself which he will reluctantly recognize as such. That with selfsame open eyes he will recognize his prudery and prurience of intellect *in extenso* and, for his own healing, will become ashamed.

Furthermore, while what I have said may cause our art to seem insignificantly small in comparison, we may easily note, in concentrating our thought upon it, that it is indissolubly a part of the larger undertaking, and in our application thereto of an analytical creative impulse phasing into a synthetic, constructive, creative impulse, we are doing our special work in connection with the greatest adventure the spirit of man ever has entered.

So let your art be of, for and by this new creative impulse of our day, that it may in due time put forth true images of man's free spirit.

NOTE: This, and the following, represent entirely new chapters, written in 1918.

LI. Optimism

And now, my dear boy, we have, substantially, rounded out our thesis. We have done so, to be sure, crudely enough, in a most sketchlike fashion. We have passed in review the phenomena of our contemporaneous American architecture. We have also taken a glance at the man of the past. From a summit laboriously reached, we have been enabled to secure a view of the man of today. Meanwhile, we have sought simple basic explanations.

We have arrived close to the ending of your primary education, and the beginning of your new, self-creative education; for our talks, in part, have been but Kindergarten Chats.

That the undertaking has been in some respects not altogether an agreeable one, is regrettable; and yet, what would you? Conditions are as they are.

If we have seen much of pessimism, it is because much pessimism exists. The same may be said of cynicism.

If we have discovered ignorance in high quarters it is because ignorance is to be found in high quarters. The same may be said of the ineptitude of the schools, of many other repellent aspects of the intellect.

If in our investigations, our search, we have come across these things, and others equally disconcerting, it is because they were there to begin with.

But having descended into this dark valley of negations, having crossed it and begun our climb out of it, we began to come across pleasanter things, and, as we trudged on, ever ascending toward the summit, we unearthed truth after truth, wholesome, immensely valuable and inspiring. And when we had reached our highest point, man, the priceless treasure, revealed himself to us and we believed in him — MAN THE CREATOR! the redeemer, the Messiah.

I have marked out for you a tenuous but secure foundation of thought, in the making of which you have bravely assisted in your enthusiasm of optimism: a basis of sanity and good will.

Let me remark in passing, what this poor word optimism has suffered at the hand of the silly, the superficial and unreflecting, and, above all, at the hand of the professional optimist. We have seen enough to know that a modern optimism must be based on a faith in things and assurances fairly well seen, rather than in a vague essence of things unseen. And among these things and assurances fairly well seen by us are man's powers: and the creative fertility of nature.

What with us savors of the essence of things unseen, but devoutly forecast, is that man, in his enlarging knowledge and understanding of man and his powers, his increasing insight into nature's processes, will arrive at an optimism completely sane, and utilize it as an interpretative, creative, constructive power for the upbuilding of his new home. Such optimism is truly worthwhile. Its basis is clear to the imaginative inquiring mind: its uses equally clear to the imaginative constructive mind.

In this sense, the beginning of an optimistic career by you may be considered well grounded, and there remains but little danger that you will decline into considering optimism of will and of character but a sentimental, fleeting or capricious attitude of mind. You will meet with difficulties, to be sure; but with patience these may be overcome by means of a thoroughly developed professional technique. Remember above all, not only that your art starts with utility, but that the foundation of utility is the sole foundation and guaranty of its expression in your hands into the beautiful. It lies with you to demonstrate the thorough-going value of optimism as imaged in results.

Now while this talk is in the nature of a farewell address . . .

Oh, say not so, I could go on forever . . .

I wish to say a few lingering words, lest it be too abrupt. So remember, and bear ever in mind in your thinking and your doings, that FORM EVER FOLLOWS FUNCTION, that this is the law — a universal truth. That the main function, so far as you will be concerned, will focus in the specific needs of those who wish to build, and that such needs are quite apt to be emotional as well as what is so generally called practical. That your share will be to investigate and assimilate these needs with the utmost care, to find in the problem, which in the aggregate they form, a true solution, and then to express in truthful terms, in satisfying beautiful forms, a creative impulse which shall conserve and not suppress.

This is perhaps all that need be said by way of caution. If you have taken to heart the substance and spirit of our various chats and experiences together, if you have thoroughly absorbed them, they will reappear in due time, newly expressed through your individual nature, tempered, colored and, I hope, amplified, by the influence of growing observation, experience and reflection, until you are completely convinced not only that architecture is A PLASTIC ART but that you have become a master of the sane and beautiful plastic art of expression; a MASTER at once of Democratic thought and Democratic art, and that thus you are inspired!

But let us not thus part. Winter is gone: the Spring is here, I feel her incense permeate the air.

Oh, let us then not part until we greet the Spring!

She comes on now apace, in all her power.

And the heart melts at the thought of her greeting; and our rejuvenescence, our resurrection, and her own. It was for her companionship I yearned I knew not why.

LII. Spring Song

They say that Love is blind, but 'tis not so — Love is clairvoyant — the loved one is blind.

They say many a thing, my lad, but 'tis not so — Where Love is not, naught else exists.

They say —well no matter what they say, Love is Love, it is the power of powers. 'Tis why we live. 'Tis our last refuge, our first hope, our unsullied and our simplest joy.

> *It is the spring, O Lord!*
> *It is the spring!*
> *Sweet fragrance fills the air,*
> *Dim censers swing,*
> *It is the spring,*
> *It is the spring!*
>
> *How languorous the gentle breeze,*
> *How suasive are the opening buds,*
> *How softly sings the spring of infancy,*
> *It is the spring!*
> *It is the spring of springs!*
> *The newborn,*
> *The delicate,*
> *The ineffable.*
> *'Tis that which melts, dissolves;*
> *'Tis that which wakens love;*
> *It is that joy which causes love to bloom forever in the garden.*
> *It is the spring,*
> *It is the dawn,*
>
> *It is the hour;*
> *Love comes to Life — Life comes to Love—*
> *The twain are one.*
> *Good is born,*
> *Power comes forth in splendor,*
> *Tenderness is here.*

An overwhelming joy awakens as Spring sings her limpid song;
We hear the melody,
And our bell sounds,
For 'tis OUR Spring that sings in the song,
While springtime listening murmurs her response;
'Tis our response to springtime's melting mood.

That which would form must melt;
The heart melts that it form;
The soul melts;
The body melts that it re-form anew.

It is the spring — the languorous, surging spring,
The sensuous, mighty spring,
The erotic spring without, within,
The spring of action — of ebullient blare,
Charged with love,
Charged with fecund passion,
Charged with infinite affection,
Charged with desire,
Surcharged with power to do.

See! in the top of yonder pine, the mocking-bird bursting his throat in love for his mate. How he sways with the bough. How he sings and sings in the breeze, singing in the springtime — singing his song of Love's ecstasy. And how well the breeze knows it. And how well the springtime knows it. And his mate on yonder tree yearning for love, yearning in the springtime of her sweet pure heart — the heart of a mocking bird!

Oh, shut not your heart to the springtime, O Man.
Shame on the prude who shuns that which is chaste, who would shut the ear to the melody of procreation.

See! how the dogwood blooms!
Shall I sometime bloom like it?

Surely! you shall — if you WILL!
The dogwood blooms in love of spring,
Love Spring — and bloom.
For Love is Life;
For Love is You;
For Love is I;
For Love is the springtime.
It is all in life;
All in religion;
All in philosophy;
And without Love — alas!
Does not the wild azalea tell you this?
Need I tell it? — I?
What am I?
It is the Spring — not I.

But where is my spring song? When shall it begin?
How raucous my treble grates within this splendor;
How pallid my wish and will against this polychrome;
How shallow I, how void of all but love.
With overflowing heart I try to sing;
And the springtime sings and sings in ecstasy — I have not lost the ear to hear — I listen and am amazed anew — such beauty, such gentleness, such fluency, such gracious pride.

Behold! the far-flung glory of the spring!
Hear her call! Hear echoing splendor everywhere!

Kindergarten Chats

Oh, for an art of spring,
A comprehending utterance.
Oh, for one mighty soul to hear and sing the song of spring:
One man to chant this hymn of hymns.
How inarticulate and hoarse are we — the while all Nature is in tune.
Oh, let there be one vibrant voice to answer, to proclaim;
To sunder the vast sky with pealing anthem;
One heart to swallow up the saturating radiance here!

Behold! Here is the volcanic warmth of life,
The mighty power of resurgent growth;
The ardent soul of ALL is here.
Oh, for one eye to see,
One will to shape!

Her sweet contagion comes so softly to my heart,
Her power seeks so winsomely an entry to the mind;
Her goodness comes so silently, so gently, toward the soul.
She knocks so timorously at the door.
It is the Spring! All hail! All hail, thou! Lovely Spring!
For mak'st thou not a dream to shape and sing now in my heart?
Would that I might wholly sing of thee in my beatitude.
Oh, take my wistful song, my famished song, my silent song if so
must be.
Take it lest I pass away;
For as I love thee, gentle Spring, with all my heart, with all my soul,
Take this pale offering of all I have.
Poor am I, yet take me, take me for my love.

How brilliantly the waters sparkle in the bay,
How softly shines the great, glad sun, which makes the waters sparkle.

So shine on me, thou gladsome Spring;
Shine on me as on waters — that I like waves may dance and gleam.

How softly moves the south breeze, coming to us from far o'er the
bay, from over broad and distant seas — come to us to join your
song, O Spring.

How every insect chirps and creaks;
How birds attune;
How flowers exhale.

It is the Spring!
It is the sweetest spring of springs;
For that arises now triumphant in my soul.
After weird winter a spring-song melts me — I am born again.

O amorous springtime!
Why art thou thus gentle in thy power?
Why art thou, sweet spirit, thus so tender: as this, my
springtime is sweet and tender — as all Nature is pellucid?

Surely God hath loved and sought thee; so thou sing'st of Him,
Then as surely will God come to me who watch and wait.
Then will He gladden my heart as He sends the sun to gladden the
water and the birds and every living thing that hails Him with no
creed but Life and Love.

The Spring is singing her gladsome song,
Hear it, all my lad:
Hear its diapason,
Hear the splendor of its flow:
Remember it forever.
There surely will another spring arise: You shall prevail!
There surely will a springtime come into the garden of the heart:
You shall prevail.

Then will come Beauty, then will come Power,
Then create! You shall prevail!
Be not self-shamed, as Spring is not self-shamed.
Be virile to the end!

Radiant Spring! Inspiring Spring!
The glory and the gentleness of her power will come to you —
Use it wisely, use it well: You shall prevail.
Enamoured and enamouring Spring!
The Spring that follows Winter of the heart:
For the heart has ever season — such as Man.

So hope, in the Spring — it is the time for hope;
So shall I believe, in Spring — it is the time to believe.
SO SHALL WE WILL, IN THE SPRINGTIME:
IT IS OUR TIME FOR WILLING!

NOW BEGIN

Additional Papers 1885-1906

Characteristics and Tendencies of American Architecture

This essay, Sullivan's first formal writing so far as is known, was delivered as an address before the Western Association of Architects in 1885.

Many who have commented upon the practice of architecture in this country have regarded the absence of a style, distinctively American, as both strange and deplorable; and with a view to betterment they have advanced theories as to the nature, and immediate realization, of such a style that evidence a lack of insight equally strange and deplorable. These theories have been for the greater part suggested by the feelings awakened in contemplating the matured beauty of Old World art, and imply a grafting or transplanting process. They have been proved empirical by the sufficient logic of time; their advocates having ignored the complex fact, that, like a new species of any class, a national style must be a growth, that slow and gradual assimilation of nutriment and a struggle against obstacles are necessary adjuncts to the purblind processes of growth, and that the resultant structure can bear only a chemical or metaphysical resemblance to the materials on which it has been nurtured.

We will, therefore, for the purposes of this paper disregard these dreams of a Minerva-like architectural splendor springing full-formed into being, and look rather for the early signs of a spontaneous architectural feeling arising in sympathy with the emotions latent or conspicuous in our people.

It is reasonable to believe that an unconquered country, peopled by colonization and natural increase, may bear in its younger and its coming generations a race whose birthright, implying freedom to receive and assimilate impressions, shall nurture emotions of rare quality and of a fruitfulness commensurate with the energy in an unexhausted soil.

It would be erroneous to assume that there will be no evidence of the activity of such emotions until as a large accumulation they break all bonds asunder. The in-

NOTE: Figs. 12-17 show examples of Sullivan's work (Figs. 12-16 by the firm, Adler and Sullivan) which in chronology, subject-matter and variety reflect the sequence of the essays.

dividual is from day to day seeking expedients by means of which to shape his immediate surroundings into a realization of his desires, and we may assume it to be quite probable that the initial impelling force, operating through the individual, has already in many cases produced significant and valuable results. These results, if not thoroughly typical, must have in them much that is eminently characteristic, and that bear the stamp of internal origin.

To test this hypothesis we have therefore but to look into the daily life of our architecture, and, in the complexion of its many fleeting phases, seek here and there for instances, some perhaps almost trivial, in which the existence of spontaneous and characteristic emotional feeling may be detected. Sometimes we shall find this impulse appearing as an element of warmth tingeing scholastic formalism; sometimes as a seemingly paradoxical inspiration in the works of the uncultivated. We may certainly expect to meet with it in the efforts of those upon whose imagination the chromatic eloquence of words and of music have taken strong hold; and above all, we are to look for it in the creations of the gifted ones whose souls are finely attuned to the touching beauty of nature and of humanity. To an apprehension of this subtle element, we may be happily guided by the suggestions of analogy. Our recent American literature comes aptly to this use. Glancing through its focusing substance, as through the lens of a camera, we may perceive an image of the abstraction we seek, and, by an extension of the process, we may fix an impression of its form and texture, to be developed at will.

Our literature is the only phase of our national art that has been accorded serious recognition, at home and abroad. The noticeable qualities of its present phases seem to be: excessive regard for minute detail, painful self-consciousness of finish, timidity and embarrassment in the delineation of all but the well-behaved and docile emotions, and a tacit fiction as to the passions: all beautifully executed with much patient, earnest labor, and diplomatically tempered to the understanding.

Exquisite, but not virile, our latter-day literature illustrates quite emphatically the quality of our tentative and provisional culture, which must ere long throw off these seedling leaves, when a higher temperature shall infuse glowing vitality into root and stem, and exuberant foliation give more certain assurance of the coming flower of our soil. Our literature, and in fact all that which we Americans complacently call our art, is too much a matter of heart and fingers, and too little an offspring of brain and soul. One must indeed have faith in the processes of nature to prophesy order eventuating upon so strange a chaos of luxuries. But to this end, transmitted knowledge must gradually be supplemented by the fresh impressions of the senses and the sensibilities, the fund so accumulated yielding richly of its own increase. This supplemental acquisition must of necessity be of slow growth, for we have all been educated to a dependence upon our artistic inheritance.

Our art is for the day, is suited to the day, and will also change as the day changes. The law of variation is an ever present force, and coordination is its goal. The first step toward a new order of things is accomplished when there appear minds receiving and assimilating fresh impressions, reaching new conclusions, and acting upon them. By this sign, we may know that such a movement is already upon us, and by the aid of the indicated literary analogy we may follow its erratic tendencies, and note its increase in strength and individuality: we may see the germ of poetry which each man has within him, slowly awakening into life, and may feel the presence of an American romanticism.

This romanticism is, in the main, also exquisite but not virile. It seeks to touch all things with softened hand. Under the influence of its warmth of feeling, hard lines flow into graceful curves, angularities disappear in a mystical blending of surfaces.

One by one the completed styles of foreign climes are passing under this hand, each in turn being quietly divested of its local charm, and clothed in a sentiment and mannerism unmistakably our own. Power laments, meanwhile, at the feet of a modern Omphale, his voice attuned to the domestic hum of the times.

Appreciation of the beauties of this romanticism is to some extent dependent upon the verbal explanation and comment of its exponents. A knowledge of their vocabulary is often of assistance in disclosing softness and refinement in many primitive expedients, and revealing beauty in barren places. Familiarity with the current phraseology of the allied arts is also useful in assisting the student to a comprehension of many things apparently incomprehensible. Metaphor and simile are rampant in this connection, a well-chosen word often serving to justify an architectural absurdity.

But overloaded as is this fabric of impulse with florid and complicated intertwinings of affection, when we examine the material thereof, we find it excellent and valuable.

Searching critically among the works executed in this feeling, we note in the varying examples, and indeed in parts of the same structure, a curious *mélange* of supersentimentalisms. Conspicuous at first glance, in some an offensive simplicity, in others a highly wrought charlatanism; further, we perceive ingenuity in device, or superb flow of spirits — all more or less leavened with stubborn common sense. After such an investigation, we may gladly become convinced that behind a somewhat uncertain vision resides a marvelous instinct.

National sensitiveness and pride, conjoined with fertility of resource, will aid as active stimuli in the development of this instinct toward a more rational and organic mode of expression, leading through many reactions to a higher sphere of artistic development.

We are now in the primary department, vaguely endeavoring to form a plastic alphabet by means of which to identify our beliefs. Progress in this respect has been very slow and results meagre: for our beliefs have still within them too much of uncertainty and diffidence to take rank as convictions. Without these latter a sufficient creating power is lacking. The formation of an alphabet, and the simplest combinations of its terms, are matters of much importance; and easy progress in this respect is seriously impeded by complications of thought. To look at things simply and clearly is quite easy, until counter influences are set at work; then comes a struggle for survival, which now and then is successful — the result being an addition, however small, to our stock of elementary forms.

The ability to develop elementary ideas organically is not conspicuous in our profession. In this respect, the architect is inferior to the business man and financier, whose capacity to expand a simple congenial idea, once fixed, into subtle, manifold and consistent ramifications is admirable, and a shining example which we have often ignored, creating thereby an undesirable impression.

This view leads us on to a consideration of the element of power. Until this element is widely introduced into our work, giving it the impress of brilliancy, intuition and great depth of feeling, that work, exhaustively considered, will remain but little more than a temporary expedient.

The presence of power, as a mental characteristic in one class of our people, augurs well for the belief that it may pervade our ranks. The beginnings of power are usually so crude and harsh as to be revolting to a refined taste, and hence it is instinctively shunned; but once subtilized, flushed with emotion and guided by clear insight, it is a worker of miracles; responsive to its ardent wooings, nature yields up her poetic secrets.

We surely have in us the germ of artistic greatness — no people on earth possessing more of innate poetic feeling, more of ideality, greater capacity to adore the beautiful, than our own people; but architects as a professional class have held it more expedient to maintain the traditions of their culture than to promulgate vitalizing thought. Here then we are weak, and should sentiment gain a pronounced ascendency, we may remain weak.

On us rests partially the responsibility, and partially on the public. We have at times individually sought to lead the public, when we more wisely should have followed it; and have, as a body, often followed, when, with beneficent results we could have led. While we may compromise for a time, through a process of local adaptation, no architectural style can become a finality, that runs counter to popular feeling. The desire at once to follow and to lead the public should be the initial attitude of our profession toward the formation of a national style. For while we conduct the technical operations, the shaping and controlling process is mainly in the hands of the public who are constantly keeping us within bounds. We cannot wholly escape this control, while we are without a national architecture fully representing the wishes of the public, and ministering to its conceptions of the beautiful and the useful. This can evidently not come to pass forthwith, for the public itself can only partially and imperfectly state its wants. Responding readily, however, to the intuition of those who anticipate its desires, it accepts provisionally year by year all the satisfaction it can get; so that while one recognized style after another shall pass through our hands to be tried and finally rejected in the search for permanent satisfaction, a modified residuum from each will doubtless be added to a fund representing our growth in emotional and spiritual wealth. The progress of this growth toward consummation in a national style, involves the lives of many generations, and need be of but little practical concern to us of today. We work at short range and for immediate results. Perhaps, however, there would be infused into our profession an abiding *esprit de corps,* should consideration of this subject and its associated themes lead to a substantial agreement upon our status, our tendencies and our policy.

If the conclusions set forth in this paper be accepted as correct, it becomes clearly evident, however, that the formative beginnings of this national style, now in progress, are of the utmost immediate interest to us, in part through feelings of patriotism, in part because of a surmise that those who approach most nearly in the substance of their work and administration to the qualities inherent to [in] our race and potential to [of] a national style, will come nearest to the hearts of our people.

Harassed though the architect may be, by the cares and responsibilities of his daily life, there exists nevertheless within him, in the midst of this turmoil, an insuppressible yearning toward ideals. These delicate promptings should be both protected and nourished, that, like the flowering plants springing by the sun's gentle persuasion from little seeds buried in the coarser elements of the soil, they also, because of the warmth of human feeling, may bloom at times by the wayside, yielding refreshing odors and the joy of color to the plodding wayfarer.

The soft beams of the full-orbed moon fall with pathetic caress upon the slumbering life of the world; paling with the dawn, her tender vigil ended, she melts into the infinite depths when the ruddy herald of day proudly summons the workers. So does the soul watch over its greater ideals until the thrilling radiance of power shall awaken them to action.

Ideal thought and effective action should so compose the vital substance of our works that they may live, with us and after us, as a record of our fitness, and a memorial of the good we may have done. Then, in the affluence of time, when a rich burden of aspiring verdure may flourish in the undulating fields of thought, wrought into fertility through the bounty of nature and the energy of the race, the mellowed spontaneity of a national style reaching its full and perfect fruition shall have come from out the very treasury of nature.

Note: The Auditorium (Figs. 13, 14) reflects many of the ideas in this essay.

"What is the Just Subordination, in Architectural Design, of Details to Mass"?

A discussion at the regular meeting of the Illinois Association of Architects, held April 2, 1887, in the form of a symposium with talks by Louis H. Sullivan, L. D. Cleveland and O. J. Pierce, and a summary by Louis H. Sullivan.

Louis H. Sullivan:

It is frequently difficult to understand that there may be two sides to a subject. It is proportionately difficult to imagine that there may be more than two, the number, indeed, mounting into the thousands. Therefore, while still in that placid and yielding state of mind, superinduced by distant and general considerations, I admit, once for all, that facets, without number, may be cut upon the rough gem which is presented as the subject of this symposium; and I further admit that each facet will reflect its share of light. I still further admit that the gem, as a whole, may be cut to suit the cutter; and taking advantage of this concession, broadly accorded to all, I shall proceed to fashion the stone after my own predilections, even as though it were the very jewel after which I longed. To approach a step nearer: If the question is a categorical one, demanding a similar reply, I can only answer, I do not know. For who shall say what is possible and what is impossible? Who shall fathom the infinite depths of creative art? Who drink up the sea, and say "all is now dry land?" I cannot do these things; I do not believe anyone can, or will ever be able. Therefore, I believe that in this regard the question is an open one, and will forever remain an open one. Assuming next that the question is not categorical, but rather general and optimistic, I may consider its scope limited within the confines of what has been done, what is for the moment uppermost in recollection, with also an underlying curiosity with regard to what may be done. This naturally makes prominent considerations of climate, locality and temperament: climate, which is the arbiter of material things; locality, with its accidental variations, superadded to those of the seasons, and both creators of temperament, which is in turn the creator and the arbiter of art. All of which makes possible as a general and qualified answer: "That depends." Storms and frost would tend to influence a softening away of detail into the general mass; localities, more or less favorable, would intensify or relax this influence, while temperament would exert its just or morbid all-controlling sway of sentiment. Similarly, countries of sunshine and flowers, or the valleys, the mountains, the seacoast, the far-reaching plains, the preponderance of heat or cold, the lakes, rivers, bleak and fertile regions, regions of snow and ice, or sultry south winds, would each, according to its rhythmic nature, simple or qualified, awaken corresponding sympathies within the heart, which, if left untrammeled by ill-fitting theories, would spontaneously evolve a coordination of mass and detail, so normal, so indigenous, that it would instinctively be recognized as literally and poetically just.

Hence, this section may be closed with the broad sentiment that all is free and open, provided the general trend is in the direction of indigenous and sincere results; that when we become justly sympathetic, ward off extraneous and irrelevant influences, and make an earnest effort to reach real and intense results, we shall probably some day find a local answer to the question — an answer which none can gainsay. As for me, I do not yet know what that answer is to be, though I believe I share with others a premonition of its nature.

Finally, assuming that the question is local, and specific in its import, and calls for merely an individual expression of opinion as to what is today and here in Chicago the just subordination of details to mass, I willingly make such an explanation as I may.

Candidly, I do not especially believe in subordination of detail in so far as the word "subordination" conveys an idea of caste or rank, with the involved suggesttion of a greater force suppressing a lesser; but I do believe in the differentiation of detail from mass (the idea of subordination occurring incidentally and as of no controlling import), because this word symbolizes to my mind an idea which is very congenial to it, namely, that of an expansive and rhythmic growth, in a building, of a single, germinal impulse or idea, which shall permeate the mass and its every detail with the same spirit, to such an extent, indeed, that it would be as difficult to determine (not, surely, as a matter of arithmetical ratio, but rather as a factor in the total complex impression on the beholder) which is the more important, which in fact subordinates, detail or mass, as it would be difficult to say of a tree, in its general impression upon us, "which is more to us, the leaves or the tree?" — a question which I believe has never arisen. For I do not know that it has occurred to anyone to ask what is the just subordination of leaves to mass in a tree? What are the just ratios of leaves, branches and trunk? Should the leaves be large, and hide the branches, as in the horse chestnut, or should they be frivolous and dainty things, coquettishly exposing the branches? Should the trunk prevail, as in the proud and mournful southern pine, or should the trunk be short and sturdy, as the oak, with powerful gnarled and spreading branches, bared and grim before the tempest? It would be interesting if someone would kindly invent a precise formula for the growth of trees, so that we might forthwith declare any tree which grew at variance with the dictum to be altogether vulgar and devoid of savoir faire. For my part, I find their thousand ways all charming, and fruitful in suggestion. I graciously permit them to grow as they will, and look on with boundless admiration. For I know that

183. *"What is the Just Subordination, in Architectural Design?"*

they are simply trees; that they have no occasion to be ill at ease, or covert, or dyspeptic with introspection; therefore I trust them, and regard them abidingly with love and veneration.

It may be said that I am at fault in comparing animate with inanimate things; but this is the very heart of a mysterious subject; for I insist strenuously, that a building should live with intense, if quiescent, life, because it is sprung from the life of its architect. On no other basis are results of permanent value to be attained.

The more I ponder the title-question, the more I am at a loss for a precise answer; the possibilities, even within the limitations of climate, are so manifold, and so native. But for the moment it suits me to favor a very simple outline, particularly at the roof, which is the part most vulnerable to the elements.

Within this simple outline, then, I prefer such subdivision of the masses into detail as is strictly called for by the utilitarian requirements of the building; and that they should comport with its size, location and purpose. That the materials of construction should largely determine the special form of details, and above all, that there shall effuse from the completed structure a single sentiment which shall be the spiritual result of a prior and perfect understanding and assimilation of all the data.

Remarks by L. D. Cleveland
Remarks by O. J. Pierce

Summary by Louis H. Sullivan:

In summing up the results of this symposium, I am at once impressed with the independence and the courtesy of my co-laborers, as well as with the fact that their comments bear out my preliminary statement that each facet cut upon this gem would reflect its share of meaning and suggestion.

Mr. Pierce's statement, that a building with a soul is a work of architecture, and Mr. Cleveland's emphasis of the fact that a building tells a wordless story, are peculiarly agreeable to me, for they are statements which carry sincerity of purpose within the words.

I substantially agree with all that these gentlemen have said; though I gather that Mr. Pierce attaches prime importance to mechanical and abstract explanations such as are implied by the words, radiation, repetition, unity in variety, etc. His right to this point of view I do not question, yet I cannot accept it, for myself, as a finality. His "masculine" and "feminine" simile, however, seems to me far-reaching in its implied analogies; recalling even the exquisite "correspondences" of Swedenborg.

Mr. Cleveland is upon catholic and humane ground when he calls for a recognition of the claims to poetic richness of the solemn and fateful work of the Druids — as indeed of the charms of story hid within the silent stones of many ages. With him I turn back thoughtfully to read the mystic and impressive volume of the past; leaving it as he does, with the heartfelt wish that we in turn may tell our story as they of old told theirs, in a language of simple and majestic fervor.

The subject of our symposium seems all bound up with general and special considerations of style — its causes and manifestations — involving naturally enough a sentiment of solicitude regarding our future development in architectural art.

It is for this reason that I wish to add a word of my own, by way of conclusion, to forcibly emphasize that which I believe seems to us three to be the inherent suggestiveness of the theme.

This conclusion I shall mold under much heavier pressure of intensity than was given to the introduction, to wit:

I value spiritual results only. I say spiritual results precede all other results, and indicate them. I can see no efficient way of handling this subject on any other than a spiritual or psychic basis.

I say present theories of art are vanity. I say all past and future theories of art were and will be vanity. That the only substantial facts which remain after all the rubbish, dust and scientific-analytic-aesthetic cobwebs are brushed away are these facts, which each man may take to himself, namely: That I am; that I am immersed in nature here with my fellow men; that we are all striving after something which we do not now possess; that there is an inscrutable power permeating all, and the cause of all.

And I say that all we see and feel and know, without and within us, is one mighty poem of striving, one vast and subtle tragedy. That to remain unperturbed and serene within this turbulent and drifting flow of hope and sorrow, light and darkness, is the uttermost position and fact attainable to the soul, the only permanent link between the finite and infinite.

On this rock I would stand. And it is because I would stand here, that I say I value spiritual results only. It is for this reason that I say all mechanical theories of art are vanity, and that the best of rules are but as flowers planted over the graves of prodigious impulses which splendidly lived their lives, and passed away with the individual men who possessed these impulses. This is why I say that it is within the souls of individual men that art reaches culminations. This is why I say that each man is a law unto himself; and that he is a great or a little law in so far as he is a great or a little soul.

This is why I say that desire is the deepest of human emotions, and that prudence is its correlative; that it is the precursor, the creator, the arbiter of all the others. That great desire and great prudence must precede great results.

This is why I say that contemplation of nature and humanity is the only source of inspiration; this is why I say that without inspiration there can be no such thing as a just coordination of mass and details. That, as there may be countless inspirations profoundly vital, so, also, there may be countless coordinations of mass and details unspeakably just. That material results are to be measured by their contained inspiration; that these results will phase as the inspiration phases.

I say that the whole inquiry as to the just subordination of details to mass, in so far as it contains the implication of a fixed rule, is simply a pedagogic scarecrow.

Nor does this signify a plea for lawlessness. On the contrary, inspiration, such as I have indicated, has too much of pathos within it, too much of the calm of nature's mysterious decadence, to permit the forgetfulness, for more than a passing moment, of this deep-down conviction, that an idea lives according solely as by its power and prudence it compromises with death.

If cultivated mediocrity is what is wanted, the title-question can be answered readily and specifically for each historic style. If the culture of action is demanded,

185. *"What is the Just Subordination, in Architectural Design?"*

then indeed we have a task before us to find an answer, which shall at best be painfully and laboriously worked out. For every problem is for us, as yet, unsolved; we are merely as pioneers in a primeval forest. Yet while our results can be but relative, they may be the fruit of great desires, and hence, may speak of greatness.

Therefore I say that each one must perforce answer the question for himself; and that his answer will be profound or superficial according to the reach of his inspiration, and the gentleness and power of his sympathy; and that this answer can be found, in tangible form, only in his works; for it is here that he records his life, and it is by his works, and not his words, that he shall be judged; for here he can hide nothing — standing to the spiritual as one naked.

Therefore, again I say, I value spiritual results only, and regard all else as vanity.

It is needless, I trust, for me to say my feet are upon the ground; though Mr. Pierce seems to hold the placing this discussion upon a psychic basis as a species of ballooning. Here I differ with him radically, for I regard spiritual or psychic facts as the only permanent and reliable facts — the only solid ground. And I believe that until we shall walk securely upon this ground we can have but little force or directness or purpose, but little insight, but little fervor, but little faith in material results.

Ornament in Architecture

This essay was published in *The Engineering Magazine*, August 1892.

I take it as self-evident that a building, quite devoid of ornament, may convey a noble and dignified sentiment by virtue of mass and proportion. It is not evident to me that ornament can intrinsically heighten these elemental qualities. Why, then, should we use ornament? Is not a noble and simple dignity sufficient? Why should we ask more?

If I answer the question in entire candor, I should say that it would be greatly for our æsthetic good if we should refrain entirely from the use of ornament for a period of years, in order that our thought might concentrate acutely upon the production of buildings well formed and comely in the nude. We should thus perforce eschew many undesirable things, and learn by contrast how effective it is to think in a natural, vigorous and wholesome way. This step taken, we might safely inquire to what extent a decorative application of ornament would enhance the beauty of our structures — what new charm it would give them.

If we have then become well grounded in pure and simple forms we will reverse them; we will refrain instinctively from vandalism; we will be loath to do aught that may make these forms less pure, less noble. We shall have learned, however, that ornament is mentally a luxury, not a necessary, for we shall have discerned the limitations as well as the great value of unadorned masses. We have in us romanticism, and feel a craving to express it. We feel intuitively that our strong, athletic and simple forms will carry with natural ease the raiment of which we dream, and that our buildings thus clad in a garment of poetic imagery, half hid as it were in choice products of loom and mine, will appeal with redoubled power, like a sonorous melody overlaid with harmonious voices.

I conceive that a true artist will reason substantially in this way; and that, at the culmination of his powers, he may realize this ideal. I believe that architectural ornament brought forth in this spirit is desirable, because beautiful and inspiring; that ornament brought forth in any other spirit is lacking in the higher possibilities.

That is to say, a building which is truly a work of art (and I consider none other) is in its nature, essence and physical being an emotional expression. This being so, and I feel deeply that it is so, it must have, almost literally, a life. It follows from this living principle that an ornamented structure should be characterized by this quality, namely, that the same emotional impulse shall flow throughout harmoniously into its varied forms of expression — of which, while the mass-composition is the more profound, the decorative ornamentation is the more intense. Yet must both spring from the same source of feeling.

I am aware that a decorated building, designed upon this principle, will require in its creator a high and sustained emotional tension, an organic singleness of idea and purpose maintained to the last. The completed work will tell of this; and if it be designed with sufficient depth of feeling and simplicity of mind, the more intense the heat in which it was conceived, the more serene and noble will it remain forever as a monument of man's eloquence. It is this quality that characterizes the great monuments of the past. It is this certainly that opens a vista toward the future.

To my thinking, however, the mass-composition and the decorative system of a structure such as I have hinted at should be separable from each other only in theory and for purposes of analytical study. I believe, as I have said, that an excellent and beautiful building may be designed that shall bear no ornament whatever; but I believe just as firmly that a decorated structure, harmoniously conceived, well considered, cannot be stripped of its system of ornament without destroying its individuality.

It has been hitherto somewhat the fashion to speak of ornament, without perhaps too much levity of thought, as a thing to be put on or omitted, as the case might be. I hold to the contrary — that the presence or absence of ornament should, certainly in serious work, be determined at the very beginnings of the design. This is perhaps strenuous insistence, yet I justify and urge it on the ground that creative architecture is an art so fine that its power is manifest in rhythms of great subtlety, as much so indeed as those of musical art, its nearest relative.

If, therefore, our artistic rhythms — a result — are to be significant, our prior meditations — the cause — must be so. It matters then greatly what is the prior inclination of the mind, as much so indeed as it matters what is the inclination of a cannon when the shot is fired.

If we assume that our contemplated building need not be a work of living art, or at least a striving for it, that our civilization does not yet demand such, my plea is useless. I can proceed only on the supposition that our culture has progressed to the stage wherein an imitative or reminiscential art does not wholly satisfy, and that there exists an actual desire for spontaneous expression. I assume, too, that we are to begin, not by shutting our eyes and ears to the unspeakable past, but rather by opening our hearts, in enlightened sympathy and filial regard, to the voice of our times.

Nor do I consider this the place or the time to inquire if after all there is really such a thing as creative art — whether a final analysis does not reveal the great artist, not as creator, but rather as interpreter and prophet. When the time does come that the luxury of this inquiry becomes a momentous necessary, our architecture shall have neared its final development. It will suffice then to say that I conceive a work of fine art to be really this: a made thing, more or less attractive, regarding which the casual observer may see a part, but no observer all, that is in it.

It must be manifest that an ornamental design will be more beautiful if it seems a part of the surface or substance that receives it than if it looks "stuck on," so to speak. A little observation will lead one to see that in the former case there exists a peculiar sympathy between the ornament and the structure, which is absent in the latter. Both structure and ornament obviously benefit by this sympathy; each enhancing the value of the other. And this, I take it, is the preparatory basis of what may be called an organic system of ornamentation.

The ornament, as a matter of fact, is applied in the sense of being cut in or cut on, or otherwise done: yet it should appear, when completed, as though by the outworking of some beneficent agency it had come forth from the very substance of the material and was there by the same right that a flower appears amid the leaves of its parent plant.

Here by this method we make a species of contact, and the spirit that animates the mass is free to flow into the ornament — they are no longer two things but one thing.

If now we bring ourselves to close and reflective observation, how evident it becomes that if we wish to insure an actual, a poetic unity, the ornament should appear, not as something receiving the spirit of the structure, but as a thing expressing that spirit by virtue of differential growth.

It follows then, by the logic of growth, that a certain kind of ornament should appear on a certain kind of structure, just as a certain kind of leaf must appear on a certain kind of tree. An elm leaf would not "look well" on a pine-tree — a pine-needle seems more "in keeping." So, an ornament or scheme of organic decoration befitting a structure composed on broad and massive lines would not be in sympathy with a delicate and dainty one. Nor should the ornamental systems of buildings of any various sorts be interchangeable as between these buildings. For buildings should possess an individuality as marked as that which exists among men, making them distinctly separable from each other, however strong the racial or family resemblance may be.

Everyone knows and feels how strongly individual is each man's voice, but few pause to consider that a voice, though of another kind, speaks from every existing building. What is the character of these voices? Are they harsh or smooth, noble or ignoble? Is the speech they utter prose or poetry?

Mere difference in outward form does not constitute individuality. For this a harmonious inner character is necessary; and as we speak of human nature, we may by analogy apply a similar phrase to buildings.

A little study will enable one soon to discern and appreciate the more obvious individualities of buildings; further study, and comparison of impressions, will bring to view forms and qualities that were at first hidden; a deeper analysis will yield a host of new sensations, developed by the discovery of qualities hitherto unsuspected —we have found evidences of the gift of expression, and have felt the significance of it; the mental and emotional gratification caused by these discoveries leads on to deeper and deeper searching, until, in great works, we fully learn that what was obvious was least, and what was hidden, nearly all.

189. *Ornament in Architecture*

Few works can stand the test of close, business-like analysis — they are soon emptied. But no analysis, however sympathetic, persistent or profound, can exhaust a truly great work of art. For the qualities that make it thus great are not mental only, but psychic, and therefore signify the highest expression and embodiment of individuality.

Now, if this spiritual and emotional quality is a noble attribute when it resides in the mass of a building, it must, when applied to a virile and synthetic scheme of ornamentation, raise this at once from the level of triviality to the heights of dramatic expression.

The possibilities of ornamentation, so considered, are marvelous; and before us open, as a vista, conceptions so rich, so varied, so poetic, so inexhaustible, that the mind pauses in its flight and life indeed seems but a span.

Reflect now the light of this conception full and free upon joint considerations of mass-composition, and how serious, how eloquent, how inspiring is the imagery, how noble the dramatic force that shall make sublime our future architecture.

America is the only land in the whole earth wherein a dream like this may be realized; for here alone tradition is without shackles, and the soul of man free to grow, to mature, to seek its own.

But for this we must turn again to Nature, and hearkening to her melodious voice, learn, as children learn, the accent of its rhythmic cadences. We must view the sunrise with ambition, the twilight wistfully; then, when our eyes have learned to see, we shall know how great is the simplicity of nature, that it brings forth in serenity such endless variation. We shall learn from this to consider man and his ways, to the end that we behold the unfolding of the soul in all its beauty, and know that the fragrance of a living art shall float again in the garden of our world.

Emotional Architecture as Compared with Intellectual:

A Study in Subjective and Objective

This essay was read before the annual convention of the American Institute of Architects, New York, October 1894; the word "Classical" appeared in the title as a misprint for "Intellectual."

How strange it seems that education, in practice, so often means suppression: that instead of leading the mind outward to the light of day it crowds things in upon it that darken and weary it. Yet evidently the true object of education, now as ever, is to develop the capabilities of the head and of the heart. He, therefore, who possesses a sound head and a responsive heart is worthy of enlightened guidance, is amenable to educational influence.

Let us now imagine a simple youth so equipped, so gifted, I am almost forced to say, an inborn poet, untaught, unschooled, and living an out-door life. So familiarly has he fared with sunshine and air and the living things, that they seem, as indeed they are, every-day and common to him.

Yet the mere community of their lives, the similarity in the experiences of the boy, the plants and the animals in that native, simple, naïf, unsullied state that we who are perhaps unduly artificial call by contrast natural, this state has drawn him very near to them all.

Breathing the same air as they, maturing in the same glowing sunshine, sustained by the same satisfying moisture, he and they expand side by side, defining themselves intimately to each other; and the boy, growing always, after a while feels himself to be not only with them but of them. His is a brotherhood with the trees; a wistful eye he softens to the flowers; he has a comely friendship for them all.

He knows that the young leaves love the dew; that the tendril reaches quietly for the twig it may cling to. He has seen the fern unfolding its brown spiral to become anon green and regular. He has splashed knee-deep in the marsh; he knows the dank fragrance very well; he parts his friends the rushes to make a way for his eyes that seek what they may devour — his eyes with a keen and endless appetite. His hands touch the warmish water: sniffing the active air, he lives as only a boy can live — his lively sensibilities always in physical touch with his surroundings, in the full and irrepressible enjoyment of his five senses.

These five senses, and they only, stand between him and nature. It is they that interpret her affection; and the ready language that they deal in keeps him in such a natural sympathy, so well in touch, so intimately at ease, that he does not for a moment realize that he is then and there doing that which education, so called, once having made inoperative in him, he will in after years, poet though he be, reacquire only with the utmost difficulty the power to do.

This something that he is doing, and the physical and psychic state that it implies, we call *Touch*: meaning not the touch of the painter, not the touch of the sculptor, not the mechanical and technical touch of the fingers only, nor quite their negligent contact with things, but the exquisite touch of the sensibilities, the warm physical touch of the body, the touch of a sound head and a responsive heart, the touch of the native one, the poet, out of doors, in spontaneous communion with Nature.

So has our youngster started easily and naturally, all alone without premeditation or guidance, upon the road to knowledge, to leadership and power. For this sensibility, this healthfulness, this touch, this directness of apprehension, this natural clearness of eyesight that is his, is the first essential prerequisite in the early analytical strivings of the mind: it is that perfect concrete analysis by the senses and the sympathies which serves as a basis for the abstract analyses of the intellect.

Let us not forget our little man, for he is to companion me in spirit through this discourse. I believe he exists somewhere, has in his breast the true architectural afflatus, and will some day come forth the Messiah of our art. For he has that early and sure understanding by the eyes that will survive the future uncertainties of the brain. He has that exalted animal sense which alone can discern the pathway to hidden knowledge; that acute and instant scent in matters objective leading to matters subjective that we call *Intuition*.

This physical endowment, this sense of touch, is, decidedly, wherever found, a generous gift of nature, but it is potent for results in so far only as it is urged into sustained and decisive action by a certain appetite or desire.

This desire, this insistence, this urgency which will not be denied; this uncomfortable hunger, this uneasy searching, this profound discontent, oh! so deep; this cry for more; this appetite, this yearning, ever unsatisfied, is not of the body alone but of the soul, and, always and everywhere, in all times and in all places, high or low, wherever found, it is the dominant characteristic of man's eminence in nature — it is the justification of the eminence of a few men among their fellows.

For appetite, in a state of nature, implies not only a keen desire and a search for the food wanted, but, as well, a rejection of all else, thus insuring a wonderful singleness of purpose, a concentration of action, a definiteness of end in the selection of that nourishment of the faculties which, when assimilated, is to become in turn thought and expression through the agency of a second desire equally great, equally intense, equally insistent, namely, the desire to act. This desire to act we call *Imagination*.

These two great desires, which are in essence the desire to absorb and the desire to emit, the desire to know and the desire to test, the desire to hear and the desire to utter, are the basis not only of a true and effective education, not only are they the wholesome body and the enchanting voice of art, but they are greater than these, for they are the animating quality of that higher purpose and significance of art that we call poetry.

Now the desire to act that in due time follows upon nutrition can assert itself tangibly and fully only by means of three agencies, the which, by virtue of its life-giving qualities, this nutritive power has called into being. All three of them must cooperate in turn in order to produce a fully rounded result. They are first, the *Imagination,* which is the very beginning of action because it is a sympathy that lives both in our senses and our intellect — the flash between the past and the future, the middle link in that living chain or sequence leading from nature unto art, and that lies deep down in the emotions and the will. It is this divine faculty which, in an illumined instant, in that supreme moment when ideas are born, reveals the end with the beginning, and liberates, as an offspring of man, that which before had rested, perhaps for untold centuries, dormant but potential in the inmost heart of nature. This is the supreme crisis. This is the summit of the soul, the fertile touch of the spirit, the smile of nature's bounty — the moment of *Inspiration!* All else is from this moment on a foregone conclusion, an absolute certainty to the master-mind: a task surely, but not a doubt.

Second in this trinity comes *Thought,* the faculty that doubts and inquires, that recognizes time and space and the material limitations, that slowly systemizes, that works by small increments and cumulation, that formulates, that concentrates, works, reworks and reviews, that goes slowly, deliberately, that makes very firm and sure, and that eventually arrives at a science of logical statement that shall shape and define the scheme and structure that is to underlie, penetrate and support the form of an art work. It is the hard, the bony structure, it is the tough, tendinous fibre; it may be at times perhaps as limber as the lips that move, yet it is never the need of smiling — never the smile.

Third, last, and the winsome one, exuberant in life and movement, copious in speech, comes *Expression,* open-armed and free, supple, active, dramatic, change-able, beautifully pensive, persuasive and wonderful. Hers it is to clothe the structure of art with a form of beauty; for she is the perfection of the physical, she is the physical itself, and the uttermost attainment of emotionality. Hers is an infinite tenderness, an adorable and sweet fascination. In her companionship, imaginative Thought, long searching, has found its own, and lives anew, immortal, filled with sensibility, graciousness and the warm blood of a fully rounded maturity.

Thus Art comes into Life! Thus Life comes into Art!

And thus by reason of a process of elaboration and growth, through the natural storage and upbuilding of the products of nutrition lifting themselves higher and higher into organization, the physical and spiritual experiences of our lives, seeking reproduction, shall find imaginative utterance, in their own image, in a *harmonious system of thinking and an equally harmonious method of expressing the thought.*

And so it shall come that when our nourishment shall be natural, our imagination therefore fervid, intense and vision-like; when our thinking and our speech shall have become as processes of nature; when, in consequence, from its mysterious abode in visible things, the invisible and infinitely fluent spirit of the universe passing to us shall have made our tongues eloquent, our utterance serene, then, and not till then, shall we possess, individually and as a people, the necessary elements of a great *Style*.

For otherwise and without this unitary impulse our expression, though delicate as a flower, our thinking as abstract as the winds that blow, our imagination as luminous as the dawn, are useless and unavailing to create: they may set forth, they cannot create.

Man, by means of his physical power, his mechanical resources, his mental ingenuity, may set things side by side. A composition, literally so called, will result, but not a great art work, not at all an art work in fact, but merely a more or less refined exhibition of brute force exercised upon helpful materials. It may be as a noise in lessening degrees of offensiveness, it can never become a musical tone. Though it shall have ceased to be vulgar in becoming sophistical, it will remain to the end what it was in the beginning: impotent to inspire — dead, absolutely dead.

It cannot for a moment be doubted that an art work to be alive, to awaken us to its life, to inspire us sooner or later with its purpose, must indeed be animate with a soul, must have been breathed upon by the spirit and must breathe in turn that spirit. It must stand for the actual, vital first-hand experiences of the one who made it, and must represent his deep-down impression not only of physical nature but more especially and necessarily his understanding of the out-working of that *Great Spirit* which makes nature so intelligible to us that it ceases to be a phantasm and becomes a sweet, a superb, a convincing *Reality*.

It absolutely must be the determination and the capacity of the artist that his work shall be as real and convincing as is his own life: as suggestive as his own eyesight makes all things to him; and yet as unreal, as fugitive, as inscrutable, as subjective, as the why and wherefore of the simplest flower that blows.

It is the presence of this unreality that makes the art work real: it is by virtue of this silent subjectivity that the objective voice of an art song becomes sonorous and thrilling.

Unless, therefore, subjectivity permeate an art work that work cannot aspire to greatness; for whatever of imagination, of thought and of expression it may possess, these as such will remain three separate things — not three phases of one thing.

An artist must necessarily, therefore, remain a more or less educated hand worker, a more or less clever sophisticator, a more or less successful framer of compromises, unless, when he was born, there was born with him a hunger for the spiritual; for all other craving avails as naught. Unless, as a child, with that marvelous instinct given only to children, he has heard the voice of nature murmuring in the woodland or afield or seaward, no after hearing can avail to catch this revelation.

And thus it is that subjectivity and objectivity, not as two separate elements but as two complementary and harmonious phases of one impulse, have always constituted and will always constitute the embodied spirit of art.

No phase of human nature can contain greater interest for the student of psychology than the history, natural, political, religious and artistic, of the successive phases for good and for ill of Objectivity and Subjectivity. *They are the two controlling elements of human endeavor.* They have caused in their internecine warfare misery and perturbation. They are ordinarily known and spoken of as the intellectual and the emotional, but they lie deeper, much deeper, than these: they lie in the very heart of Nature. Coming into man's being, they have been antagonistic because of the fanaticism and one-sidedness of human nature, because of its immobility. Because from the beginning man has been beset by beautiful, by despicable, illusions. Because one set of men have believed in what they could see and another set have believed in what they could not see. Because it has too often happened that the man who could see with the outer eye could not see with the inner eye; because the other man, rhapsodizing with the clear insight of faith, had no thought for the things of this world. Neither has believed in the virtue of the other. Neither has inferred, from the presence of the other, the necessary existence of a balancing but hidden power. Now and then through the ages they have come twin-born in the bosom of an individual man — upon whose brow the generations have placed the wreath of immortality.

So vast, so overwhelming is the power of a great, a properly balanced subjectivity, so enormously does it draw on the spiritual nutrition and stored-up vitality of the world, that, soon sapping this up, and still craving, the man possessed of it, urged by it, goes straight to the unfailing bounty of nature, and there, by virtue of his passionate adoration, passing the portals of the objective, he enters that extraordinary communion that the sacred writers called to "walk with God."

There can be no doubt that the most profound desire that fills the human soul, the most heartfelt hope, is the wish to be at peace with Nature and the Inscrutable Spirit; nor can there be a doubt that the greatest Art Work is that which most nearly typifies a realization of this ardent, patient longing. All efforts, of the body, all undertakings of the mind, tend, consciously or unconsciously, toward this consummation, tend toward this final peace: the peace of perfect equilibrium, the repose of absolute unity, the serenity of a complete identification.

When, therefore, turning from this our contemplation we compare the outworking of the vital processes of nature with the so-called creative activity of the average man of education and culture, we wonder at the disparity, we seek its cause.

When, after having with joy observed the quality of identity and singleness that Nature imparts to her offspring, when with aroused expectancy, with a glowing sense of the richness, fullness and variety that might and should come from the man's brain with the impulse of nature's fecundity flowing through it, we seek — we are amazed to find in this man's work no such thing.

When we, in place of a fertile unity which we had hoped for, come suddenly upon miscellany and barrenness, we are deeply mortified, we are rudely shocked.

We are dismayed at this: that man, Nature's highest product, should alone have gone awry, that with remarkable perversity he should have strayed — that for the simple and obvious he should substitute the factitious, the artificial.

The cause needs not a long searching, it is near at hand. It lies precisely in that much glorified, much abused word "education."

To my view no word in the entire vocabulary of the English language contains so much of pathos, so much of tragedy as this one pitiful word "education," for it

195. *Emotional Architecture as Compared With Intellectual*

typifies a fundamental perversity of the human soul, a willful blindness of the mind, a poverty of the heart.

For one brain that education has stimulated and strengthened, it has malformed, stupefied and discouraged thousands. Only the strongest, only the masterful, can dominate it, and return to the ownership of their souls.

For it is education's crime that it has removed us from Nature. As tender children it took us harshly away with stern words, and the sweet face of our natural mother has faded in the unspeakable past, whence it regards us at times, dimly and flittingly, causing in us uneasy and disturbing emotion.

And thus it is through a brutish and mean system of guidance, through the density of atmosphere that we have breathed, that we are not what our successors may easily become, a race filled with spiritual riches in addition to the vast material wealth.

That in place of a happy people, open-eyed children of Nature teeming with beautiful impulses, we are a people lost in darkness, groping under a sooty and lurid sky sinister with clouds that shut out the sunshine and the clear blue heavens.

Yet the murky materialism — the fierce objectivity, the fanatical selfishness — of this dark age of ours, in this sense the darkest of all dark ages, is so prodigious, so grotesque, so monstrous, that in its very self it contains the elements of change: from its own intensity, its own excess, its complex striving, it predetermines the golden age of the world.

The human mind in all countries having gone to the uttermost limit of its own capacity, flushed with its conquests, haughty after its self-assertion upon emerging from the prior dark age, is now nearing a new phase, a phase inherent in the nature and destiny of things.

The human mind, like the silk-worm oppressed with the fullness of its own accumulation, has spun about itself gradually and slowly a cocoon that at last has shut out the light of the world from which it drew the substance of its thread. But this darkness has produced the chrysalis, and we within the darkness feel the beginning of our throes. The inevitable change, after centuries upon centuries of preparation, is about to begin.

Human development, through a series of vast attractions and perturbations, has now arrived at a materialism so profound, so exalted as to prove the fittest basis for a coming era of spiritual splendor.

To foresee this necessity, consider but a moment the richness of our heritage from the past, its orderly sequence, its uplifting wave of power, its conservation of force.

Think of the Hindu, with folded hands, soaring in contemplation, thousands of years ago — think of what he has left us. Think of the Hebrew man coming out of Ur of the Chaldees, to find for us the One Great Spirit. Think of the sombre Egyptians, those giants who struggled so courageously with fate — think of the stability they have given to us. Think of the stars of Israel, singing in the morning's dawn. Think of the lonely man of Nazareth breathing a spirit of gentleness of which the world had never heard before. Think of the delicately objective Greeks, lovers of the physical, accurate thinkers, the worshippers of beauty. Think that in them the Orient, sleeping, was born anew. Think of the Goth, and with him the birth of emotion as we know it. Think of modern Science which has taught us not to fear. Think of modern Music, arising in glory as the heart took wings — *a new thing under the sun.* Think deeply of the French Revolution and Democracy — the utterance of freedom, the beginning of the Individual Man. Think now of our own age with its machinery, its steam power, its means of communication, its annihilation of distance. Think of the humanitarianism of our day. Think, as we stand here, now, in a new land, a Promised Land that at last is ours, think how passionately latent, how marvelous to contemplate is America, our country. *Think that here destiny has decreed there shall be enacted the final part in the drama of man's emancipation — the redemption of his soul!*

Think of these things, think of what they signify, of what they promise for us, and think then that as architects it peculiarly behooves us to review our own special past, to forecast our future, to realize somewhat our present status.

Summoned to answer before an enlightened judgment seat, how shall we now give other, alas, than a wretched accounting of our stewardship! How shall we excuse our sterility? We surely need to inquire, for we must need explain the emaciation of our art in the midst of plenty, its weakness in the midst of strength, its beggarly poverty in the midst of abundance.

By what glamour or speciousness of words shall we persuade a wrathful judgment toward kindness? How can our vapid record be made to plead for us?

Shall we summon the clear-eyed, intellectual Greek or the emotional and introspective Goth to bear witness that we stand as ambassadors in their names — we would surely be repudiated.

Shall we call to the fateful Egyptian or the dashing, polished Assyrian — one would scorn us, the other would flout us.

Who are we then, and how shall we explain our sinister condition, our mere existence?

Shall we claim we are second cousins to Europe, or must we, before we can ourselves behold the truth, so far abase our heads in the ashes as to acknowledge that we of the great and glorious ending of the nineteenth century are the direct lineal descendants of the original bastards and indiscretions of architecture?

Or, still seeking excuses in our fin-de-siècle pocket, shall we plead in the language of myth that our art, like Brünnehilde, lies sleeping: that she awaits a son of nature, one without fear, to penetrate the wall of flame, to lift her helmet's visor?

Dreading the storm, shall we seek shelter under the spreading plea that poets are born, not made; that, if Nature for all these centuries has not brought forth a great master-spirit in the architectural art, it must be for very good reasons of her own — for reasons definitely interwrought with the beneficence of her own rhythmical movements? That, with her endless fecundity, there must be a profoundly significant reason for this barrenness.

Or, perhaps, shall we simply say that men have now turned to other gods, that they have forgotten the ancient deities?

That there has arisen in our land a new king who knows not Joseph; that he has set o'er us taskmasters to afflict us with burdens.

All these pleadings may be true, yet after all they do not explain why we make easy things very difficult, why we employ artificial instead of natural processes, why we walk backwards instead of forwards, why we see cross-eyed instead of straight-eyed, why we turn our minds inside out instead of letting them alone; they do not explain why we are so vulgarly self-conscious, so pitifully bashful, so awkward in our art, so explanatory, so uncertain that we know anything at all or are anybody in particular, so characterless, so insipid, so utterly without savor. They do not explain why the intellectual and emotional phases of the architectural mind do precisely the wrong thing when the right thing is quite attainable.

No! I pretend to advocate the real, the true cause of my generation, of my art. I do not wish to abase them except in so far as he who loveth chasteneth. I know that the secret of our weakness lies not only in our plethoric dyspepsia, in our lack of desire, in our deficiency of gumption and moral courage, but that it lies primarily in the utterly purposeless education we have received.

I know that the architectural schools teach a certain art or method of study in which one is made partly familiar with the objective aspects and forms of architecture. I know that this, as far as it goes, is conscientiously and thoroughly done. But I also know that it is doubtful, in my mind, if one student in a thousand emerges from his school possessed of a fine conception of what architecture really is in form, in spirit and in truth: and I say this is not primarily the student's fault. I know that before entering his architectural school he has passed through other schools, and that they began the mischief: that they had told him grammar was a book, algebra was a book, geometry another book, geography, chemistry, physics, still others: they never told him, never permitted him, to guess for himself how these things were actually intense symbols, complex ratios, representing man's relation to Nature and his fellow man; they never told him that his mathematics, etc. etc., came into being in response to a *desire* in the human breast to come nearer to nature — that the full moon looked round to the human eye ages before the circle was dreamed of.

Our student knows, to be sure, as a result of his teaching that the Greeks built certain-shaped buildings, that the Goths built certain-shaped buildings, and that other peoples built other buildings of still other shapes. He knows, moreover, if he has been a conscientious hewer of wood and drawer of water, a thousand and one specific facts concerning the shapes and measurements and ratios of the whole and the parts of said buildings, and can neatly and deftly draw and color them to scale. He moreover has read in the philosophies or heard at lectures that the architecture of a given time gives one an excellent idea of the civilization of that time.

This, roughly speaking, is the sum total of his education, and he takes his architectural instruction literally, just as he has taken every other form of instruction literally from the time he was a child — because he has been told to do so, because he has been told that architecture is a fixed, a real, a specific, a definite thing, that it's all done, that it's all known, arranged, tabulated and put away neatly in handy packages called books. He is allowed to believe, though perhaps not distinctly so taught, that, to all intents and purposes, when his turn comes, if he wishes to make some architecture for Americans or for this generation at large, he can dip it out of his books with the same facility that dubs a grocer dipping beans out of a bin. He is taught by the logic of events that architecture in practice is a commercial article, like a patent medicine, unknown in its mixture and sold to the public exclusively on the brand.

He has seriously been told at the school, and has been encouraged in this belief by the endorsement of people of culture, that he can learn all about architecture if he but possess the attributes of scholarship and industry. That architecture is the name of a system of accredited, historical facts as useful, as available and as susceptible to inspection as the books of a mercantile house.

Everything literal, formal and smart in his nature has been encouraged — the early and plastic glow to emotion and sensibility has been ignored.

He has been taught many cold and dead things, but the one warm living thing that he has not been taught and apparently never will be taught is the stately and all-comprehending truth that architecture, wherever it has appeared and reached a spontaneous culmination, is not at all what we so stupidly call a reality, but, on the contrary, it is a most complex, a glowing and gloriously wrought metaphor, embodying as no other form of language under the sun can do, the pure, clean and deep inspiration of the race flowing as a stream of living water from its well-spring to the sea.

He has not been taught that an architect, to be a true exponent of his time, must possess first, last and always the sympathy, the intuition of a poet; that this is the one real, vital principle that survives through all places and all times.

This seeking for a natural expression of our lives, of our thoughts, our meditations, our feelings, is the architectural art as I understand it: and it is because I so understand it, that, ignoring the viciousness of the past, I gladly make an appeal to the good that is in human nature — that goodness of heart and soundness of head, that ready and natural response of the soul in which I have always trusted and shall always trust. It is to this sane and wholesome quality that I plead for the abiding sincerity and nobility of our art. It is to this *manliness* that I call to come before the judgment seat and make an answer for us.

I know very well that our country will in due time possess a most interesting, varied, characteristic and beautiful architecture; that the time will begin whenever we take as our point of the departure the few and simple elements of architecture and not its complex forms. That this time will come just as soon as the young are relieved of the depressing weight of a factitious education, the benumbing influence of an instruction that insulates them from the vitalizing currents of nature. Just so soon as those having them in charge, coming to the full sense of the fact, realizing how truly dangerous a thing is a little knowledge, a partial knowledge, dreading to assume the responsibility for stunted, for imperfectly developed natures, feeling how deeply necessary it is that a technical or intellectual training be supplemented by a full, a rich, a chaste development of the emotions, shall say to the young that they are free, that from the musty school they may fly to the open air, to the sunshine, to the birds, the flowers, and, wanton and joyous in their own fancies, face to face with the integrity of nature, they shall substitute for the arbitrary discipline of the school the natural, the easy self-control of a dignified manhood, to the end that not books but personal feeling, personal character and personal responsibility shall form the true foundation of their art.

It has, alas, for centuries been taught that the intellect and the emotions were two separate and antagonistic things. This teaching has been firmly believed, cruelly lived up to.

How depressing it is to realize that it might have been taught that they are two beautifully congenial and harmonious phases of that single and integral essence that we call the soul. That no nature in which the development of either is wanting can be called a completely rounded nature.

That, therefore, classical architecture, so called (meaning the Greek), was one-sided and incomplete because it was almost exclusively intellectual. That the emotional architecture (meaning especially the Gothic) was likewise one-sided and incomplete, however great and beautiful its development of feeling, because of the almost total absence of mentality. That no complete architecture has yet appeared in the history of the world because men, in this form of art alone, have obstinately sought to express themselves solely in terms either of the head or of the heart.

I hold that architectural art, thus far, has failed to reach its highest development, its fullest capability of imagination, of thought and expression, because it has not yet found a way to become truly plastic: it does not yet respond to the poet's touch. That it is today the only art for which the multitudinous rhythms of outward nature, the manifold fluctuations of man's inner being have no significance, no place.

That the Greek Architecture, unerring as far as it went — and it went very far indeed in one direction — was but one radius within the field of a possible circle of expression. That, though perfect in its eyesight, definite in its desires, clear in its purpose, it was not resourceful in forms: that it lacked the flexibility and the humanity to respond to the varied and constantly shifting desires of the heart.

It was a pure, it was a noble art, wherefore we call it classic; but after all it was an apologetic art, for, while possessing serenity, it lacked the divinely human element of mobility: the Greek never caught the secret of the changing of the seasons, the orderly and complete sequences of their rhythm within the calmly moving year. Nor did this selfsame Greek know what we now know of Nature's bounty, for music in those days had not been born: this lovely friend, approaching man to man, had not yet begun to bloom as a rose, to exhale its wondrous perfume.

That the Gothic architecture, with sombre ecstatic eye, with its thought far above with Christ in the heavens, seeing but little here below, feverish and overwrought, taking comfort in gardening and plant life, sympathizing deeply with Nature's visible forms, evolved a copious and rich variety of incidental expressions but lacked the unitary comprehension, the absolute consciousness and mastery of pure form that can come alone of unclouded and serene contemplation, of perfect repose and peace of mind.

I believe, in other words, that the Greek knew the statics, the Goth the dynamics, of the art, but that neither of them suspected the mobile equilibrium of it: neither of them divined the movement and the stability of nature. Failing in this, both have forever fallen short, and must pass away when the true, the *Poetic Architecture* shall arise — that architecture which shall speak with clearness, with eloquence, and with warmth, of the fullness, the completeness of man's intercourse with Nature and with his fellow men.

Moreover, we know, or should by this time know, that human nature has now become too rich in possessions, too well equipped, too magnificently endowed, that [for] any hitherto architecture can [to] be said to have hinted at its resources, much less to have exhausted them by anticipation.

It is this consciousness, this pride, that shall be our motive, our friend, philosopher and guide in the beautiful country that stretches so invitingly before us.

In that land, the schools, having found the object of their long, blind searching, shall teach directness, simplicity, naturalness: they shall protect the young against palpable illusion. They shall teach that, while man once invented a process called composition, Nature has forever brought forth organisms. They shall encourage the love of Nature that wells up in every childish heart, and shall not suppress, shall not stifle, the teeming imagination of the young.

They shall teach, as the result of their own bitter experience, that conscious mental effort, that conscious emotionality, are poor mates to breed from, and that true parturition comes of a deep, instinctive, subconscious desire. That true art, springing fresh from Nature, must have in it, to live, much of the glance of an eye, much of the sound of a voice, much of the life of a life.

That Nature is strong, generous, comprehensive, fecund, subtile: that in growth and decadence she continually sets forth the drama of man's life.

That, thro' the rotating seasons, thro' the procession of the years, thro' the march of the centuries, permeating all, sustaining all, there murmurs the still, small voice of a power that holds us in the hollow of its hand.

The Tall Office Building Artistically Considered

This essay was first published in *Lippincott's,* March 1896.

The architects of this land and generation are now brought face to face with something new under the sun —namely, that evolution and integration of social conditions, that special grouping of them, that results in a demand for the erection of tall office buildings.

It is not my purpose to discuss the social conditions; I accept them as the fact, and say at once that the design of the tall office building must be recognized and confronted at the outset as a problem to be solved — a vital problem, pressing for a true solution.

Let us state the conditions in the plainest manner. Briefly, they are these: offices are necessary for the transaction of business; the invention and perfection of the high-speed elevators make vertical travel, that was once tedious and painful, now easy and comfortable; development of steel manufacture has shown the way to safe, rigid, economical constructions rising to a great height; continued growth of population in the great cities, consequent congestion of centers and rise in value of ground, stimulate an increase in number of stories; these successfully piled one upon another, react on ground values — and so on, by action and reaction, inter-action and inter-reaction. Thus has come about that form of lofty construction called the "modern office building." It has come in answer to a call, for in it a new grouping of social conditions has found a habitation and a name.

Up to this point all in evidence is materialistic, an exhibition of force, of resolution, of brains in the keen sense of the word. It is the joint product of the speculator, the engineer, the builder.

Problem: How shall we impart to this sterile pile, this crude, harsh, brutal agglomeration, this stark, staring exclamation of eternal strife, the graciousness of those higher forms of sensibility and culture that rest on the lower and fiercer passions? How shall we proclaim from the dizzy height of this strange, weird, modern housetop the peaceful evangel of sentiment, of beauty, the cult of a higher life?

This is the problem; and we must seek the solution of it in a process analogous to its own evolution — indeed, a continuation of it — namely, by proceeding step by step from general to special aspects, from coarser to finer considerations.

It is my belief that it is of the very essence of every problem that it contains and suggests its own solution. This I believe to be natural law. Let us examine, then, carefully the elements, let us search out this contained suggestion, this essence of the problem.

The practical conditions are, broadly speaking, these:

Wanted — 1st, a story below-ground, containing boilers, engines of various sorts, etc. — in short, the plant for power, heating, lighting, etc. 2nd, a ground floor, so called, devoted to stores, banks, or other establishments requiring large area, ample spacing, ample light, and great freedom of access. 3rd, a second story readily accessible by stairways — this space usually in large subdivisions, with corresponding liberality in structural spacing and expanse of glass and breadth of external openings. 4th, above this an indefinite number of stories of offices piled tier upon tier, one tier just like another tier, one office just like all the other offices — an office being similar to a cell in a honey-comb, merely a compartment, nothing more. 5th, and last, at the top of this pile is placed a space or story that, as related to the life and usefulness of the structure, is purely physiological in its nature — namely, the attic. In this the circulatory system completes itself and makes its grand turn, ascending and descending. The space is filled with tanks, pipes, valves, sheaves, and mechanical etcetera that supplement and complement the force-originating plant hidden below-ground in the cellar. Finally, or at the beginning rather, there must be on the ground floor a main aperture or entrance common to all the occcupants or patrons of the building.

This tabulation is, in the main, characteristic of every tall office building in the country. As to the necessary arrangements for light courts, these are not germane to the problem, and as will become soon evident, I trust need not be considered here. These things, and such others as the arrangement of elevators, for example, have to do strictly with the economics of the building, and I assume them to have been fully considered and disposed of to the satisfaction of purely utilitarian and pecuniary demands. Only in rare instances does the plan or floor arrangement of the tall office building take on an æsthetic value, and this usually when the lighting court is external or becomes an internal feature of great importance.

As I am here seeking not for an individual or special solution, but for a true normal type, the attention must be confined to those conditions that, in the main, are constant in all tall office buildings, and every mere incidental and accidental variation eliminated from the consideration, as harmful to the clearness of the main inquiry.

The practical horizontal and vertical division or office unit is naturally based on a room of comfortable area and height, and the size of this standard office room as naturally predetermines the standard structural unit, and, approximately, the size of window openings. In turn, these purely arbitrary units of structure form in an equally natural way the true basis of the artistic development of the exterior. Of course the structural spacings and openings in the first or mercantile story are required to be the largest of all; those in the second or quasi-mercantile story are of

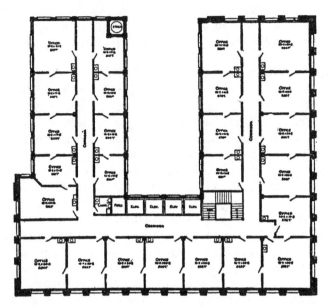

12. Plans of First and Sixth Floors, Wainwright Building, St. Louis (See also Fig. 16)

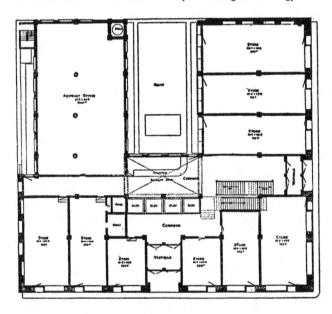

a somewhat similar nature. The spacings and openings in the attic are of no importance whatsoever (the windows have no actual value), for light may be taken from the top, and no recognition of a cellular division is necessary in the structural spacing.

Hence it follows inevitably, and in the simplest possible way, that if we follow our natural instincts without thought of books, rules, precedents, or any such educational impedimenta to a spontaneous and "sensible" result, we will in the following manner design the exterior of our tall office building — to wit:

Beginning with the first story, we give this a main entrance that attracts the eye to its location, and the remainder of the story we treat in a more or less liberal, expansive, sumptuous way — a way based exactly on the practical necessities, but expressed with a sentiment of largeness and freedom. The second story we treat in a similar way, but usually with milder pretension. Above this, throughout the indefinite number of typical office tiers, we take our cue from the individual cell, which requires a window with its separating pier, its sill and lintel, and we, without more ado, make them look all alike because they are all alike. This brings us to the attic, which, having no division into office-cells, and no special requirement for lighting, gives us the power to show by means of its broad expanse of wall, and its dominating weight and character, that which is the fact — namely, that the series of office tiers has come definitely to an end.

This may perhaps seem a bald result and a heartless, pessimistic way of stating it, but even so we certainly have advanced a most characteristic stage beyond the imagined sinister building of the speculator-engineer-builder combination. For the hand of the architect is now definitely felt in the decisive position at once taken, and the suggestion of a thoroughly sound, logical, coherent expression of the conditions is becoming apparent.

When I say the hand of the architect, I do not mean necessarily the accomplished and trained architect. I mean only a man with a strong, natural liking for buildings, and a disposition to shape them in what seems to his unaffected nature a direct and simple way. He will probably tread an innocent path from his problem to its solution, and therein he will show an enviable gift of logic. If he have some gift for form in detail, some feeling for form purely and simply as form, some love for that, his result in addition to its simple straightforward naturalness and completeness in general statement, will have something of the charm of sentiment.

However, thus far the results are only partial and tentative at best; relatively true, they are but superficial. We are doubtless right in our instinct but we must seek a fuller justification, a finer sanction, for it. [See Figs. 12, 16]

I assume now that in the study of our problem we have passed through the various stages of inquiry, as follows: 1st, the social basis of the demand for tall office buildings; 2nd, its literal material satisfaction; 3rd, the elevation of the question from considerations of literal planning, construction, and equipment, to the plane of elementary architecture as a direct outgrowth of sound, sensible building; 4th, the question again elevated from an elementary architecture to the beginnings of true architectural expression, through the addition of a certain quality and quantity of sentiment.

But our building may have all these in a considerable degree and yet be far from that adequate solution of the problem I am attempting to define. We must now heed the imperative voice of emotion.

It demands of us, what is the chief characteristic of the tall office building? And at once we answer, it is lofty. This loftiness is to the artist-nature its thrilling aspect. It is the very open organ-tone in its appeal. It must be in turn the dominant chord in his expression of it, the true excitant of his imagination. It must be tall, every inch of it tall. The force and power of altitude must be in it, the glory and pride of exaltation must be in it. It must be every inch a proud and soaring thing, rising in sheer exultation that from bottom to top it is a unit without a single dissenting line — that it is the new, the unexpected, the eloquent peroration of most bald, most sinister, most forbidding conditions.

The man who designs in this spirit and with the sense of responsibility to the generation he lives in must be no coward, no denier, no bookworm, no dilettante. He must live of his life and for his life in the fullest, most consummate sense. He must realize at once and with the grasp of inspiration that the problem of the tall office building is one of the most stupendous, one of the most magnificent opportunities that the Lord of Nature in His beneficence has ever offered to the proud spirit of man.

That this has not been perceived — indeed, has been flatly denied — is an exhibition of human perversity that must give us pause.

One more consideration. Let us now lift this question into the region of calm, philosophic observation. Let us seek a comprehensive, a final solution: let the problem indeed dissolve.

Certain critics, and very thoughtful ones, have advanced the theory that the true prototype of the tall office building is the classical column, consisting of base, shaft and capital — the moulded base of the column typical of the lower stories of our building, the plain or fluted shaft suggesting the monotonous, uninterrupted series of office-tiers, and the capital the completing power and luxuriance of the attic.

Other theorizers, assuming a mystical symbolism as a guide, quote the many trinities in nature and art, and the beauty and conclusiveness of such trinity in unity. They aver the beauty of prime numbers, the mysticism of the number three, the beauty of all things that are in three parts — to wit, the day, subdividing into morning, noon, and night; the limbs, the thorax, and the head, constituting the body. So they say, should the building be in three parts vertically, substantially as before, but for different motives.

Others, of purely intellectual temperament, hold that such a design should be in the nature of a logical statement; it should have a beginning, a middle, and an ending, each clearly defined — therefore again a building, as above, in three parts vertically.

Others, seeking their examples and justification in the vegetable kingdom, urge that such a design shall above all things be organic. They quote the suitable flower with its bunch of leaves at the earth, its long graceful stem, carrying the gorgeous single flower. They point to the pine-tree, its massy roots, its lithe, uninterrupted trunk, its tuft of green high in the air. Thus, they say, should be the design of the tall office building: again in three parts vertically.

Others still, more susceptible to the power of a unit than to the grace of a trinity, say that such a design should be struck out at a blow, as though by a blacksmith or by mighty Jove, or should be thought-born, as was Minerva, full grown. They accept the notion of a triple division as permissible and welcome, but non-essential. With them it is a subdivision of their unit: the unit does not come from the alliance of the three; they accept it without murmur, provided the subdivision does not disturb the sense of singleness and repose.

All of these critics and theorists agree, however, positively, unequivocally, in this, that the tall office building should not, must not, be made a field for the display of architectural knowledge in the encyclopædic sense; that too much learning in this instance is fully as dangerous, as obnoxious, as too little learning; that miscellany is abhorrent to their sense; that the sixteen-story building must not consist of sixteen separate, distinct and unrelated buildings piled one upon the other until the top of the pile is reached.

To this latter folly I would not refer were it not the fact that nine out of every ten tall office buildings are designed in precisely this way in effect, not by the ignorant, but by the educated. It would seem indeed, as though the "trained" architect, when facing this problem, were beset at every story, or at most, every third or fourth story, by the hysterical dread lest he be in "bad form"; lest he be not bedecking his building with sufficiency of quotation from this, that, or the other "correct" building in some other land and some other time; lest he be not copious enough in the display of his wares; lest he betray, in short, a lack of resource. To loosen up the touch of this cramped and fidgety hand, to allow the nerves to calm, the brain to cool, to reflect equably, to reason naturally, seems beyond him; he lives, as it were, in a waking nightmare filled with the disjecta membra of architecture. The spectacle is not inspiriting.

As to the former and serious views held by discerning and thoughtful critics, I shall, with however much of regret, dissent from them for the purpose of this demonstration, for I regard them as secondary only, non-essential, and as touching not at all upon the vital spot, upon the quick of the entire matter, upon the true, the immovable philosophy of the architectural art.

This view let me now state, for it brings to the solution of the problem a final, comprehensive formula.

All things in nature have a shape, that is to say, a form, an outward semblance, that tells us what they are, that distinguishes them from ourselves and from each other.

Unfailingly in nature these shapes express the inner life, the native quality, of the animal, tree, bird, fish, that they present to us; they are so characteristic, so recognizable, that we say, simply, it is "natural" it should be so. Yet the moment we peer beneath this surface of things, the moment we look through the tranquil reflection of ourselves and the clouds above us, down into the clear, fluent, unfathomable depth of nature, how startling is the silence of it, how amazing the flow of life, how absorbing the mystery. Unceasingly the essence of things is taking shape in the matter of things, and this unspeakable process we call birth and growth. Awhile the spirit and the matter fade away together, and it is this that we call decadence, death. These two happenings seem jointed and interdependent, blended into one like a bubble and its iridescence, and they seem borne along upon a slowly moving air. This air is wonderful past all understanding.

Yet to the steadfast eye of one standing upon the shore of things, looking chiefly and most lovingly upon that side on which the sun shines and that we feel joyously to be life, the heart is ever gladdened by the beauty, the exquisite spontaneity, with which life seeks and takes on its forms in an accord perfectly responsive to its needs. It seems ever as though the life and the form were absolutely one and inseparable, so adequate is the sense of fulfillment.

Whether it be the sweeping eagle in his flight or the open apple-blossom, the toiling work-horse, the blithe swan, the branching oak, the winding stream at its base, the drifting clouds, over all the coursing sun, form ever follows function, and this is the law. Where function does not change form does not change. The granite rocks, the ever-brooding hills, remain for ages; the lightning lives, comes into shape, and dies in a twinkling.

It is the pervading law of all things organic, and inorganic, of all things physical and metaphysical, of all things human and all things superhuman, of all true manifestations of the head, of the heart, of the soul, that the life is recognizable in its expression, that form ever follows function. This is the law.

Shall we, then, daily violate this law in our art? Are we so decadent, so imbecile, so utterly weak of eyesight, that we cannot perceive this truth so simple, so very simple? Is it indeed a truth so transparent that we see through it but do not see it? Is it really then, a very marvelous thing, or is it rather so commonplace, so everyday, so near a thing to us, that we cannot perceive that the shape, form, outward expression, design or whatever we may choose, of the tall office building should in the very nature of things follow the functions of the building, and that where the function does not change, the form is not to change?

Does this not readily, clearly, and conclusively show that the lower one or two stories will take on a special character suited to the special needs, that the tiers of typical offices, having the same unchanging function, shall continue in the same unchanging form, and that as to the attic, specific and conclusive as it is in its very nature, its function shall equally be so in force, in significance, in continuity, in conclusiveness of outward expression? From this results, naturally, spontaneously, unwittingly, a three-part division, not from any theory, symbol, or fancied logic.

And thus the design of the tall office building takes its place with all other architectural types made when architecture, as has happened once in many years, was a living art. Witness the Greek temple, the Gothic cathedral, the medieval fortress.

And thus, when native instinct and sensibility shall govern the exercise of our beloved art; when the known law, the respected law, shall be that form ever follows function; when our architects shall cease struggling and prattling handcuffed and vainglorious in the asylum of a foreign school; when it is truly felt, cheerfully accepted, that this law opens up the airy sunshine of green fields, and gives to us

13. Auditorium Building, from the East, Chicago *(Chicago Architectural Photograph. Co.)*

14. Auditorium Theatre, proscenium and "Golden Arches" *(Chicago Historical Society)*

15. Getty Tomb, bronze doors and entrance arch, Chicago *(Chicago Architectural Photograph. Co.)*

16. Wainwright Building, St. Louis *(Keystone View Co.)*

17. Carson Pirie Scott Store, Chicago *(Chicago Architectural Photograph. Co.)*

a freedom that the very beauty and sumptuousness of the outworking of the law itself as exhibited in nature will deter any sane, any sensitive man from changing into license, when it becomes evident that we are merely speaking a foreign language with a noticeable American accent, whereas each and every architect in the land might, under the benign influence of this law, express in the simplest, most modest, most natural way that which it is in him to say; that he might really and would surely develop his own characteristic individuality, and that the architectural art with him would certainly become a living form of speech, a natural form of utterance, giving surcease to him and adding treasures small and great to the growing art of his land; when we know and feel that Nature is our friend, not our implacable enemy — that an afternoon in the country, an hour by the sea, a full open view of one single day, through dawn, high noon, and twilight, will suggest to us so much that is rhythmical, deep, and eternal in the vast art of architecture, something so deep, so true, that all the narrow formalities, hard-and-fast rules, and strangling bonds of the schools cannot stifle it in us — then it may be proclaimed that we are on the high-road to a natural and satisfying art, an architecture that will soon become a fine art in the true, the best sense of the word, an art that will live because it will be of the people, for the people, and by the people.

The Young Man in Architecture

This essay was read before the annual convention of the Architectural League of America, Chicago, June 1900.

It is my premise that the Architectural League of America has its being in a sense of discontent with conditions now prevailing in the American malpractice of the architectural art; in a deep and wide sense of conviction that no aid is to be expected from the generation now representing that malpractice; and in the instinctive feeling that, through banding together, force, discretion and coherence may be given to the output of these feelings which are, in themselves, for the time being, vague and miscellaneous, however intensely they may be felt.

Did I not believe that this statement substantially represents the facts, I should be the last to take an interest in your welfare. I would be indifferent concerning what you did or what you did not.

That you have abundant reason for discontent needs no proof; let him read who runs through the streets.

That you have cause for discontent is evident. That you should feel discontent gives one a delightfully cynical sense of shock, and a new-born desire to believe in the good, the true, the beautiful and the young.

American architecture is composed, in the hundred, of ninety parts aberration, eight parts indifference, one part poverty and one part Little Lord Fauntleroy. You can have the prescription filled at any architectural department-store, or select architectural millinery establishment.

As it is my desire to speak from the viewpoint that architecture should be practised as an art and not strictly as a commercial pursuit, and as I am assuming that you agree with me in this respect, we may now pertinently inquire wherein does this American architecture differ from the architecture of the past.

It differs in little, if in anything, provided we except the few great epochs.

Human nature has changed but little since the time man was slaughterer or the slaughtered of the great white bear.

Seldom, in the past, has man thought of aught but war, which menaced his life;

religion, which menaced his soul; hunger, which threatened his stomach; or love, which concerned his progeny.

From time to time this tempestuous human sky has calmed, for a divine moment, and the glory of man has shone forth upon a fertile land. Then came again the angry elements —and the sun departed.

This, in brief, is the recurrent history of man from the beginning. You may change the values in the formula to suit the epoch, the century or the generation.

Ninety-nine years of the hundred the thoughts of nine hundred and ninety-nine people of the thousand are sordid. This always has been true. Why should we expect a change?

Of one hundred so-called thoughts that the average man thinks (and thus he has ever thought), ninety-nine are illusions, the remaining one a caprice.

From time to time in the past, these illusions have changed their focus and become realities, and the one caprice has become an overwhelming desire.

These changes were epoch-making.

And the times were called golden.

In such times came the white-winged angel of sanity.

And the great styles arose in greeting.

Then soon the clear eye dimmed.

The sense of reality was lost.

Then followed architectures, to all intents and purposes quite like American architecture of today:

Wherein the blind sought much discourse of color.

The deaf to discuss harmonics.

The dry of heart twaddled about the divinity of man.

The mentally crippled wrought fierce combats in the arena of logic.

And so it has come about that the white-winged angel has been on a far journey these six hundred years.

Now, insisting for the moment, in spite of the hierarchy, that this white-winged absence is of gentle sex, I entreat your close attention:

Let radiant and persuasive Youth lure her back again to earth!

For that she hovers in the visible blue of your firmament I can prove to you beyond a gossamer of doubt.

That she awaits with eager ear the spring-enthralling voice of adolescence, the clear sweet morning-call of a pure heart, the spontaneity and jocund fervor of a bright and winning mind, the glance of a modest and adoring eye!

That she awaits.

That she has so long awaited.

That she cannot make herself first known to you —

Alas, 'tis of her enchantment that she is invisible and dumb!

Perhaps this is enough of poesy —

Let us say, enough likewise of the prevailing cacophony; of

The howling of the vast and general horde of Bedlamites.

The purring of the select company of Ruskinites.

The gasping of the Emersonites.

The rasping of the Spencerites.

The moaning of the Tennysonites.

The whimper of the æsthetes.

The yowling of the reformers.

The yapping of strenuous livers.

The rustle of the rustlers.

The hustle of the hustlers.

The howl of the taxpayers.

And the clang of the trolley car —

All, "signs, omens and predictions" of our civilization.

We are commanded to know that there is much of mystery, much of the esoteric, in the so-called architectural styles. That there is a holiness in so-called "pure art" which the hand of the Modern may not profane.

So be it.

Let us be the Cat.

And let the pure art be the King.

We will look at him.

And we will also look at the good king's good children, the great styles.

And at his retinue of bastards, the so-called "other styles."

There is, or at least there is said to be, a certain faculty of the mind, whereby the mind or the faculty, as you choose, is on the one hand enabled to dissolve a thing into its elements, and, on the other hand, to build up these or similar elements into the same or a similar thing. This process is, I believe, called Logic — the first operation going by the name, analysis, and the second, synthesis. Some men possess the half-faculty of separating; others the half-faculty of upbuilding. When the whole faculty exists in one man, in a moderate degree, he is said to be gifted. When he has it in a high degree, he is said to be highly gifted; and when in the highest degree he is called a genius or a master mind. When a man has neither the one half-faculty nor the other half-faculty he is mentally sterile.

I fear lest the modern architect be placed in this category, by reason of his devious ways.

Let us suppose ourselves, nevertheless, moderately gifted and apply our analysis to the great styles:

Presto — dissolve!

We have as residuum, two uprights, and a horizontal connecting them.

We have two bulky masses and an arch connecting them.

Revolve your arches and masses and you have a dome.

Do the trick a few times more with a few other "styles" and you have the Elements of Architecture.

We approach in the same way a master mind — and all speedily disappears — leaving insoluble Desire.

The architectural elements, in their baldest form, the desire of the heart in its most primitive, animal form, are the foundation of architecture.

They are the dust and the breathing spirit.

All the splendor is but a gorgeous synthesis of these.

The logic of the books, is, at best, dry reading; and, morover, it is nearly or quite dead, because it comes at second hand.

The human mind, in operation, is the original document.

Try to read it.

If you find this for the moment too difficult and obscure, try to study a plant as it grows from its tiny seed and expands toward its full fruition. Here is a process, a spectacle, a poem, or whatever you may wish to call it, not only absolutely logical in essence, because exhibiting in its highest form the unity and the quality of analysis and synthesis, but which is of vastly greater import, vital and inevitable: and it is specifically to this phenomenon that I wish to draw your earnest attention — if it be true and I sincerely hope that such is the fact, that you wish to become real architects, not the imitation brand. For I wish to show to you, or at least intimate to you, how naturally and smoothly and inevitably the human mind will operate if it be not harassed or thwarted in its normal and instinctive workings.

Some day, watch the sun as he rises, courses through the sky, and sets.

Note what your part of the earth does meanwhile.

Ponder the complex results of this simple single cause.

Some year, observe how rhythmically the seasons follow the sun. Note their unfailing, spontaneous logic; their exquisite analysis and synthesis; their vital inevitable balance.

When you have time or opportunity, spare a moment to note a wild bird, flying; a wave, breaking on the shore. Try to grasp the point that, while these things are common, they are by no means commonplace.

Note any simple thing or act whatsoever provided, only, it be natural, not artificial — the nearer undisturbed nature the better; if in the wilderness, better still, because wholly away from the perverting influence of man.

Whenever you have done these things attentively and without mental bias or preoccupation, wholly receptive in your humor, there will come to your intelligence a luminous idea of simplicity, and equally luminous idea of a resultant organic complexity, which, together, will constitute the first significant step in your architectural education, because they are the basis of rhythm.

There will gently dawn in your mind an awakening of something vital, something organic, something elemental that is urging things about you through their beautiful, characteristic rhythms, and that is holding them in most exquisite balance.

A little later you will become aware with amazement that this same impulse is working on your own minds, and that never before had you suspected it. This will be the second step in your architectural education.

Later you will perceive, with great pleasure, that there is a notable similarity, an increasing sympathy between the practical workings of your own minds and the workings of nature about you.

When this perception shall have grown into a definite clear-cut consciousness, it will constitute the closing of the first chapter and the opening of all the remaining chapters in your architectural education, for you will have arrived at the basis of organized thinking.

You will have observed doubtless, that, thus far, while endeavoring to lead you toward a sane and wholesome conception of the basis of the architectural art, I have said not a word about books, photographs or plates. I have done this advisedly, for I am convinced beyond the shadow of a doubt that never can you acquire from books, or the like, alone, even a remote conception of what constitutes the real, the living, architectural art. It has been tried for generations upon generations with one unvarying result: dreary, miserable failure.

To appreciate a book at its just value, you must first know what words signify, what men signify, and what nature signifies.

Books, taken in their totality, have one ostensible object, one just function: namely, to make a record of Man's relation to his fellow men and to Nature, and the relation of both of these to an all-prevading, Inscrutable Spirit.

To these relations, Mankind, in its prodigious effort to define its own status, has given thousands upon thousands of names.

These names are called words.

Each word has a natural history.

Each word is not the simple thing it appears, but, on the contrary, it is a highly complex organism, carrying in its heart more smiles, more tears, more victories, more downfalls, more bloody sweats, more racial agonies than you can ever dream of.

Some of these words are very old —

They still cry with the infancy of the race.

Therefore, should I begin by putting into your hands a book or its equivalent, I would, according to my philosophy, be guilty of an intellectual crime.

I would be as far from the true path as I now most heartedly regard most teachers of the architectural art to be.

I would be as reckless and brutal as my predecessors.

But I would not be as unconscious of it as they appear to be.

Therefore, I say with emphasis, begin by observing.

Seek to saturate your minds by direct personal contact with things that are natural — not sophisticated.

Strive to form your own judgments, at first in very small things, gradually in larger and larger things. Do not lean upon the judgment of others if it is reasonably within your power to form your own.

Thus, though you may often stumble and wander, such experiences will be valuable because personal; it is far better that they occur in youth rather than in maturer years. Gradually by virtue of this very contact with things you will acquire that sure sense of physical reality which is the necessary first step in a career of independent thinking.

But strive not, I caution you, after what is called originality. If you do you will be starting in exactly the wrong way. I wish distinctly to impress upon you that what I am advocating, and what I am in turn striving to point out to you, is the normal development of your minds. That if the mind is properly nurtured, properly trained, and left free to act with spontaneity, individuality of expression will come to you as naturally as the flower comes to the plant — for it is nature's law.

When you begin to feel the flow and stimulation of mind which are first fruits of wholesome exercise of the faculties, you may begin to read the books. Read them carefully and cautiously, not superciliously.

Bear in mind that books, generally speaking, are composed mainly of sophistries, assumptions, borrowings, stealings, inadequate presentations or positive perversions of truth.

The author, too frequently, is posing, masquerading or ambuscading. His idea is to impress you. He himself well knows how little he has to say that can in strictness be classed as truth in his possession only.

You will soon have no trouble in discerning the exception —and the exceptions, by their value, will conclusively prove the rule.

Later you may turn from the documents called books to the documents called buildings, and you will find that what I have said of books applies with equal force to buildings and to their authors. Soon you will be enabled to separate the wheat from the chaff.

Thus, one after the other, you may pass in review the documents called Music, Painting, Sculpture, Agriculture, Commerce, Manufactures, Government, etc.

You will find them, for your purposes, much alike.

You will, ere long, acquire an inkling of the fullness and the emptiness of these documents, if, as I advise, you keep closely in touch with nature.

When you know something more of the working of the human mind than you now know (and the day will not be long in coming if you follow the program I am indicating), you will not be greatly surprised, when taking a backward glance, that those in high places today seemingly believe or profess to believe that the fruit need bear no relation to the tree.

You will be no more amused than I am at the psychological irony presented by the author of a callously illogical building declaring in solemn tones that it is the product of a logical mind.

You will smile with wonderment when you recall that it is now taught, or appears now to be taught, that like does not beget like; whereas you will know that nature has for unnumbered ages and at every instant proclaimed that like can beget nothing but its like:

That a logical mind will beget a logical building.

That an illogical mind will beget an illogical building.

That perversity will bring forth perversity.

That the children of the mind will reveal the parent.

You will smile again when you reflect that it was held in your youth that there was no necessary relationship between function and form. That function was one thing, form another thing.

True, it might have seemed queer to some if a pine-tree had taken on the form of a rattlesnake, and, standing vertically on its tail, had brought forth pine cones; or that a rattlesnake, vice versa, should take on the form of a pine-tree and wriggle along the ground biting the heel of the passer-by.

Yet this suggestion is not a whit queerer than are some of the queer things now filling the architectural view, as, for instance, a steel frame function in a masonry form —

Imagine, for instance:

Horse-eagles.

Pumpkin-bearing frogs.

Frog-bearing pea vines.

Tarantula-potatoes.

Sparrows in the form of whales, picking up crumbs in the streets.

If these combinations seem incongruous and weird, I assure you in all seriousness that they are not a whit more so than the curiosities encountered with such frequency by the student of what nowadays passes for architecture.

With this difference, only, that, inasmuch as the similarity is chiefly mental, it can produce no adequate impression on those who have never felt the sensitizing effect of thought.

You will remember that it was held that a national style must be generations in forming — and that the inference you were to draw from this was that the individual should take no thought for his own natural development because it would be futile so to do — because, as it were, it would be an impertinent presumption.

I tell you exactly the contrary: Give all your thought to individual development, which it is entirely within your province and power to control; and let the nationality come in due time as a consequence of the inevitable convergence of thought.

If anyone tells you that it is impossible within a lifetime to develop and perfect a complete individuality of expression, a well-ripened and perfected personal style, tell him that you know better and that you will prove it by your lives. Tell him with little ceremony, whoever he may be, that he is grossly ignorant of first principles — that he lives in the dark.

It is claimed that the great styles of the past are the sources of inspiration for this architecture of the present. This in fact is the vehement assertion of those who "worship" them.

Would you believe it? Really, would you believe it!

So it appears that like can beget its unlike after all. That a noble style may beget, through the agency of an ignoble mind, an ignoble building.

It may be true that a blooded male may beget, through a mongrel female, a cur progeny. But the application of this truth to the above instance wherein occurs the great word Inspiration implies a brutal perversion of meaning and a pathetic depravity in those who use that word for their sinister ends.

For inspiration, as I conceive it, is the intermediary between God and man, the pure fruition of the soul at one with immaculate nature, the greeting of noble minds.

To use this word in a tricky endeavor to establish a connection legitimizing the architecture of the present as the progeny of the noblest thought in the past is, to my mind, a blasphemy, and so it should appear to yours.

In truth the American architecture of today is the offspring of an illegitimate commerce with the mongrel styles of the past.

Do not deceive yourselves for a moment as to this.

It is a harsh indictment.

But it is warranted by the facts.

Yet let us not be too severe. Let us remember and make what allowance we may for the depressing, stultifying, paralyzing influence of an unfortunate education.

After all, every American man has had to go to school. And everything that he has been taught over and above the three R's has been in essence for his mental undoing.

I cannot possibly emphasize this lamentable fact too strongly.

And the reason, alas, is so clear, so forcible, so ever present — as you will see.

We live under a form of government called Democracy. And we, the people of the United States of America, constitute the most colossal instance known in history of a people seeking to verify the fundamental truth that self-government is Nature's law for Man.

It is of the essence of Democracy that the individual man is free in his body and free in his soul.

It is a corollary therefrom, that he must govern or restrain himself, both as to bodily acts and mental acts — that, in short, he must set up a responsible government within his own individual person.

It implies that highest form of emancipation — of liberty physical, mental and spiritual, by virtue whereof man calls the gods to judgment, while he heeds the divinity of his own soul.

It is the ideal of Democracy that the individual man should stand self-centered, self-governing — an individual sovereign, an individual god.

Now who will assert, specifically, that our present system of higher architectural education is in accord with this aspiration? That the form, Education, bears any essential relation other than that of antagonism to the function Democracy?

It is our misfortune that it does not.

We as a people are too youthful. We are too new among the world forces. We are too young. We have not yet had time to discover precisely the trouble, though we feel in our hearts that something is amiss. We have been too busy.

And so comes about the incongruous spectacle of the infant Democracy taking its mental nourishment at the withered breast of Despotism.

To understand it from our point of view, examine: These are the essential points:

We are to revere authority.

We are to take everything at second hand.

We are to believe measurements are superior to thought.

We are advised not to think.

We are cautioned that by no possibility can we think as well as did our predecessors.

We are not to examine, not to test, not to prove.

We are to regard ourselves as the elect, because, forsooth, we have been instructed by the elect.

We must conform.

We are not to go behind the scenes.

We are to do as we are told and ask no foolish questions.

We are taught that there is a royal road to our art.

We are taught hero-worship —

We are not taught what the hero worshipped.

We are taught that nature is one thing, man another thing.

We are taught that God is one thing, man another thing.

Does this conform to the ideal of Democracy?

Is this a fitting overture to the world's greatest drama?

Is it not extraordinary that we survive it even in part?

Is it a wonder that our representative architecture is vapid, foolish, priggish, insolent and pessimistic?

Manifestly you cannot become truly educated in the schools.

Ergo, you must educate yourselves.

There is no other course, — no other hope.

For the schools have not changed much in my generation; they will, I fear, not change much in your generation — and soon it will be too late for you.

Strive, strive therefore, while you are young and eager, to apply to your mental development the rules of physical development.

Put yourselves in training, so to speak.

Strive to develop in your minds the agility, flexibility, precision, poise, endurance and judgment of the athlete.

Seek simple, wholesome, nourishing food for the mind.

You will be surprised and charmed with the results.

The human mind in its natural state, not drowsed and stupefied by a reactionary education, is the most marvelously active agency in all nature.

You may trust implicitly in the results of this activity if its surroundings are wholesome.

The mind will inevitably reproduce what it feeds upon.

If it feeds upon filth, it will reproduce filth.

If it feeds upon dust, it will reproduce dust.

If it feeds upon nature, it will reproduce nature.

If it feeds upon man, it will reproduce man.

If it feeds upon all of these, it will reproduce all of these.

It will reproduce infallibly whatever it is fed upon.

It is a wonderful machine — its activity cannot wholly be quenched except by death. It may be slowed down or accelerated — it cannot be stopped.

It may be abused in every conceivable way, but it will not stop, even in insanity, even in sleep.

So beware how you tamper with this marvelous mechanism, for it will record inevitably, in all its output, whatever you do to it.

The human mind is the summation of all the ages. It holds in trust the wisdom and the folly of all the past.

Beware what you do to it, for it will give you bad for your bad, good for your good —

It is a mechanism of such inconceivable delicacy and complexity.

Man through his physical infancy is most carefully nurtured.

His delicate and fragile, helpless little body is tenderly watched with all the solicitude of parental affection.

Indeed, under the law he is still a child until the age of twenty-one.

But his mind! Who cares for his mind?

After he has passed from the simple, beautiful ministrations at his mother's knee, who guards this ineffably delicate impressionable organism?

Oh, the horror of it!

Oh, ye gods, where is justice, where is mercy, where is love!

To think that the so-called science of political economy is so futile, so drugged with feudalism, that it has not noted this frightful waste, this illogical interruption of the happiness of the human family, this stark, staring incongruity in our education.

That it does not perceive, in its search for the sources of wealth, the latent richness of the human mind, its immense wealth of practical possibilities, the clearly marked indications of enormous productiveness — a productiveness sane and of vital consequence to the public welfare: so much for a science which regards man as a mechanical unit.

It is typical in a measure of the learning we have donned as a misfit garment.

You have every reason to congratulate yourselves that you are young — for you have so much the less to unlearn, and so much the greater fund of enthusiasm.

A great opportunity is yours. The occasion confronts you. The future is in your hands — will you accept the responsibility or will you evade it?

That is the only vital question I have come here to put to you.

I do not ask an answer now.

I am content with putting the question.

For it is the first time that the question ever has been put squarely to you.

I ask only that you consider this:

Do you intend, or do you not intend, do you wish or do you not wish, to become architects in whose care an unfolding Democracy may entrust the interpretation of its material wants, its psychic aspirations?

In due time doubtless you will answer in your own way.

But I warn you the time left for an answer in the right way is acutely brief.

For young as you are, you are not as young as you were yesterday —

And tomorrow?

Tomorrow!

Education

This essay was read before the annual convention of the Architectural League of America, Toronto, in 1902; published here for the first time.

After the long night, and longer twilight, we envisage a dawn-era: an era in which the minor law of tradition shall yield to the greater law of creation, in which the spirit of repression shall fail to repress.

Man at last is become emancipated, and now is free to think, to feel, to act — free to move toward the goal of the race.

Humanitarianism slowly is dissolving the sway of utilitarianism, and an enlightened unselfishness is on its way to supersede a benighted rapacity. And all this, as a deep-down force in nature awakens to its strength, animating the growth and evolution of democracy.

Under the beneficent sway of this power, the hold of illusion and suppression is passing; the urge of reality is looming in force, extent and penetration, and the individual now is free to become a man, in the highest sense, if so he wills.

There is no estoppel to his imagination.

No limitation to the workings of his mind.

No violence to the dignity of his soul.

The tyranny alike of church and state has been curbed, and true power is now known to reside where forever it must remain — in the people.

Rapidly we are changing from an empirical to a scientific attitude of mind; from an inchoate to an organic trend of thinking. Inevitably we are moving toward the larger significances of life and the larger relations of the individual to that life as embodied in the people.

Truly we are face to face with great things.

The mind of youth should be squarely turned to these phenomena. He should be told, as he regards them, how long and bitterly the race has struggled that he may have freedom.

His mind should be prepared to cooperate in the far-reaching changes now under way, and which will appear to him in majestic simplicity, breadth and clearness when the sun of democracy shall have arisen but a little higher in the firmament of the race, illumining more steadily and deeply than now the mind and will of the individual, the minds and wills of the millions of men — his own mind and his own will.

He should be shown, as a panorama, as a great drama, the broad sweep and flow of the vast life in which he is a unit, an actor; and, that of a vital necessity, fundamental principles must nourish the roots of his lifework and permeate its branches; just as they must animate the work and life of the neighbor — for the general harmony, the good of all.

He should be shown what the reality of history shows, namely, that optimism is an abiding emotion in the heart of the race: an emotion arising from the constant pressure of aspiring democracy seeking its own.

He must be imbued with that pride, that sure quality of honor which are the ethical flower of self-government and the sense of moral responsibility. He must be distinctly taught his responsibility to his fellow men.

He should be taught that a mind empty of ideals is indeed an empty mind, and that there will be demanded of him, if not self-sacrifice, at the least self-restraint, self-denial, and that the highest of ideals is the ideal of democracy.

To this end, history must be illumined for him, and the story of his own day clarified.

To this end he must be inspired first and always with a clear, full conception of what democracy truly means, what it has signified and now signifies for the emancipation of man; what it costs [has cost] in time, blood and sorrow, that it might emerge from the matrix of humanity; how priceless is it as a heritage — the most priceless of heritages; and how valiantly, how loyally, how jealously should he, as copartner in its beneficence, cherish its superb integrity. He, born into democracy, and therefore especially apt to deem it negligible, must be taught with persistent, untiring assiduity, by constant precept, warning and eulogy, that its existence, its perpetuation, its development, is as necessary to the fullness of life as is the physical air he breathes.

The beauty of nature should most lovingly be shown to him, and he be encouraged to venerate and to prize that beauty.

He should be taught that he and the race are inseparably a part of nature and that his strength must come of her bounty.

His mind and heart should be opened to the inspiration of nature, his eye directed to the borderland of that infinite and unknown toward which she leads the thoughtful view, that he may know how great is man and yet how fragile; so will he see life in its momentous balance.

He should be taught that the full span of one's life is but a little time in which to accomplish a worthy purpose; and yet should he be shown what men have done, what man can do.

An art of expression should begin with childhood, and the lucid use of one's mother tongue should be typical of that art.

The sense of reality should be strengthened from the beginning, yet by no means at the cost of those lofty illusions we call patriotism, veneration, love.

He should be taught that high ideals make a people strong.

225. *Education*

That decay comes when ideals wane.

He should be taught that civilization has a higher reach than the goal of material things, that its apex lies in the mind and the heart.

He should be taught common honesty and that there is but one standard of honesty.

He should be taught to despise hypocrisy and cant.

This, in my view, is the fundamental of education, because it leads straight to manhood, because it makes for the moral and mental vigor of the race, because it leads toward a constantly expanding sense of humanity, because under its aegis a true art may flourish.

I am not of those who believe in lackadaisical methods. On the contrary, I advocate a vigorous, thorough, exact mental training which shall fit the mind to expand upon and grasp large things and yet properly to perceive in their just relation the significance of small ones — to discriminate accurately as to quantity and quality — and thus to develop individual judgment, capacity and independence.

But at the same time I am of those who believe that gentleness is a greater, surer power than force, and that sympathy is a safer power by far than is intellect. Therefore would I train the individual sympathies as carefully in all their delicate warmth and tenuity as I would develop the mind in alertness, poise and security.

Nor am I of those who despise dreamers. For the world would be at the level of zero were it not for its dreamers — gone and of today. He who dreamed of democracy, far back in a world of absolutism, was indeed heroic, and we of today awaken to the wonder of his dream.

How deep this dreamer saw into the heart of man!

So would I nurse the dreamer of dreams, for in him nature broods while the race slumbers.

So would I teach the art of dreaming, as I would teach the science of thinking, as I would teach the value of action.

He who knows naught of dreaming can, likewise, never attain the heights of power and possibility in persuading the mind to act.

He who dreams not creates not.

For vapor must arise in the air before the rain can fall.

The greatest man of action is he who is the greatest, and a life-long, dreamer. For in him the dreamer is fortified against destruction by a far-seeing eye, a virile mind, a strong will, a robust courage.

And so has perished the kindly dreamer — on the cross or in the garret.

A democracy should not let its dreamers perish. They are its life, its guaranty against decay.

Thus would I expand the sympathies of youth.

Thus would I liberate and discipline all the constructive faculties of the mind and encourage true insight, true expression, real individuality.

Thus would I concentrate the powers of will.

Thus would I shape character.

Thus would I make good citizens.

And thus would I lay the foundations for a generation of real architects — real, because true, men, and dreamers in action.

What Is Architecture: *A Study in the American People of Today*

This, a revised form of the essay, was published first in the *American Contractor,* January 1906.

The intellectual trend of the hour is toward simplification. The full powers of the modern scientific mind are now directed, with a common consent, toward searching out the few and simple principles that are believed to underlie the complexity of Nature, and such investigation is steadily revealing a unitary impulse underlying all men and all things.

This method of analysis reveals a curious aspect of Man, namely: that as he thinks, so he acts; and, conversely, one may read in his acts what he thinks — his real thoughts, be it understood, not what he avows he thinks. For all men think, all men act. To term a man unthinking is a misuse of words; what really is meant is that he does not think with accuracy, fitness and power. If, then, it be true that as a man thinks so must he act in inevitable accordance with his thought, so is it true that society, which is but a summation of individuals, acts precisely as it thinks. Thus are the thoughts of a people to be read in the acts of a people, as clearly as words are read upon the printed page.

If, in like manner, we apply this method of analysis to the complex spread of historical and contemporaneous architecture, we perceive, clearly revealed in their simplicity, its three elementary forms, namely, the pier, the lintel and the arch. These are the three, the only three letters, from which has expanded the Architectural Art as a great and superb language wherewith Man has expressed, through the generations, the changing drift of his thoughts. Thus, throughout the past and the present, each building stands as a social act. In such act we read that which cannot escape our analysis, for it is indelibly fixed in the building, namely, the nature of the thoughts of the individual and the people whose image the building is or was.

Perhaps I should not leave the three elements, pier, lintel and arch, thus baldly set forth. It may not appear to the reader that the truth concerning them is as clear and simple as I state it. He may think, for example, that there was a marked difference between the Egyptian and the Greek Architectures, even though both were based on pier and lintel only. There was a marked difference. The difference that existed between the Egyptian and the Greek minds. The Egyptian animated pier and lintel with his thought — he could not do otherwise; and the Egyptian temple took form as an Egyptian act — it could not be otherwise. So Greek thought, clearly defined, took form in the Greek temple, clearly defined, and the Greek temple stood clearly forth as a Greek act. Yet both were as simply pier-and-lintel as I, in setting one brick upon two separated other bricks, simply expose the principles of pier and lintel.

Similarly the Roman aqueduct and the medieval cathedral were both in the pier-and-arch form. But what a far cry from Roman thought to medieval thought! And how clearly is that difference in thought shown in the differences in form taken on in each case by pier and arch, as each structure in its time stood forth as an act of the people. How eloquently these structures speak to us of the militant and simple power of Roman thought, of the mystic yearning of medieval thought.

But, you may say, these structures were not acts of the people, rather, in one case the act of an emperor, in the other case an act of the church. Very well; but what really was the emperor but an act of the people — expressing the thought of the people; and what was the church but similarly the thought of the people in action? When the thought of the Roman people changed, the vast Roman fabric disintegrated; when the thought of the medieval people changed, the vitality of the church subsided exactly in proportion as the supporting thought of the people was withdrawn. Thus every form of government, every social institution, every undertaking, however great, however small, every symbol of enlightenment or degradation, each and all have sprung and are still springing from the life of the people, and have ever formed and are now as surely forming images of their thought. Slowly by centuries, generations, years, days, hours, the thought of the people has changed; so with precision have their acts responsively changed; thus thoughts and acts have flowed and are flowing ever onward, unceasingly onward, involved within the impelling power of Life. Throughout this stream of human life, and thought, and activity, men have ever felt the need to build; and from the need arose the power to build. So, as they thought, they built; for, strange as it may seem, they could build in no other way. As they built, they made, used and left behind them records of their thinking. Then, as through the years new men came with changed thoughts, so arose new buildings in consonance with the change of thought — the building always the expression of the thinking. Whatever the character of the thinking, just so was the character of the building. Pier, lintel and arch changed in form, purpose and expression, following, with the fidelity of Life, Man's changing thoughts as he moved in the flow of his destiny — as he was moved ever onward by a drift unseen and unknown — and which is now flowing and is still unseen and unknown.

This flow of building we call Historical Architecture. At no time and in no instance has it been other than an index of the flow of the thought of the people — an emanation from the inmost life of the people.

Perhaps you think this is not so; perhaps you think the feudal lord built the fortified castle. So he did, ostensibly. But where did his need and power so to build come from? From his retainers. And whence came the power of his retainers? From the people. As the people thought, so they acted. And thus the power of the feudal lord rested upon the thought, the belief of the people; upon their need and upon their power. Thus all power rests upon the consent of the people, that is, upon their thought. The instant their thought begins to change, that instant the power, resting upon it and sanctioned by it, begins its waning. Thus the decay of the old and the formation of the new are synchronous effects of one cause. That single cause is: Thought. Thus we perceive that the simplest aspect of all human activity is change.

To analyze the influences that cause thought to change would take me, now, too far afield. Suffice it to say that thought, once having undergone change, does not again become the same — however great the lapse in time. Thus is there ever new birth, never rebirth.

It may now become clear to my reader that we ought, in viewing historic Architecture, to cease to regard it under the artificial classification of styles, as is now the accepted way, and to consider (as is more natural and more logical) each building of the past and the present as a product and index of the civilization of the time, also, as the product and index of the thought of the people of the time and place. In this way we shall develop in our minds a much broader, clearer panorama of the actual living flow of Architecture through the ages; and grasp the clear, simple, accurate notion, that Architecture always has been, and still is, a simple impulse of which the manifestation in varied form is continuously changing.

I should add, perhaps, that, in speaking of the people, I do not use the word in the unhappy sense of the lower classes, so-called. I mean all the people; and I look upon all the people as constituting a social organism.

I am quite aware that these are views not generally held among architects. Indeed you will not find a thesis of this kind set forth in books or taught in schools. For the prevailing view concerning Architecture is strangely artificial and fruitless, as indeed are the current American ideas concerning almost any phase of the welfare of all the people. That is to say; in our democratic land, ideas, thoughts, are weirdly, indeed destructively, undemocratic — an aspect of our current civilization which, later, I shall consider.

I therefore ask my reader, for the time being at least, to repose sufficient confidence in my statements, that he may lay aside his existing notions concerning Architecture, which are of necessity traditional, and, as such, acquired habits of thinking, unanalyzed by him; and thus lay his mind open to receive and consider the simple and more natural views which make up my paper, to the end that he may perceive how far astray we are from an Architecture natural, truthful and wholesome, such as should characterize a truly democratic people. I ask this because the welfare of democracy is my chief concern in life; and because I have always regarded Architecture, and still so regard it, as merely one of the activities of a people, and, as such, necessarily in harmony with all the others. For as a people thinks concerning Architecture, so it thinks concerning everything else; and as it thinks concerning any other thing, so it thinks concerning Architecture; for the thought of a people, however complicated it may appear, is all of-a-piece, and represents the balance of heredity and environment at the time.

I trust, further, that a long disquisition is not necessary in order to show that the attempt at imitation, by us of this day, of the by-gone forms of building, is a procedure unworthy of a free people; and that the dictum of schools, that Architecture is finished and done, is a suggestion humiliating to every active brain, and, there-fore, in fact, a puerility and a falsehood when weighed in the scales of truly demo-cratic thought. Such dictum gives the lie, in arrogant fashion, to healthful human experience. It says, in a word: The American people are not fit for democracy. Perhaps they are not. If so, we shall see how and why. We shall see if this alleged unfitness is really normal and natural, or if it is a feudal condition imposed upon the people by a traditional system of inverted thinking. We shall see if those whom we have entrusted with leadership in our matters educational have or have not misled us. We shall see, in a larger sense, if we, as a people, not only have betrayed each other, but have failed in that trust which the world-spirit of democracy placed in our hands, as we, a new people, emerged to fill a new and spacious land.

All of this we shall presently read in our current Architecture, and we shall test the accuracy of that reading by a brief analysis of the thought and activities of the American people as they are expressed in other ways. For, be sure, what we shall find in our Architecture, we shall as surely find elsewhere and everywhere.

If it is assumed that the art of reading is confined to the printed page, we cannot go far. But if we broaden and quicken our sense of reading until it appears to us, in its more vital aspect, as a science, an art of interpretation, we shall go very far in-deed. In truth, there will be no ending of our journey; for the broad field of nature, of human thought and endeavor, will open to us as a book of life, wherein the great-est and the smallest, the most steadfast and the most fleeting, will appear in their true value. Then will our minds have ecsaped slavery to WORDS and be at liberty, in the open air of reality, freely and fully to deal with THINGS.

Indeed, most of us have, in less or greater measure, this gift of reading things. We come into it naturally; but, curiously enough, many are ashamed because it does not bear the sanction of authority, because it does not bear the official stamp of that much misunderstood word scholarship, a stamp, by the way, which gives currency to most of the notions antagonistic to the development of our common thinking powers. It is this same scholastic fetichism, too, that has caused an illogical gap between the theoretical and the practical. In right thinking such gap cannot exist. A true method of education, therefore, should consist in a careful and complete de-velopment of our common and natural powers of thinking, which, in reality, are vastly greater, infinitely more susceptible to development than is generally assumed. Indeed, the contumacy in which we habitually underrate the latent powers of the average human mind is greatly to our discredit. It constitutes, in fact, a superstition. A superstition whose origin is readily traceable to the scholasticism of past centuries, and to the tenacious notion of social caste. It is definitely the opposite of the modern and enlightened view now steadily gaining ground, that the true spirit of democratic education consists in searching out, liberating and developing the splendid but ob-scured powers of the average man, and particularly those of his children.

It is disquieting to note that the system of education on which we lavish funds with such generous, even prodigal, hand, falls short of fulfilling its true democratic function; and that particularly in the so-called higher branches its tendency appears daily more reactionary, more feudal.

It is not an agreeable reflection that so many of our university graduates lack the trained ability to see clearly, and to think simply, concisely, constructively; that there is perhaps more showing of cynicism than good faith, seemingly more distrust of men than confidence in them, and, withal, no consummate ability to interpret things.

In contrast, we have the active-minded but "uneducated" man, he who has so large a share in our activities. He reads well those things that he believes concern him closely. His mind is active, practical, superficial; and, whether he deals with small things or large, its quality is nearly the same in all cases. His thoughts almost always are concerned with the immediate. His powers of reflection are undeveloped, and thus he ignores those simple, vital things which grow up beside him, and with which, as a destiny, he will some day have to reckon, and will then find himself unprepared. The constructive thinking power of such men, the imaginative reach, the incisive intuition, the forceful will, sometimes amaze us. But when we examine closely we find that all this is but a brilliant superstructure, that the hidden foundation is weak because the foundation-thought was not sought to be placed broad, deep and secure in the humanities. Thus we have at the poles of our thinking two classes of men, each of which believes it is dealing with realities, but both in fact dealing with phantoms; for between them they have studied everything but the real thoughts and the real hearts of the people. They have not sufficiently reckoned with the true and only source both of social stability and of social change. If, in time, such divergence of thought, as it grows in acuteness, shall lead to painful readjustments, such will be but the result, natural and inexorable, of a fatal misunderstanding, the outgrowth of that fatal defect in our system of thinking which is leading us away from our fellows.

If I say that these aspects of our thought are readable in our current Architecture, I am not saying too much, for acts point surely to the parent thoughts, and in everything that men do they leave an indelible imprint of their minds. If this suggestion be followed out, it will become surprisingly clear how each and every building reveals itself naked to the eye; how its every aspect, to the smallest detail, to the lightest move of the hand, reveals the workings of the mind of the man who made it, and who is responsible to us for it. Everything is there for us to read, to interpret; and this we may do at our leisure. The building has not means of locomotion, it cannot hide itself, it cannot get away. There it is, and there it will stay — telling more truths about him who made it, who thought it, than he in his fatuity imagines; revealing his mind and his heart exactly for what they are worth, not a whit more, not a whit less; telling, plainly, the lies he thinks; telling with almost cruel truthfulness of his bad faith, his feeble, wabbly mind, his impudence, his selfish egoism, his mental irresponsibility, his apathy, his disdain for real things. Is it cruelty to analyze thus clearly? Is it vivisection thus to pursue, step by step, to uncover nerve after nerve, dispassionately to probe and test and weigh act after act, thought after thought, to follow every twist and turn of the mind that made the building, sifting and judging it until at last the building says to us: "I am no more a real building than the thing that made me is a real man!"

If so, then it must, correspondingly, be a pleasure and a genuine beneficence to recognize and note, in some other building, the honest effort of an honest man, the kindly willingness and frankness of a sincere mind to give expression to simple, direct, natural thinking, to produce a building as real as the man who made it.

And is it not, as naturally, helpful to recognize and note in still another building a mind perhaps not too well trained, perhaps not very sure of itself, but still courageously seeking a way; the building showing where the mind stumbles and tries again, showing just where the thought is not immanent, not clear, not self-centered?

Is it not the part of wisdom to cheer, to encourage such a mind, rather than to dishearten it with ridicule? To say to it: Learn that the mind works best when allowed to work naturally; learn to do what your problem suggests when you have reduced it to its simplest terms; you will thus find all problems, however complex, taking on a simplicity you had not dreamed of; accept this simplicity, boldly, and with confidence, do not lose your nerve and run away from it, or you are lost, for you are here at the point men so heedlessly call genius — as though it were necessarily rare; for you are here at the point no living brain can surpass in essence, the point all truly great minds seek — the point of vital simplicity — the point of view which so illuminates the mind that the art of expression becomes spontaneous, powerful and unerring, and achievement a certainty; so, if you would seek and express the best that is in yourself, you must search out the best that is in your people; for they are your problem, and you are indissolubly a part of them; it is for you to affirm that which they really wish to affirm, namely, the best that is in them, and they as truly wish you to express the best that is in yourself; if the people seem to have but little faith it is because they have been tricked so long; they are weary of dishonesty, much more weary than you know, and in their hearts they seek honest and fearless men, men simple and clear of mind, loyal to their own manhood and to the people. The American people are now in a stupor; be on hand at the awakening. The lion is now in the net, or the larva in the cocoon — take the simile you prefer.

But to simplify the mind is, in fact, not so easy. Everything is against you. You are surrounded by a mist of tradition which you, alone, must dispel. The schools will not help you, for they too, are in a mist. So, you must develop your mind as best you can. The only safe method is to take nothing for granted, but to analyze, test and examine all things, for yourself, and determine their true values; to sift the wheat from the chaff, and to reduce all thoughts, all activities, to the simple test of honesty. You will be surprised, perhaps, to see how matters that you once deemed solid, fall apart; and, how things that you once deemed inconsequential, take on a new and momentous significance. But in time your mind will clarify and strengthen, and you will have moved into that domain of intellectual power wherein thought discriminates, with justice and clarity, between those things which make for the health, and those which make for the illness of a people. When you have done this, your mind will have reached its balance; you will have something to say, and you will say it with candor.

In the light of the preceding statements, the current mannerisms of architectural criticism must often seem trivial. For of what avail is it to say that this is too small, that too large, this too thick, that too thin, or to quote this, that or the other precedent, when the real question may be: Is not the entire design a mean evasion, a parasitic growth? Why magnify this, that or the other little thing, if the entire scheme of thinking, that the building stands for, is false, and puts a mask upon the people, who want true buildings, but do not know how to get them so long as architects betray them with architectural phrases?

Why have we not more of vital architectural criticism? Is it because our professional critics lack penetration? Because they lack courage? Is it because they, who should be free, are not free? Is it because they, who should know, do not know? Do they not see, or will they not? Do they know such buildings to be lies, and refrain from saying so? Or are they, too, inert of mind? Are their minds, too, benumbed with culture, and their hearts, thus, made faint?

How is a people to know what, for them, a real and fitting Architecture may mean, if it is not first made clear to them that the current and accepted Architecture with which their minds are rapidly being distorted — is false to them! To whom are we to look if not to our trusted critics? And if these fail us, what then?

But — the cynic may observe — what if they do fail us! They write merely in the fashion. For everybody else betrays everybody else. We are all false; and why should a false people expect other than a false Architecture? A people always gets what it deserves, neither more or less. It's up to the people, anyway. If they want a real Architecture, let them become real, themselves. If they do not wish to be betrayed, let them quit betraying. If they really wish loyalty, let them be loyal. If they really wish thinkers, let them so think. If they really do not wish humbug Architecture, let them cease being humbugs themselves. There is so much of truth in this discouraging view, that I shall later clarify it.

For the moment, however, it is significant in passing to note, concerning our architectural periodicals. They float along, aimlessly enough, drifting in the tide of heedless commercialism — their pages filled with views of buildings, buildings, like "words, words, words." Buildings in this "style," that and the other; false always, except now and then and here and there in spots, where the "style" has been dropped in spots, and where, in consequence, the real building appears in spots; or where the architect, under "compulsion," has had to let the "style" go — and do something sensible; or, rarely, where the architect, of his own free will, has chosen to be clean, and has expressed himself with feeling and simple, direct eloquence. The publishers may well say: Make the Architecture and we will publish it; we are but mirrors of the times. If our pages are filled with pretentious trash, it is because architects make it. We publish what our critics write, such as it is, and what architects write, such as it is. We give our readers, who are mostly architects, what they give us. If they want better, they will let us know. We are willing.

And a word concerning "Handbooks on Architecture." All that need be said of them is that they are the blind leading the blind.

Concerning more ambitious works: while they contain certain, or rather uncertain, attempts at philosophy, such discussion is left in the air as a vapor; it is not condensed into terms of vital, present use.

Thus, it happens that the would-be searcher after architectural reality finds no air, no comfort. He is led into a jungle within whose depths his guides are lost, and he is left without compass and without a star. And why is this so? The answer is at hand: Because it has long and tacitly been assumed, by our would-be mentors, that the Architectural Art is a closed book, that the word FINIS was written centuries ago, and that all, obviously, that is left for us moderns is the humble privilege to select, copy and adapt. Because it has not been assumed that ALL buildings have arisen, have stood, and stand as physical symbols of the psychic state of the people.

Because no distinction has been made between WAS and IS. And — what is most dispiriting — this lunacy continues its erratic parade in plain open view of the towering fact that modern science, with devoted patience of research, has evolved, is perfecting and has placed freely at our service the most comprehensive, accurate and high-powered system of organic reasoning that the world has known. These methods and powers, the breadth and fertility of this supreme search for the all-life-process, this most fruitful function of democracy, is, by those connected with the Architectural Art and its teaching, today regarded vacantly. Strangely they undervalue that which for us all, in all truth, in the serenity of human hope, heralds a sunrise for the race. Truly, procreant modern thought, clothed in all its radiance of good will, is a poet, a teacher and a prophet not known in the land of these.

Confronting this ignoble apathy of those we have trusted, let us assume, if it be but in fancy, a normal student of Nature and of Man. Let us assume a virile critic, human and humane, sensitive to all, and aware of this modern daybreak. He will have been a life-seeker of realities. His compass pointing ever to the central fact that all is life; his drinkwater, the knowledge that act and thought are fatefully the same; his nourishing food, the conviction that pure democracy is the deepest-down, the most persistent, while the most obscured desire within the consciousness of man — so equipped, he will have traversed the high seas and the lands, from poles to equator, all latitudes and longitudes of the prolific world of repressed but aspiring humanity. He will hold history, as a staff, in his hand. He will weigh the Modern Man in a just balance, wherein he will set against that man his accountability to all the people. He, as dispassionately, will weigh the people, collectively, against their manifest responsibility and accountability to the child and to the man.

Let us suppose him, now, in his wandering, to have come into Our Land. That he views our Architecture, weighs it, evaluates it; then, turning in thought, looks out upon us, as a people, analyzes us, weighs us, takes our measure, appraises us; that he then places People and Architecture in the great balance of History, and thoughtfully weighs, carefully appraises; then places the people, with all their activities, in the new balance of Democracy, again to weigh, again to appraise; and then puts us with our self-called Common Sense into the serene balance of Nature; and, at the last, weighs Us and Our All, in the fateful balance of All-Encompassing Life — and makes the last appraisement! What, think you, will be his revaluing of our valuations of things, of thoughts, of men? What, in the sifting, would prove wheat, what, in the weighing, would have substance, what in this refiner's fire would be the dross? After his reflections, what will he say? What will he say, after weighing us against our broad, fertile land, with its many waters, its superb and stimulating air, its sumptuous and placid beauty? How will he define us when he shall have searched our minds and hearts? For we cannot hide! What will he say when he shall come to hold us in a close accounting of our stewardship of the talent, Liberty, the treasure that the world has paid so dear in sorrow to transmit to us?

What he might say, would prove a new and most dramatic story.

But surely he might, in part, speak thus:
As you are, so are your buildings; and, as are your buildings, so are you. You and your Architecture are the same. Each is the faithful portrait of the other. To

read the one is to read the other. To interpret the one is to interpret the other. Arising from both, as a miasma: What falsity! What betrayal of the present and the past! Arising from both, as the most thrilling, the more heart-piercing of refrains, as the murmur of a crowd, I hear the cry: "What is the use?" that cry begun in frivolity, passing into cynicism, and, now, deepening into pessimism. That cry which in all time and in all peoples became the cry of death or of revolution, when from frivolity it had merged through pessimism — into an utterance of despair! Your buildings, good, bad and indifferent, arise as warning hands in the faces of all — for they are what you are. Take heed! Did you think Architecture a thing of books — of the past? No! Never! It WAS, ALWAYS, OF ITS PRESENT AND ITS PEOPLE! It, NOW, IS OF THE PRESENT, AND OF YOU! This Architecture is ashamed to be natural, but is not ashamed to lie; so, you, as a people, are ashamed to be natural but are not ashamed to lie. This Architecture is ashamed to be honest, but it is not ashamed to steal; so, then, by the unanswerable logic of Life, you are ashamed to be honest but are not ashamed to steal. This Architecture is filled with hypocrisy and cant. So, likewise, are you, but you say you are not. This Architecture is neurasthenic; so have you burned the candle at both ends. Is then this Democracy? This Architecture shows, ah, so plainly, the decline of Democracy, and a rank new growth of Feudalism — sure sign of a people in peril! This Architecture has no serenity — sure symbol of a people out of balance. This Architecture reveals no lucid guiding principle — nor have you yet evolved a lucid guiding principle, sorely though you now need it! This Architecture shows no love of Nature — you despise Nature. In it is no joy of living — you know not what the fullness of life signifies — you are unhappy, fevered and perturbed. In these buildings the Dollar is vulgarly exalted — and the Dollar you place above Man. You adore it twenty-four hours each day: it is your God! These buildings show lack of great thinkers, real men, among your architects; and, as a people, you are poor in great thinkers, real men — though you now, in your extremity, are in dire need of great thinkers, real men. These buildings show no love of country, no affection for the people. So have you no affection for each other, but secretly will ruin each and any, so much do you love gold, so wantonly will you betray not only your neighbor but yourselves and your own children, for it!

Yet, here and there, a building bespeaks integrity — so have you that much of integrity. All is not false — so are you not wholly false. What leaven is found in your buildings — such leaven is found in you. Weight for weight, measure for measure, sign for sign — as are your buildings, so are you!

A colossal energy is in your buildings, but not true power — so is found in you a frenzied energy, but not the true power of equipoise. Is this an indictment? Not unless you yourselves are an indictment of yourselves. There stand the buildings, they have their unchanging physiognomy. Look! See! Thus, this is a reading, an interpretation.

Here and there are buildings, modest, truthful and sincere: products of a genuine feeling existing in you. They are not truly ashamed where you are not ashamed; they are natural where you are natural; they are democratic where you are democratic. Side by side they stand against the false and feudal — all intermixed. So are your thoughts and acts intermixed, democratic and feudal, in a strange and sinister drift.

Your buildings show no philosophy. So have you no philosophy. You pretend a philosophy of common sense. Weighed in the balance of your acts, your common sense is light as folly: a patent-medicine folly; an adulterated-food folly, a dyspeptic folly, the folly of filth and smoke in your cities, and innumerable every-day follies quite the reverse of that common sense which you assume to mean clear-cut and sturdy thinking in the affairs of daily life. You boast a philosophy of Success. It has long been your daily harangue. But, weighed in the balance of Democracy, your successes are but too clearly, in the main, feudal. They are pessimisms, not optimisms. You did not think to count the cost; but you are beginning now to catch a corner of its masked visage. The sight of the true full cost will stagger you — when the mask is fully drawn aside, and it stands clearly revealed! You would not foresee a crisis, BUT CRISIS FORESAW YOU, AND NOW IS UPON YOU.

You tacitly assumed philosophy to be an empty word, not a vital need; you did not inquire; and in so blindfolding your minds, you have walked straight to the edge of an abyss.

For a Sound Philosophy is the Saving Grace of a Democratic People! It means, very simply, a balanced system of thinking, concerning the vital relations of a people. It is intensely practical. Nothing can be more so. For it saves waste. It looks far behind and far ahead. It forestalls Crisis. It nurtures, economizes and directs the vitality of a people. It has for its sole and abiding objective, their equilibrium, hence their happiness.

Thus, foibles and follies have usurped in your minds the vacant seat of Wisdom. Thus, has your Dollar betrayed you, as it must. And thus, has NOT been given to the World that which was and still remains your highest office, and your noblest privilege to give, in return for that Liberty which was once yours, and which the world gave to you: A sane and pure accounting of Democracy; a philosophy founded upon Man — thereby setting forth, in clear and human terms, the integrity, the responsibility and the accountability of the individual — in short, a new, a real Philosophy of the People.

It is not yet too late.

Let such philosophy be the spiritual first-fruit of your fair and far-flung land. For you must now think quickly, and with a penetration, concentration, simplicity, accuracy and nerve, the necessity of which you have hitherto belittled and denied. Your one splendid power and reserve lies in your resourceful intelligence when forced by your distress into a crisis. Your Architecture hints at this in its many-sided practicalities. Your history in this land has proved it. Use this power at once!

Again, this Architecture, in the large sense, is barren of poetry; yet, strangely enough it faintly contains in its physiognomy a latent suggestion, which bespeaks dramatic, lyric, eloquent and appealing possibilities. In fine, it expresses obscurely the most human qualities you as a people possess, and which, such is your awkward mental bashfulness, you are ashamed to acknowledge, much less to proclaim. One longs to wash from this dirty face its overlay of timidity and abasement; to strip from its form the rags of neglect and contumely, and to see if indeed there be not beneath its forlorn and pitiful aspect, the real face and form of unsuspected Cinderella.

I surmise — or is it a hope born of visible possibilities? A sense of not negligible probabilities? For, truly, what in all the world is more sweet, in the last analysis, however fickle and at times childishly cruel, than is the American heart!

On this foundation, deeper and stronger than you suspect, I would, if I were you, build a new superstructure, really truer to yourselves, and more enduring, than that which now is crumbling upon its weak support of over-smartness and fundamental untruth.

Fortunate, indeed, are you, that your corruption has been so crude; for you can still survive the surgery of its eradication.

It is on this sound heart, and that still better part of it as yet unmatured and un-revealed to your own consciousness, that I would build anew and aright.

For he who knows even a genuinely little of Mankind knows this truth: The heart is greater than the head. For, in the heart, is Desire; and, from it, comes forth Courage and Magnanimity.

To be sure, you had assumed that poetry meant verses; and that reading such was an unworthy weakness for men of brains and hard-headed business. You have held to a fiction, patterned upon your farcical common sense, that sentiment has no place in affairs. Again you did not inquire; you assumed, took for granted — as is your heedless way. You have not looked into your own hearts. You have looked only at the vacancy of convention from which realities have long since departed. Only the husks remain there, like the shells of beetles upon the bark of a living tree.

You have not thought deeply enough to know that the heart in you is the woman in man. You have derided your femininity, where you have suspected it; whereas, you should have known its power, cherished and utilized it, for it is the hidden well-spring of Intuition and Imagination. What can the brain accomplish without these two! They are the man's two inner eyes; without them, he is stone blind. For the mind sends forth their powers both together. One carries the light, the other searches; and between them they find treasures. These they bring to the brain, which first elaborates them, then says to the will, "Do" — and Action follows.

Poetically considered, as far as the huge, disordered resultant mass of your Archi-tecture is concerned, Intuition and Imagination have not gone forth to illuminate and search the hearts of the people. Thus are its works stone blind. If such works be called masculine, this term will prove but a misuse of neuter. For they are empty of procreant powers. They do not inspire the thoughtful mind, but much do they depress it; they are choked with inarticulate cries which evoke pathos in the hearer.

Consider, now, that poetry is not verse — although some verse may be poetic. Consider, now, poetry as apart from words and as resident in things, in thoughts, in acts. For if you persist in regarding print or language as the only readable or hearable things — you must, indeed, remain dull interpreters of the voices of Na-ture, and of the acts and thoughts of the men of the present and the past, in their varied, but fundamentally alike activities. No; poetry, rightly considered, stands for the highest form of intellectual scope and activity. Indeed, it were truer to say psychic activity, if it be known what realities lie behind the mask of that word.

And, be it said in passing, most words are masks. Habit has accustomed you to this company of masks, beautiful some of them, repellent others, but you seldom draw aside a word-mask to see, for yourselves, the countenance of reality which it may both reveal and conceal. For, as I have said, you do not inquire, you are prone to take things for granted. You have seen masks since childhood, and have assumed and still assume them to be real, because, since childhood, you have been told they were, and are, real, by those to whose selfish interest it was, and is, that you cherish the illusion. Latterly, however, you have sufficiently awakened to draw aside the mask-word "Respectability."

You dearly love the mask-word, "Brains," which means physical action; and sniff at the word "Intellect," which stands for clear, powerfully constructive reflection. Therefore, as this is your thought, naturally enough, you are the victims of your impulsive acts, and of your apathy toward far-reaching, inevitable, yes, inexorable, consequences.

It is vitally with realities that poetry deals. But you say it does not; so that settles the matter as far as you are concerned — at least you think it does — in reality it settles you — it keeps you self-bound.

You say that poetry deals only with metaphor and figures of speech. What is your daily talk but metaphor and figures of speech! Every word, genuinely used, is a picture; whether used in conversation or in literary production. Mental life, indeed physical life, is almost entirely a matter of eyesight.

Now poetry, properly understood, means the most highly efficient form of mental eyesight. That is to say, it is that power of seeing and doing which reveals to Man's inner self the fullness and the subtle power of Life.

Poetry, as a living thing, therefore, stands for the most telling quality that man can impart to his thoughts and his acts. Judged by this test, your buildings are dreary, empty places.

Further, these buildings reveal no genuine art of expression — and neither have you as a people genuinely expressed yourselves. You have sniffed at this, too; for you are very cynical, and very pert, and very cocksure. The leer is not long absent from your eyes. You have said in substance: "What do we want of an art of expression? We cannot sell it!" Perhaps not. But you can and have sold yourselves.

You have assumed that an art of expression is a fiction, something apart from yourselves; as you have assumed almost all things, of genuinely preservative value, to be fictions, apart from yourselves — things negligible, to be put on or off like a coat.

Therefore look at your body of laws —complicated, grotesque and inefficient, spiked with "jokers," as guns are spiked. Look at your Constitution. Does that now really express the sound life in you, or is there a "joker" in that, too, that is surely strangling you? Look at your business. What is it become but a war of extermination among cannibals? Does it express Democracy? Are you, as a People, now really a Democracy? Do you still possess the power of self-government of a people, by a people, for a people? Or is it now perished, as your Abraham Lincoln, on the field of Gettysburg, hoped it might not, and as hoped a weary and heartsick people at the close of an awful struggle to preserve Democracy in its integrity, to preserve that fundamental art of expression whereby a people may, unhampered, give voice and form to the aspiration of their lives, their hopes, as they press onward toward the enjoyment of their birthright, the birthright of every man — the right to happiness!

Do you realize with what caustic accuracy this stupor is shown in your buildings?

They, too, stand for the spiked laws of an art of expression. For what is there to express but the true life of a people? What is there, in a Democracy, but All the People? By what right does any man say: "I am! I own! I am therefore a law unto myself!" How quickly among you has I LEAD! BECOME —I POSSESS! I BETRAY! How glibly have you acquiesced! With what awful folly have you assumed selfish egotism to be the basis of Democracy!

How significant is it, that, now, a few rough hands are shaking you, a few sharp shrill voices calling: "Awake before it is too late!"

"But," I hear you say, testily, "we are too young to consider these accomplishments. We have been so busy with our material development that we have not found the time to consider them."

Know then, that, to begin with, they are not accomplishments but necessaries. And, to end with, you are old enough, and have found the time to succeed in nearly making a fine art of — Betrayal, and a science of — Graft!

Know, that you are as old as the race. That each man among you has in him the accumulated power of the race, ready at hand for use, in the right way, when he shall conclude it better to think straight and hence act straight, rather than, as now, to act crooked and pretend to be straight.

Know, that the test, plain, simple HONESTY (and you all know, every man of you knows, exactly what that means), is always at your hand.

Know, that as all complex manifestations have a simple basis of origin, so the vast complexity of your national unrest, ill health, inability to think clearly and accurately concerning simple things, really vital things, is easily and swiftly traceable to the single, actual, active cause — Dishonesty; and that this points with unescapable logic and in just measure to each INDIVIDUAL MAN!

The Remedy: INDIVIDUAL HONESTY.

A conclusion as logical and as just!

"But," you may say, "how absurdly simple."

Doubtless it is absurd, if you think it is, and will so remain, as far as you are concerned, just so long as you think it is — and no longer. But just so long will your social pains and aches and unrest continue; and these you do not consider absurd.

When Newton saw the apple fall, he saw what you might likewise call an absurdly simple thing. Yet with this simple thing he connected up the Universe.

Moreover, this simple thing, Honesty, stands in the Universe of Human Thought and Action, as its very Center of Gravity, and is our human mask-word behind which abides all the power of Nature's Integrity, the profoundest FACT which modern thinking has persuaded Life to reveal.

What folly, then, for Man to buck against the stupendous FLOW of LIFE; instead of voluntarily and gladly placing himself in harmony with it, and thus transferring to himself Nature's own creative energy and equipoise.

"But," you say, "All this is above our heads."

No it is not! IT IS CLOSE BESIDE YOUR HAND! And therein lies its power.

Again you say: "How can honesty be enforced?"

It cannot be enforced.

"Then how will the remedy go into effect?"

It cannot GO into effect. It can only COME into effect.

"Then how can it come?"

Ask Nature.

"And what will Nature say?"

Nature is always saying: "I center at each man, woman and child. I knock at the door of each heart, and I wait. I wait in patience — ready to enter with my gifts."

"And is that all that Nature says?"

That is all.

"Then how are we to receive Nature?"

By opening wide the door of your minds! For your greatest crime against yourselves is that you have locked the door in Her face, and have thrown away the key! Now you say: "There is no key!"

"Then how shall we make a new key?"

First: Care scrupulously for your individual and collective physical health. Beware of those who are undermining it; they are your deadliest danger. Beware of yourselves if you are undermining it, for you are then your own deadliest enemy. Thus will you achieve the first vital preliminary — a quiet, strong and resilient nervous system. Thus will your five senses become accurate interpreters of your physical surroundings; and thus, quite naturally, will the brain resume, in you, its normal power to act and react.

Second: Begin at once the establishment of a truly democratic system of education. The basis of this must be CHARACTER; and the mind must be so trained in the sense of reality that it may reach the fullness of its power to weigh all things, and to realize that the origin and sustenance of its power comes from without, and is Nature's bounteous, unstinted gift to all men.

Such system of education will result in equilibrium of body, mind and heart. It will therefore develop real men and women — as is Nature's desire.

It will produce social equilibrium in every aspect of human affairs. It will so clearly reveal the follies that have cursed you, that you will abandon them forever. For you will then recognize and gladly accept the simple, central truth that the individual grows in power only as he grows in integrity, and that the unfailing source of that integrity lies in the eternal integrity of Nature and of that Infinite Serenity of which Nature is but a symbol.

Thus will you make of Democracy a religion — the only one the world will have developed — befitting freemen — free in the integrity of their bodies, free in the integrity of their thought.

So doing, all aspects of your activities will change, because your thoughts will have changed. All of your activities will then take on organic and balanced coherence, because all of your thoughts will have a common center of gravity in the integrity of individual Man.

And, as the oak-tree is ever true to the acorn from which it sprang, and propagates true acorns in its turn, so will you then give true expression and form to the seed of Democracy that was planted in your soil, and so spread in turn the seeds of true Democracy.

Thus, as your thoughts change, will your civilization change. And thus, as Democracy takes living and integral shape within your thought, will the Feudalism, now tainting you, disappear. For its present power rests wholly upon your acquiescent and supporting thought. Its strength lies wholly in you, not in itself. So, inevitably, as the sustaining power of your thought is withdrawn, this Feudalism will crumble and vanish!

So have you no need of Force, for force is a crude and inefficient instrument. THOUGHT is the fine and powerful instrument. Therefore, HAVE THOUGHT FOR THE INTEGRITY OF YOUR OWN THOUGHT. For all social power, for good, or for ill, rests upon the thought of the People. THIS IS THE SINGLE LESSON IN THE HISTORY OF MANKIND THAT IS REALLY WORTH THE WHILE.

Naturally, then, as your thoughts thus change, your growing Architecture will change. Its falsity will depart; its reality will gradually appear. For the integrity of your thought, as a People, will then have penetrated the minds of your architects.

THEN, TOO, AS YOUR BASIC THOUGHT CHANGES WILL EMERGE A PHILOSOPHY, A POETRY, AND AN ART OF EXPRESSION IN ALL THINGS: FOR YOU WILL HAVE LEARNED THAT A CHARACTERISTIC PHILOSOPHY, POETRY AND ART OF EXPRESSION ARE VITAL TO THE HEALTHFUL GROWTH AND DEVELOPMENT OF A DEMOCRATIC PEOPLE.

As a People you have enormous latent, unused power.

Awaken it.

Use it.

Use it for the common good.

Begin now!

For it is as true today as when one of your wise men said it:—"THE WAY TO RE-SUME IS TO RESUME!"

Appendix A

Tear-sheets of the original Kindergarten Chats as they appeared in *The Interstate Architect and Builder* were preserved in a scrapbook (now in the Avery Library, Columbia University, New York) by Lyndon P. Smith, a friend of Sullivan's, who collaborated on the Bayard Building, in New York City. Very little further information has been obtained concerning Lyndon P. Smith: he owned a house at Palisades, New York, where, according to notations in the scrapbook, several chapters of *Kindergarten Chats* were written; he wrote an article on the Schlesinger and Mayer Building (now Carson Pirie Scott) which was published in *Architectural Record*, vol. 16, no. 1, July 1904; he died ca. 1936.

Into the scrapbook Smith inserted several letters received from Sullivan, here published from manuscript, with the original punctuation:

LOUIS H. SULLIVAN

ARCHITECT

1600 AUDITORIUM TOWER

CHICAGO

Dec. 13th 1900

Dear Lyndon: Yes I have read the circulars [unidentified], and must have neglected to acknowledge same————The number sent will suffice.

It may interest you to know that I have arranged to write 52 articles on American architecture for the *Interstate Architect & Builder* of Cleveland. Publication to begin about March 1st 1901————In reality the 52 articles will constitute *one* argument and will all be interrelated. I have completed two, up to date, and I think the "style" of them will interest you. They will be called "Kindergarten Chats."

Yours

Louis

LOUIS H. SULLIVAN

ARCHITECT

1600 AUDITORIUM TOWER

CHICAGO

Feb. 18 1901

My dear Lyndon

I should like to have the "Kindergarten Chats" circulated as extensively as possible among the *laity*. The architects will not understand much of what is in them, but the laity, more open-minded, will.

Please send to
E. C. Kelly
    Mgr. Interstate Publishing Co.
      Chamber of Commerce Bldg.
        Cleveland   Ohio

as copious a list as you can of those who might be interested in reading these articles, and he can send them notices and a subscription blank———It is among the *people* that we want to work. The composition of the articles is going along merrily. I have 27 written. In the 24th I get the "young man" out of doors on a hot summer's day, and the *awakening* begins.

Let me know, from time to time your impressions of the articles, as they appear. How is everything with you and yours?

Truly

Sullivan

....

LOUIS H. SULLIVAN

ARCHITECT

1600 AUDITORIUM TOWER

CHICAGO

Feb. 22nd 1901

My dear Lyndon:

The "Kindergarten Chats" will strike deeper than you are inclined to imagine. As a psychological study they will be far and away beyond anything I have hitherto attempted. The key to them, you will find, as the development proceeds, slowly but elaborately,—in the development of the character and artistic nature of the young man, *from within.*

It will be the first serious attempt ever made to test architecture by human nature and democracy———Don't let a certain flippancy of treatment mislead you. Try to spread them as far as you can among the laity, for they will be free from technicalities. I am writing for the people, not for architects.

Kelly is a rough diamond. He deserves great credit for his nerve and foresight, and a certain vague but strong desire to make his journal an educational power. He insisted that I should write absolutely with a free hand. It is a pretty heavy money investment for him and he ought to be backed up with subscriptions. I have 27 of the articles written, so I have my "curve" all right.

Yours

Louis

....

LOUIS H. SULLIVAN

ARCHITECT

1600 AUDITORIUM TOWER

CHICAGO

Jan. 11th 1902

Dear Lyndon:

I find your charming Xmas note upon my return from the South where I spent the holidays with Margaret [Sullivan's wife]. All you say from the kindness of your heart we reciprocate in full measure. We had a most delightful Xmas — lunch on the gallery, etc. — temp. 72° — birds singing — waters sparkling — a perfect Ocean Springs day [Sullivan had built a house at Ocean Springs, Miss.]———Margaret remains in the South for a while and I miss her terribly———I am working now on the last of the K.C.'s — #52 — "Springsong". I worked upon it until 5 ³⁰ yesterday morning — but the pace I took in the poem is so extremely high-keyed that I don't dare publish it — after writing 30 pages of manuscript I found I had scarcely made an introduction to my theme———So I must lower the temperature———I shall work on it again tonight — for I wish to get through. These K.C.'s have been a pretty heavy strain on me———Business is picking up a little, and the weather is mild———I send my very best wishes to you both: Margaret would join me were she here.

Louis

Sullivan's estimate of Kelly is borne out by some editorial paragraphs in *The Interstate Architect and Builder*, February 8, 1902:

"The last article of the series under the head of Kindergarten Chats by Louis H. Sullivan appears in this issue of the Interstate Architect and Builder.

"For a year Mr. Sullivan has written strongly, sometimes fiercely, but always in an original vein on principles underlying architecture and its practice. He is not the kind of man who calls a thing which he dislikes by the smoothest and softest name he can find; on the contrary, he applies the roughest words in his vocabulary to things offensive to his ideas.

"For his originality, vigor and boldness in writing who can help liking him? He exhibits a brand of manhood that Americans especially admire.

"Though Mr. Sullivan has bitterly attacked some of the architectural schools, his motive has always been corrective in principle.

"He has persistently urged a higher standard for the profession to which he belongs. Who of us does not speak vehemently and passionately of the wrong-teaching or wrong-doing which to his mind seems to exist? He would be a wishy-washy style of man who would do otherwise.

"We do not all think alike. What appears wrong to one is right to another. So some of Mr. Sullivan's brethren do not agree with him in his argument. Nevertheless he has set them to thinking and he has said things that will benefit every person who has read them. . . . ."

Sullivan also set forth his purpose in writing *Kindergarten Chats* in a letter to Claude F. Bragdon which is quoted in the Introduction to the Scarab edition, as follows:

"A young man who has 'finished his education' at the architectural schools comes to me for a post-graduate course — hence a free form of dialogue.

"I proceed with his education rather by indirection and suggestion than by direct precept. I subject him to certain experiences and allow the impressions they make on him to infiltrate, and, as I note the effect, I gradually use a guiding hand. I supply the yeast, so to speak, and allow the ferment to work in him.

"This is the gist of the whole scheme. It remains then to determine carefully the kind of experiences to which I shall subject the lad, and in what order, or logical (and especially psychological) sequence. I begin, then, with aspects that are literal, objective, more or less cynical, and brutal, and philistine. A little at a time I introduce the subjective, the refined, the altruistic; and by a to-and-fro, increasingly intense rhythm of these two opposing themes, worked so to speak in counterpoint, I reach a preliminary climax; of brutality tempered by a longing for nobler, purer things.

"Hence arise a purblind revulsion and yearning in the lad's soul; the psychological moment has arrived, and I take him at once into the *country* — (Summer: The Storm). This is the first of the four-out-of-door scenes, and the lad's first real experience with nature. It impresses him crudely but violently; and in the tense excitement of the tempest he is inspired to temporary eloquence; and at the close is much softened. He feels in a way but does not know that he has been a participant in one of Nature's superb dramas. (Thus do I insidiously prepare the way for the notion that creative architecture is in essence a dramatic art, and an art of eloquence: of subtle rhythmic beauty, power and tenderness.)

"Left alone in the country the lad becomes maudlin — a callow lover of nature — and makes feeble attempts at verse. Returning to the city he melts and unbosoms — the tender shaft of the unknowable Eros has penetrated his heart — Nature's subtle spell is on him, to disappear and reappear. Then follow discussions, more or less didactic, leading to the second out-of-door scene (Autumn Glory). Here the lad does most of the talking and shows a certain lucidity and calm of mind. The discussion of Responsibility, Democracy, Education, etc., has inevitably detached the lurking spirit of pessimism. It has to be: Into the depths and darkness we descend, and the work reaches the tragic climax in the third out-of-door scene — Winter.

"Now that the forces have been gathered and marshalled, the true, sane movement of the work is entered upon and pushed at high tension, and with swift, copious modulations, to its foreordained climax and optimistic peroration in the fourth and last out-of-door scene as portrayed in the Spring Song. The *locale* of this closing number is the beautiful spot in the woods, on the shore of Biloxi Bay — where I am writing this."

245. *A*

Appendix B

A letter to the editor, *The Interstate Architect and Builder,* May 11, 1901:

I have been reading with much interest and considerable edification, I trust, the series of Kindergarten Chats by Mr. Louis H. Sullivan. I do not say this to praise Mr. Sullivan nor to compliment your enterprising journal, but only to show you that the criticism which follows is not born of a spirit of general hostility to Mr. Sullivan and his ideas.

It is my opinion that Mr. Sullivan allowed his strong convictions (I admire him for his strong convictions) to lead him into error and indefensible grounds in paper No. 10 (on a Roman Temple) in your issue of April 20. In general I agree heartily with his criticism of the "Roman Temple" and would feel nothing but complacence as he toasted the perpetrator for lack of ability, but it certainly is a violation of all teachings of ethics and moral philosophy to say that a man who makes a mistake in judgment is as bad as a defaulter. Surely there can be no justice in arraigning incapacity as a crime. It may be deplorable, but it gives us no moral shock. The idiot would scarcely be hired by us to fill a responsible position, if we knew it, but if we did hire him and he betrayed his trust we could not charge him with crime.

Maybe Mr. Sullivan wants to be credited with the belief that all architects who build badly know better but build badly from "pure cussedness." Of course if this be his position, I have nothing more to say except that I hardly believe it.

A.L.F.

Sullivan's reply, in the May 18, 1901, issue:

To the editor,

The letter of your correspondent, A.L.F., in the issue of May 11 is so reasonable in tone that I wish, in a measure, to reply. I cannot discuss with him the ethical issue he raises. I will only suggest for the benefit of himself and of those who think with him, that the Kindergarten Chats are not intended to be a series of disconnected weekly articles, but a *thesis,* gradually and organically developed. This thesis will grow and unfold in its own way, and in due time will put forth its flower. When complete it must, as must any work of art, take its chances of survival. I do not specifically object to criticism. Why should I? I propose for myself to criticize with the utmost freedom and without reserve. Why then should I deny that right for others concerning my own work? I do not, but I am writing this merely as a suggestion to your correspondent that when he shall have read up to and including the 52nd article he may find an explanation, not only of the 10th, but of all the others, and the 52nd will be explained by the other 51, and each article will be justified by its 51 companions.

When my thesis shall be completed then you may turn on all the artillery of criticism that you please. A philosophy that will not withstand rough usage is no philosophy, and by this standard, which I hereby accept in advance, my philosophy must either survive and triumph, as I think it should, and in which case there will come, by a natural process, a complete and world-wide regeneration of the architectural art or — it must go by the board. I ask no favor and give none. I ask no quarter and I give none. The time has come when a vital issue must be fought to a finish. Whether a false education is to dominate us, or whether we are to evolve from ourselves and from the conditions of democracy a true education, is that issue.

Louis H. Sullivan

Appendix C

Sullivan had deleted (in his revision) the sentence: "And yet this man was none other than a president of the A.I. of A. and he voiced this stupid, paltry sentiment in a presidential address."

At the annual convention of the A.I.A. in 1900, in Washington, D.C., the president, Robert S. Peabody, remarked: ". . . . It is charged, that, as a body, we do not encourage original work, and that architecture, as understood by those influential in our affairs, is only a repetition of old forms and well worn ornaments, applied without reason and as veneers to absolutely new constructive methods. Even if varied opinions assert themselves, it is said that most of us produce nothing but imitations, more or less feeble and inappropriate, of Parisian work, of Medieval England, of Italy in the fifteenth century, or of Classic Rome itself. Perhaps the professors of architecture are worse than the architects themselves. They are described as 'brooding like a blight over their schools,' as lauding 'symbols and figments,' as 'hearkening to echoes,' as pilfering 'the spontaneity and charm of youth,' and as setting up 'the infallibility of tradition' . . . . Happily, as I think, the horror of adapting to our uses ornamental forms endeared by long association is not widespread. Most of us shudder to think what our land would be if subjected to 'a liberation of the creative impulse'."

The phrases ironically quoted by Peabody, are from an essay, by Sullivan, "Reality in the Architectural Art," printed in the *Chicago Tribune* and later published by *The Interstate Architect and Builder,* (vol. 2, no. 25, August 11, 1900): "It is clearly recognized that educational methods, hitherto, have been criminally false, bewildering and destructive, and an eager desire is abroad to loosen the husk of classic, of medieval and of monarchical artificiality from the natural man, that he may come into his own. . . . . Toward this aspiration, educators, with few exceptions, are lending strenuous and enlightened aid to youth.

"Among the exceptions, notably, are the professors of architecture, brooding, like blight, over their schools. They ingest the subtle hypodermic of I and Thou—the pharisaism of mental pride. They foster the sense of dilettantism. They extol the artificial, the unreal. They laud symbols and figments. They hearken to echoes.

"In so doing they assert that they teach the architectural art, whereas, in fact, not only do they obscure the reality of that art, but, quickly and surely, they repress and pilfer the spontaneity and charm of youth, the sanity, the higher usefulness of the future man. . . . .

"The remedy is self-evident — a return to natural, simple, wholesome and sympathetic ways of thinking; a liberation of the creative impulse. . . . ."

Robert S. Peabody, of the Boston firm, Peabody and Stearns, designed public buildings and residences in New England, New York City, etc., and the Hall of Machines at the Exposition in Chicago, 1893.

Appendix D

The Gold Medal of the American Institute of Architects was presented to Louis H. Sullivan, at the annual convention, May 10, 1946, in Miami, with the following citation, by Hugh Morrison:

To Louis Sullivan we render honor:

His profession of Architecture was a lifetime dedication of all his energies of mind and spirit.

By esteeming practical requirements as aesthetic responsibilities he unfolded a new discipline of design.

He believed that the dimensions of American architecture are the dimensions of American life, and thus directed us to an art of, by, and for our own people.

He approached each task afresh, believing that each problem contains and suggests its own solution.

He demanded of himself an emotional and spiritual expenditure to endow each building with its own identity of beauty.

He attacked entrenched beliefs.

He repudiated false standards.

He scorned the stylistic gods of the market-place.

He fought almost alone in his generation, lived unhappily, and died in poverty.

But because he fought, we today have a more valiant conception of our art. He helped to renew for all architects the freedom to originate and the responsibility to create. The standards he set have contributed much to the achievement of today and will augment the promise of tomorrow.

We render to Louis Sullivan this grateful tribute, highest honor of our profession, the Gold Medal of the American Institute of Architects.

(By courtesy of the *Journal of the American Institute of Architects*)

The medal was accepted by George Grant Elmslie with the following response, which was read in Mr. Elmslie's absence:

It is with deep emotion that I accept the posthumous Gold Medal Award to Louis Henri Sullivan by this Institute; its highest award. It is as representative and guardian that I accept it and will cherish it in memory of other days. I was closely associated with Mr. Sullivan for many years and while he was in his creative prime.

It is now twenty-two years past in April since this great American passed away, and the intervening years have tended to clarify his position and define his stature as a leader of men, not only in the field of his beloved architecture but in the avenue of our ever widening Democratic Vista. The public and the architectural profession are more aware of the leavening value of his spirit now than ever before, and, in that sense, the Award is timely.

As a man he was essentially a lyric poet. An unpublished work of his called "The Master" is truly a lyric poem and reveals the character of the man in his most subjective moments; and criticism of his life should consider this vital factor in appraisement of his accomplishments.

Stalwart and vital he stood, four-square to the world of his day and never faltered in his efforts to liberate architecture from the scholastic thralldom involved in traditional architectural forms and in our relics of feudalism with their many inhibitions relative to what he believed to be the normally creative spirit of man. All this was done in the face of savage and witless criticism abroad the land, which continued during many years of his life.

Perhaps it may not be amiss to relate some of my experiences with him. Mr. Sullivan was a gracious and animating preceptor to all who cared for independent thinking and to those who had the privilege of being under his eye in the drawing room on top of his great Auditorium Tower. In criticism of work being done he was broad and stimulating in his approach; seldom censorious or arbitrary. To the men of ideas he was especially encouraging.

As a draughtsman he had few equals, and it was an object-lesson to see him in action with his extraordinary deftness and precision. His designs were all previously conceived in communion with the problems themselves and far away from paper and pencil contact—a mental and spiritual method of approach that he never ceased stressing.

Many people have read his *Autobiography of an Idea,* published by the A. I. A., but few have read his *Kindergarten Chats* on Architecture, Education and Democracy. A new and enlarged edition of this book, embracing some heretofore unpublished essays, is coming out this year as arranged by me as his literary executor. It may also be of interest to you to know, for the younger men and students of architecture, that there is a collection of Mr. Sullivan's manuscripts, drawings and other material in the Burnham Library of the Chicago Art Institute, placed there as of historical significance.

I deeply regret not being able to be present in person at this accolade to Louis Sullivan, a leader in the Arts as well as in a way of life.

It is fitting to close this response by quoting a paragraph from one of his essays:

"Before my vision as I go, opens a bewitching landscape—wherein abides an architecture of peace, of wit and of sanity—an architecture that shall take on such natural and shapely shapes that it would seem as though Nature made it; for it will arise graciously from the mind, the heart, the soul of man; an architecture which shall seem as though the Lord God made it, for into it will have been breathed the breath of life—yet will it be an architecture made by Men —for men will then have become Men."

Appendix E

Manuscripts and editions of *Kindergarten Chats*

A   Holograph manuscript, in pencil; in the Avery Library, Columbia University (Chs. 31 & 32 missing). A holograph list of chapters, in diagram form, with the corresponding dates of publication in *Interstate Architect & Builder*, is pasted in a scrapbook made by Lyndon P. Smith and bequeathed to the Avery Library.

B   Typed manuscript of A prepared for printer (hypothetical) — carbon copies of this were known to exist.

C   Serialization in *Interstate Architect & Builder*, February 8, 1901 to February 16, 1902. This text varies from that of A only in minor changes of words and in deletions of brief phrases.

D   Manuscript revised by Sullivan (June-October 1918): this consists of a carbon copy of B with interlineations in pencil, mostly printed, and with extensive cuts. Six chapters were rewritten on separate sheets of paper and have been lost, except for two (31 — in the Avery — and 32), given to the editor of edition F by Mr. George G. Elmslie. The original revised manuscript is in the Burnham Library, The Art Institute, Chicago, to which it was presented by Mr. Elmslie, who received it about 1936. In the revision, Sullivan had cut the text from approximately 130,000 to approximately 100,000 words.

E   Typed copy of D, presented to the Burnham Library by Mr. Charles H. Whitaker. This lacks the foreword written by Sullivan for D.

F   Scarab Fraternity Press limited edition, 1934, edited and with an introduction by Claude F. Bragdon, who prepared the text from back numbers of *Interstate Architect & Builder* (and two manuscript chapters noted under D). Mr. Bragdon's introduction explains the nature and extent of his editing and quotes at length a letter from Sullivan concerning the purpose of *Kindergarten Chats* (see App. A); one conclusion is invalidated by the existence of manuscript D: "Several attempts were made, both before and after Sullivan's death in 1924, to have the essays issued in book form, but all proved abortive . . . for publication in book form, emendations and excisions were imperative. Sullivan refused to perform this task himself, nor would he submit to anyone else's editorship."

G   The present edition, prepared directly from D, with the missing chapters supplied from E.